LITTLE HOUSE
IN THE
OZARKS

Books by the Author

Little House in the Big Woods
Farmer Boy
Little House on the Prairie
On the Banks of Plum Creek
By the Shores of Silver Lake
The Long Winter
Little Town on the Prairie
These Happy Golden Years
The First Four Years, edited by Roger Lea MacBride
On the Way Home with Preface by Rose Wilder Lane
West From Home: Letters of Laura Ingalls Wilder, San Francisco 1915, edited by Roger Lea MacBride
The Little House Sampler, edited by William Anderson
Little House in the Ozarks, edited by Stephen W. Hines

LITTLE HOUSE
IN THE
OZARKS

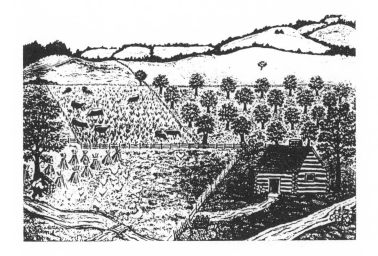

A Laura Ingalls Wilder Sampler
The Rediscovered Writings

LAURA INGALLS WILDER
EDITED BY STEPHEN W. HINES

Published in Nashville, Tennessee, by Thomas Nelson, Inc., and distributed in Canada by Lawson Falle, Ltd., Cambridge, Ontario.

Printed in the United States of America.

Scripture quotations noted NKJV are from THE NEW KING JAMES VERSION. Copyright © 1979, 1980, 1982, Thomas Nelson, Inc., Publishers.

Other Scripture quotations are from the King James Version of the Bible.

The article titled "Whom Will You Marry?" was originally published in *McCall's* magazine, June 1919.

Library of Congress Cataloging-in-Publication Data

Wilder, Laura Ingalls, 1867–1957.
    Little house in the Ozarks : a Laura Ingalls Wilder sampler : the rediscovered writings / by Laura Ingalls Wilder : edited by Stephen W. Hines.
        p.   cm.
    ISBN 0-8407-7597-0
    1. Wilder, Laura Ingalls, 1867–1957—Homes and haunts—Ozark Mountains. 2. Authors, American—20th century—Biography. 3. Ozark Mountains—Social life and customs. 4. Ozark Mountains—Literary collections. I. Hines, Stephen W. II. Title.
PS3545.I342Z414   1991
813'.52—dc20   91–10820
                                                                      CIP

For Mom and Dad, loving and affectionate parents; and for Gwendolyn, my loving and affectionate wife

Acknowledgments

First of all I would like to acknowledge the invaluable aid of my wife, Gwen, in this undertaking. Her persistence in proofreading, titling of chapters, and all-around general good advice made this project flow much more smoothly than it would have otherwise.

And my thanks to:

Carolyn B. Cuany, my mother-in-law, for her help in rooting out an obscure article of Laura Wilder's in *McCall's* magazine.

Gordon R. Cuany, my brother-in-law, for his considerable efforts in seeking to make me computer literate (he failed) and for obtaining material for me through interlibrary loan.

Jackie Dana, graduate student in history, for her determined research efforts.

Patricia Timberlake, librarian, for early work over the phone that greatly forwarded my research.

June DeWeese, librarian, for making it possible for me to review highly fragile periodicals in a dismaying state of decay.

Margaret Howell, librarian, for providing access to the material I needed from special collections.

Laurel Boeckman, librarian, for assisting Jackie Dana in her work.

Marie Concannon, librarian, for her flexibility and good humor in dealing with the requests, often seemingly nonsensical, that were made of her.

Suzanne Lippard, library clerk, for her fund of personal information about Laura Wilder and about the people still living who had known her.

Marian Bond, library assistant, for invaluable help in speeding my research.

Dwight Miller, librarian, for help in tracking down archival material.

Robin L. Coreas and Rosemary K. Panzenbeck, bibliographers in the Reference and Bibliography section of the Library Congress, for the useful information they provided.

Connie Tidwell, Curator of the Laura Ingalls Wilder-Rose Wilder Lane Museum and Home, for a pleasant and informative day at the museum.

Irene V. Lichty Le Count, first Curator of the Laura Ingalls Wilder-Rose Wilder Lane Museum and Home, for invaluable information about Laura's Iowa years.

Vivian Glover, Secretary of the Laura Ingalls Wilder Memorial Society, De Smet, South Dakota, for her valuable assistance in obtaining material on Laura's life in and around "The Little Town on the Prairie."

William Anderson, Laura Ingalls Wilder authority, for his guidance in searching for material by Laura in *Youth's Companion,* a magazine of the Congregational Church (ceased publication, 1929).

Jim Schall, Vice President of Church Engineering, who provided much of the computer hardware that greatly aided in my putting this book together.

And last, but not least, thanks to Bruce Barbour, Publisher of Trade Books at Thomas Nelson Publishers, for backing the lengthy efforts of this project; and thanks to Bill Watkins, Senior Editor, for his alert eye in going over the manuscript.

If I have forgotten anyone in these acknowledgments, I do regret the oversight.

Contents

Long ago and far away 15

Chapter One—**Her husband's partner** 19
Let's Visit Mrs. Wilder 21
Our Little Place in the Ozarks 24
When Is a Settler an Old Settler? 28
The March of Progress 30
My Dream House 34
How to Furnish a Home 36
Rocky Ridge Farm 38
We Revel in Water! 41
My Apple Orchard 44
Heirs of the Ages 47

Chapter Two—**Nothing new under the sun** 49
Sweet Williams 51
The Findleys Strive for an Education 53
"A Spirit of Sadness Over It All" 56
Classed As Illiterates 58
Our Next President 60
Our Brains—and Providence 62
Home 64
The Man of the Place 65
Kind Hearts 68
The Wanton Destruction of Trees 69
Be True to Yourself 71
Love of Home 73
Far in the Future 75
The Great Woods Have Been Destroyed 76
Income and Expenses 78
Compensations 79

Chapter Three—**The garden of our lives** 81
I Don't Know What the World Is Coming To 83
Make Your Garden! 85
Parable of Wild Fruit 87

Are You Your Children's Confidant? 89
Kinfolks or Mere Relations? 91
Troubles Grow As We Talk About Them 93
We Keep Right on Eating 95
Keep Journeying On 96
Getting the Worst of It 98
The Source of Improvement 100
A Man's Word Is All He Has 102
The Helping Hand of Helpfulness 103
Growing Older 105

Chapter Four—**Have you seen any fairies lately?** 107
Fairies Still Appear to Those with Seeing Eyes 109
Where Sunshine Fairies Go 110
Naughty Four O'Clocks 111
The Fairy Dew Drop 112
When Sunshine Fairies Rest 112
The Fairies in the Sunshine 113
Lesson from an Irish Fable 114

Chapter Five—**The rush of work** 115
Tired to Death with Work 117
Going After the Cows 119
Mrs. Jones Takes the Rest Cure 120
Let's Not Depend on Experts 122
When Proverbs Quarrel 124
Farmers—Need More Wives? 126
Does It Pay to Be Idle? 128
Join 'Don't Worry' Club 131
A Fool and His Son Are Soon Parted 134
A Day Off Now and Then 135
About Work 137
When the Blues Descend 138
Life Is an Adventure 140

Chapter Six—**A great many interesting things** 145
The Hard Winter 147
The Friday Night Literary 149
On Chickens and Hawks 151

Times and Things 152
When Grandma Pioneered 153
Make a New Beginning 155
Having a Family Motto 156
The First Frost 157
Our Fair and Our Fancy 159
Chasing Thistledown 161
What Became of the Time We Saved? 163
Just a Question of Tact 165
The Old Dash Churn 167
Christmas When I Was Sixteen 169

Chapter Seven—**Give me just one logical reason** 171
Five Dollar Prize for Women 173
Dear Farm Women 174
    Why Should I Stay? 174
    Church and School Privileges 175
    Here's Hope Deferred 176
Pioneering on an Ozark Farm 178
Whom Will You Marry? 183

Chapter Eight—**A new day for women** 191
Shorter Hours for the Farm Home Manager 193
A Woman's Power and the Vote 197
The Woman's Place 199
Two Heads Are Better Than One 200
Women's Work? 202
Women's Duty at the Polls 204
Daily Tasks Are Not Small Things 206
Thoughts on the Role of Women and Divorce 208
The Home Beauty Parlor 211
What Women Can Add to Politics 214
This and That—A Neighborly Visit with Laura 215
New Day for Women 218

Chapter Nine—**If we would but open our eyes** 221
The Creative Chemistry of Life 223
The Light We Throw 225
A Few Minutes with a Poet 226

Success 228
Good Neighbors 229
A Constant Friend 231
What Would You Do? 233
Opportunity 235
To Stand by Ourselves 237
Challenges 239
An Autumn Day 240

Chapter Ten—**The war, the terrible** 243
Each in His Place 245
Left Out and Pushed About 247
The War, the Terrible 249
Getting Down to First Causes 251
Are We Too Busy? 253
Make Every Minute Count 255
A Wish for the Present 257
Glory! What Days in Which to Live! 259
Our Code of Honor 261
When the War Ended 263
Peace on Earth 264

Chapter Eleven—**Surely worth the effort** 267
Administer Advice in Small Doses 269
Keeping Friends 271
We Always Pay for That "Need" 273
Learning Something New 275
The Hidden Cost of Getting What We Want 276
Early Training Counts 278
Don't Call on the Government All of the Time 280
Pies and Poetry 282
Simplify, Simplify 283
Think for Yourself 285
The Blessings of the Year 286

Chapter Twelve—**The greatness and goodness of God** 287
Everyday Implications of the Golden Rule 289
Thanks for Benefits Bestowed 291
Thanks for the Harvest 292

Harvest of the Soul 293
A Dog's a Dog for A' That 295
Let Us Be Just 297
Do the Right Thing Always 299
The Armor of a Smile 301
Laura and Mary Quarrel at Thanksgiving 302
Not So Bad Off 304
Swearing 305
Honor and Duty 307
If We Only Understood 309
The Things That Matter 311
Mother 313
"Mother Passed Away" 315

Long Ago and Far Away

On February 10, 1957, one of the most popular—if not *the* most popular children's author of all time—passed away at the age of ninety on her beloved Rocky Ridge Farm near the small town of Mansfield, Missouri. Laura Ingalls Wilder had survived the "Man of the Place," her husband, Almanzo James Wilder (the subject of *Farmer Boy*), by a little over eight years. They had been husband and wife, partners and pioneers, for sixty-four years.

At about the time of Laura's passing I was just discovering, as a farm boy of ten or eleven, that she had ever lived. I believe that the first book of her famous "Little House" series I ever read was perhaps the most famous one, *Little House on the Prairie*. The book was a sensation for me; I felt that I had discovered a wonderful author and a wonderful series of books that no one else even knew of. They were special to me because they reflected the same feelings I had about my own family—the deep love that was there even though we might fight like cats and dogs. And millions of childhood fans of those "Little House" books feel the same way.

In Laura Ingalls Wilder I had found a friend who knew and understood my world, though she was a girl from long ago and far away. Times had changed so much; yet they hadn't changed so much after all: the meadowlarks still rose to sing in the morning while the dew freshened the grass; the cows still grazed in the furthest corner of the pasture from which they must be driven to give their milk at the barn and eat the sweet smelling hay from the loft above them.

Her landscape and my landscape, despite all those years, weren't that different after all.

* *

Laura's stories were as good as fiction; but they were real, of course, the true stories of her fascinating childhood, the true stories of a pioneer girl who literally grew up with America (1867–1957). But like all stories—whether true or not—her's had an end. There were eight books, then no more for the longest time. Then there was a ninth book in 1971, and even though I was an adult, *The First Four Years* still saddened me, not only because it *is* a sad book, but also because I read that there would be no more books from Laura to read.

I am happy to report that my fears were unfounded.

In 1989 I discovered that Laura actually had quite a long apprenticeship in writing, being in the early part of this century not only a pioneer farmer's wife but also a pioneer woman journalist. For twenty years before she ever took up her pen to write the first "Little House" book, she was already doing their fascinating *sequel* by writing for then contemporary Missouri farm papers and even national magazines.

And this material wasn't just a curiosity, though it happily gives us a wonderful record of those times. In some ways this material, 90 percent of which has never been available to her present-day audience, tells us as much or more about Laura as we get from her justly famous books.

We learn for the first time that Laura had a truly marvelous sense of humor, as you will read in "The Old Dash Churn" and "Just a Question of Tact." We learn that there is a "strong" and there is a "tender" Laura, as in "Don't Call on the Government All of the Time" and "Growing Older." The virtues of self-reliance and love of home and home-oriented values are much extolled, being major themes of her entire life and writings.

Still perhaps I should further justify why I feel that this volume is a true "sequel" to Laura's "Little House" series. After all, I have just admitted that these approximately 150 articles and essays were written *before* Laura became famous.

For that justification we have to look at the last of the books in the honored "Little House" series, *The First Four Years*. Those who have read it have all noted its honest, unremitting grimness in detailing disaster after disaster in Laura and Almanzo's early married life: the death of a boy child, a week later the loss of their home in a fire, the loss of Almanzo's robust health owing to a stroke following diphtheria that nearly killed them both, and finally the loss of their little farm claim altogether owing to many years of crop failure.

Early in that book Laura warns Almanzo that she does not believe in blindly obeying her husband. And she further reveals that she doesn't want to be a farmer's wife. She lays down an ultimatum to the optimistic, as yet un-scarred Almanzo: If the farm isn't turning a profit in three years, they will move to town for the sake of an easier life.

It is an ultimatum, you will learn as you read this sequel volume, that she never kept. This collection, *Little House in the Ozarks,* tells you why; for two diverse threads act to unify all that she wrote prior to the 1930s. First, for Laura, no matter how tough farming was, if a woman didn't give up, she could become *equal* partners with her husband and share in the self-respect and re-wards that this sort of status brought. It was a great thing to be a *partner* with your man; and from Laura's time and perspective there was virtually no other occupation, commonly open to women, that brought this possibility within reach.

Second, the farm was a natural setting for the upholding of the home values she so admired and loved from her own childhood. Laura held the teachings of her mother and father dear throughout her ninety years of life.

Modern times may be modern times—there may be a war to deal with in

1917–1918 (and Laura deals with it); and there may be an aftermath to follow that leads people to think things won't come right side up again; and there may be more worries from the outside world as motor cars become more prevalent and the radio brings the world's bad news into even remote Ozark homes; but Laura is sure, as she says so well, that certain things will remain constant.

"At the long last, I am beginning to learn that it is the sweet, simple things of life which are the real ones after all.

"We heap up around us things that we do not need as the crow makes piles of glittering pebbles. We gabble words like parrots until we lose the sense of their meaning; we chase after this new idea and that; we take an old thought and dress it out in so many words that the thought itself is lost in its clothing, like a slim woman in a barrel skirt, and then we exclaim, 'Lo, the wonderful new thought I have found!'

"'There is nothing new under the sun,' says the proverb. I think the meaning is that there are just so many truths or laws of life, and no matter how far we may think we have advanced, we cannot get beyond those laws. However complex a structure we build of living, we must come back to those truths, and so we find we have traveled in a circle.

". . . It is the simple things of life that make living worthwhile, the sweet fundamental things such as love and duty, work and rest. . . ."

As you can see from these comments, Laura's perspective on life was shaped not only by pioneer virtues of self-reliance but also by a simple Christian faith. Irene Lichty Le Count, Laura's friend of many years, writes of a troubled time in Laura's girlhood when, out of that trouble, she encountered the presence of God.

"One night when Laura was saying her prayers, which she always did before going to bed, the feeling of worry . . . was worse than usual. Gradually she had a feeling of a hovering, encompassing Presence, of a Power comforting and sustaining her and she thought in surprise, 'This is what men call God!'" The family's financial crisis passed, and the Ingalls moved to South Dakota. (See *The Ingalls Family: from Plum Creek to Walnut Grove via Burr Oak, Iowa.*)

Yes, you will find some material here that has the quaint dress of other times, conditions and urgencies of another day; but it is my hope that you will grin at some of them and ponder others and come to conclude with Laura that things really don't change that much in the end. Past and present—they are bound much more together than we know.

✳✳✳

Finally, just a comment about the editing. Grammar, punctuation, and spelling have been modernized. Otherwise, this is Laura's book. Points of ellipsis have been used where truly out of date or irrelevant material did exist, and series of asterisks have been used to indicate breaks in thought.

But enough. Now for a feast!

Stephen W. Hines, 1991

CHAPTER 1

Her husband's partner

Let's Visit Mrs. Wilder
February 1918
by John F. Case

Missouri farm folks need little introduction before getting acquainted with Mrs. A. J. Wilder of Rocky Ridge Farm. During the years that she has been connected with this paper*—a greater number of years than any other person on the editorial staff—she has taken strong hold upon the esteem and affections of our great family. Mrs. Wilder has lived her life upon a farm. She knows farm folks and their problems as few women who write know them. And having sympathy with the folks whom she serves, she writes well.

---

*"She is her husband's partner
in every sense."*

"Mrs. Wilder is a woman of delightful personality," a neighbor tells me, "and she is a combination of energy and determination. She always is cheery, looking on the bright side. She is her husband's partner in every sense and is fully capable of managing the farm. No woman can make you feel more at home than can Mrs. Wilder, and yet, when the occasion demands, she can be dignity personified. Mrs. Wilder has held high rank in the Eastern Star. Then when a Farm Loan Association was formed at Mansfield, she was made secretary-treasurer. When her report was sent to the Land Bank officials, they told her the papers were perfect and the best sent in." As a final tribute, Mrs. Wilder's friends said this: "She gets eggs in the winter when none of her neighbors gets them."

Born in Wisconsin

"I was born in a log house within four miles of the legend-haunted Lake Pepin in Wisconsin," Mrs. Wilder wrote when I asked for information about her. "I remember seeing deer that father had killed hanging in the trees about our forest home. When I was four years old, we traveled to the Indian Territory—Fort Scott, Kansas, being our nearest town.** My childish memories hold the sound of the war whoop, and I see pictures of painted Indians."

Looking at the picture of Mrs. Wilder, which was recently taken, we find it

---

*Part of the Arthur S. Capper Chain of farm papers.
**Actually, Laura's memory failed her here; she lived near Independence, Kansas.

---

difficult to believe that she is old enough to be the pioneer described. But having confided her age to the editor (not for publication), we must be convinced that it is true. Surely Mrs. Wilder, who is the mother of Rose Wilder Lane, talented author and writer, has found the fountain of youth in the Ozark hills. We may well believe that she has a "cheerful disposition" as her friend asserts.

"I was a regular little tomboy," Mrs. Wilder confesses, "and it was fun to walk the two miles to school." The folks were living in Minnesota then, but it was not long until Father Ingalls, who seems to have had a penchant for moving about, had located in Dakota. It was at De Smet, South Dakota, that Laura Ingalls, then eighteen years old, married A. J. Wilder, a farmer boy.

"Our daughter, Rose Wilder Lane, was born on the farm," Mrs. Wilder informs us, "and it was there I learned to do all kinds of farm work with machinery. I have ridden the binder, driving six horses. And I could ride. I do not wish to appear conceited, but I broke my own ponies to ride. Of course, they were not bad, but they were broncos." Mrs. Wilder had the spirit that brought success to the pioneers.

Mr. Wilder's health failed and the Wilders went to Florida. "I was something of a curiosity, being the only 'Yankee girl' the inhabitants ever had seen," Mrs. Wilder relates. The low altitude did not agree with Mrs. Wilder, though, and she became ill. It was then that they came to Rocky Ridge Farm near Mansfield, Wright County [Mo.], and there they have lived for twenty-five years.

Only forty acres were purchased, and the land was all timber except a four-acre, worn-out field. "Illness and traveling expenses had taken our surplus cash, and we lacked $150 of paying for the forty acres," Mrs. Wilder writes. "Mr. Wilder was unable to do a full day's work. The garden, my hens, and the wood I helped saw and which we sold in town took us through the first year. It was then I became an expert at the end of a cross-cut saw, and I still can 'make a hand' in an emergency. Mr. Wilder says he would rather have me help than any man he ever sawed with. And, believe me, I learned how to take care of hens and to make them lay."

Intelligent industry brings its own reward. Mr. and Mrs. Wilder not only paid for the forty acres, but they have added sixty acres more, stocked the farm to capacity, and improved it and built a beautiful modern home. "Everything sold by the Wilders brings a good price," their neighbor tells me, "because it is standard goods. It was by following strict business methods that they were enabled to build their beautiful home. Most of the material used was found on the farm. Fortunate indeed are those who are entertained at Rocky Ridge."

One may wonder that so busy a person, as Mrs. Wilder has proved to be, can find time to write. "I always have been a busy person," she says, "doing my own housework, helping the Man of the Place when help could not be obtained; but I love to work. And it is a pleasure to write. And, oh, I do just love to play! The days never have been long enough to do the things I would like to do. Every year has held more of interest than the year before." Folks who possess that kind of spirit get a lot of joy out of life as they travel the long road.

Joined the Family in 1911

Mrs. Wilder has held numerous important offices, and her stories about farm life and farm folks have appeared in the best farm papers. Her first article printed [for us] appeared in February 1911. It was a copy of an address prepared for Farmer's Week. So for seven years she has been talking to Missouri women through these columns, talk that always has carried inspiration and incentive for worthwhile work.

Reading Mrs. Wilder's contributions, most folks doubtless have decided that she is a college graduate. But "my education has been what a girl would get on the frontier," she informs us. "I never graduated from anything and only attended high school two terms."

Folks who know Mrs. Wilder though, know that she is a cultured, well-educated gentlewoman. Combined with inherent ability, unceasing study of books has provided the necessary education, and greater things have been learned from the study of life itself.

As has been asserted before, Mrs. Wilder writes well for farm folks because she knows them. The Wilders can be found ready to enter wholeheartedly into any movement for community betterment, and the home folks are proud of the reputation that Mrs. Wilder has established. They know that she has won recognition as a writer and state leader because of ability alone.

Our Little Place in the Ozarks
December 1923

When we came to Missouri in 1894, we were looking for a place where the family health might make a good average, for one of us was not able to stand the severe cold of the North, while another could not live in the low altitude and humid heat of the Southern states.

It was before the days of "Tin Can Tourists," and we traveled with a team and covered wagon. It was rather unpleasant journeying in the heat of summer; but as we climbed into the hills this side of Springfield, the air grew fresher and more invigorating the farther we went until, in Wright County, we found the place we were seeking. It was far enough south so that the winters were mild, high enough for the air to be pure and bracing, sheltered in the hills from the strong winds of the West, yet with little breezes always blowing among them, with plenty of wood for fuel and timber and rocks for building, with low lands for cultivation and upland bluegrass pastures for grazing, with game in the woods and fish in the rivers, and springs of pure, cold, mountain water everywhere.

*We found the place we were
seeking . . . far enough south
so that the winters were mild,
high enough for the air to be pure
and bracing, sheltered in the hills
from the strong winds
of the West.*

Atop the Ozarks

Here on the very peak of the Ozark watershed are to be found good health, good homes, a good living, good times, and good neighbors. What more could anyone want?

Wright County is the highest part of the state south of the Missouri River. Its surface is a broad plateau broken by hills rising from it and by valleys and ravines through which flow the numerous spring branches, creeks, and rivers seeking the waters of the Missouri and the Mississippi.

The rolling hills and fertile valleys are beautifully wooded, except where cleared for agricultural purposes. The trees are of many different kinds—black oak, white oak, blackjack, maple, cherry, ash, elm, sycamore, gum, hickory, walnut, butternut, persimmon, redbud, and linden—and give great variety to the forest foliage and furnish timber for every use.

A peculiarity of the country is that springs break out near the tops of the hills as well as on lower ground, and wells of good water on the high lands are only from forty to sixty feet deep.

In the early days, all the large game lived here, except buffalo. Deer fed on the hills and in the valleys; bears and panthers denned in the many caves, while wolves and foxes hunted their prey where they might find it. Even yet a panther or wildcat appears now and then, while at times wolves are reported killing the sheep.

There is no record of an Indian settlement in Wright County, but the Delawares, Shawnees, and Pinkashaws wandered over it hunting and fishing. Their stone arrowheads and clubs are still frequently found.

The first Americans to settle in Wright County came from Tennessee, Kentucky, and the Carolinas. The first settlement was made in 1836, and there were seventy slaves in the county at the beginning of the Civil War.

Wright County was organized January 29, 1841, and the courthouse was built in December 1849. The county was named for Silas Wright, a leading New York politician; and the guiding spirit of the life of Bart Baynes, the hero of *The Light in the Clearing.**

The first vote of the county was taken in 1844, the total number of ballots being 583; 97 for Henry Clay and 486 for James K. Polk.

The first church was organized in 1842 and the first school in 1848. The first road through the county was the old trail from Union to the Fulbright settlement, and the pioneer newspaper was *The Southwest News* established at Hartville in 1869.

There are many amusing stories told of Wright County's earlier law courts, one being of a certain judge who adjourned without observing the proper formalities and, when one of the lawyers protested, exclaiming, "You can't do that! You can't do that!" the judge replied. "Well, by —— I have done it!"

This is the spirit in which many things have been done in Wright County, until what seemed impossible of accomplishment has become a commonplace.

We were told that motor cars could never be used in our hills; now nearly every farmer owns and runs one.

We were told that we never could have good roads, but there are now fifty-three miles of state roads in good condition and more building. The very best of materials for permanent roads lie all along the highways and are being used in the construction of these roads.

We have no large city within our boundaries, but our towns are good trad-

*A novel by Irving Bacheller, published in 1917 by Bobbs Merrill of Indianapolis, Indiana.

ing points and are developing on a sound basis with the country around them.

Hartville, the county seat, is an inland town on the beautiful Gasconade River. It is an old town with a history that includes several battles of the Civil War. The fine courthouse and tree-shaded courthouse square give the town its distinctive character.

Mountain Grove, Mansfield, Norwood, Cedar Gap, and Macomb are railroad shipping points.

Mansfield is the heaviest shipping point, save one, for cream between Springfield and Memphis, shipping in the last three months 2,812 cans of cream. Other farm products are shipped in proportion.

In three months there were shipped from Mountain Grove 68 cars of eggs, valued at $275,000; 14 cars of poultry, $48,000; 45 cars of lumber, $60,000; 47 cars of ties, $13,000; 26 cars of hogs, cattle, and mules, $30,000; 1 car of apples, $6,000; 1 car of butter, $8,000; making a total of $404,600.

There are several farmers exchanges in the county, and the one at Mountain Grove did a business last year of $182,640, paying dividends and interest back to the farmers of more than $11,000. For the first half of this year, they have returned $5,400 to the 400 members.

The soil of Wright County is a deep gravelly, clay loam, with a red clay sub-soil, having an admixture of gravel which makes it porous and gives good drainage for plant roots.

On the lowlands along the Gasconade River—and its branches, Beaver, Elk, Whetstone, and Clark's Creek—are many fine bottom farms, while, on the up-lands, cattle are grazing on a thousand hills rich in many kinds of grasses.

Conditions in the whole country are ideal for the raising of poultry and fruit.

Land of the Big Red Apple

Wright County is in the heart of the "Land of the Big Red Apple" and, be-sides apples, grows peaches, pears, plums, cherries, persimmons, grapes, strawberries, huckleberries, dewberries, and currants. We have fruit the year around, for apples keep well in the cellar until strawberries are plentiful, and then there is a great variety as well as an unbroken succession of fresh fruit.

. . . .

One particularly attractive thing about our county is that while so much has been done and though, by date of settlement, it is an old county, still, it is practically a new country; for its resources and possibilities have only been touched. There is still plenty of opportunity for young and old on the land and in the openings for factories and manufacturing plants to care for our products and furnish us the things we need.

There are several wholesale houses and a few manufactures in our towns, and at Cedar Gap are the Erb Fruit Farms, with their own packing house, cold storage, and vinegar plant. These and our canning factories, busily canning and shipping tomatoes and fruits, show what can be done along these lines and point the way to larger things.

The growing of tomatoes and grapes is on the increase, the conditions of soil and climate being particularly favorable for them and also for the growing of sorghums—our sorghum molasses having an especially fine flavor.

And besides all these things, Wright County has valuable mines of lead, zinc, coal, and onyx, which though not fully developed, are worked at times.

With such diversity of products, so many different branches of agriculture, Wright County offers to everyone a chance to follow their own especial taste in farming—poultry, dairying, fruits, beef cattle, horses and mules, sheep, goats, hogs, grain, hay, and bees—one can make his own choice of what he will specialize in or, by raising all on the same place as is usually done, there is the finest sort of diversified farming one could wish; and each member of a family may work at the thing he likes best.

. . . .

We play as well as work in Wright County and do it with much enthusiasm, having all the materials at hand for this also.

Our diversity is not confined to our agriculture and amusements but extends to our people. From Wright County have gone many who have distinguished themselves in various ways. Among these are Cleveland Newton who was sent to Congress, where he made good, and from there went to his law office in St. Louis where he still is making good; William H. Hamby, noted writer of books, magazine stories, and photoplays; Rose Wilder Lane, writer and world traveler whose books and short stories are published in the United States and England and have been translated into foreign languages; and Carl Mays, famous pitcher for the Yankees who has been called the greatest pitcher in the world.

Not all of us can become famous, but nowhere are there better neighbors or truer friends. If misfortune, sickness, or sorrow comes to one, the neighbors rally to help with a wholehearted good fellowship that makes living worthwhile and dying easier.

If you have thoughtfully read this little story, you will know that I am proud of Wright County because of its healthful, pleasant climate and its natural features, which make possible a happy combination of work and play, and because of the spirit of its people, which is the American pioneer spirit of courage, jollity, and neighborly helpfulness.

When Is a Settler an Old Settler?
June 1916

"Why, you are an old settler," said a newcomer to us recently. "Yes," I replied proudly, "we consider ourselves natives," yet when we drove into the Ozarks twenty years ago, [1894; see *On the Way Home*] with a covered hack and a pony team, we found the "old settler" already here. In conversation with us he made the remark: "My father was an old settler here. He came up from Tennessee before the war."* Since then in working the fields we have found now and then a stone arrow or spearhead made by a settler older still.

When we came to the Ozarks, a team of fairly good horses would trade for forty acres of land. The fences were all rail fences and a great many of the houses were built of logs. The country was a queer mixture of an old and a new country. A great many of the fields had been cropped continually since the war and were so worn out that as one of the neighbors said, "You can't hardly raise an umbrella over it." Aside from these old fields, the land was covered with timber and used for range. The "old settlers" told us that the thick growth of timber was comparatively a new thing; that before the country was so thickly settled, there were only a few scattering large trees. The fires were allowed to run, and they kept down the young growth of timber. Wild grass grew rankly over all the hills and cattle pastured free.

When Mrs. Cleaver protested, I suppose in a rather frantic way, she was driven from the courthouse, with a horsewhip, by the sheriff.

It has always been a great pleasure to hear the tales of earlier days. A neighbor, Mrs. Cleaver, told us stories of her experience in war times and the days, equally as bad, which immediately followed. Her husband did not go to war, but one night a band of men came and took him away. She never knew what became of him. Then came hard days for her and her young stepson. They raised a little crop and a hog or two for their living, but whenever they had stored a little corn or meat, some of the lawless bands of raiders that infested the Ozark hills would come and take it from them. When the war ended, some of the leaders of these lawless bands continued their depredations, only

*The Civil War.

in a little different fashion. Through the machinations of one of them, Mrs. Cleaver's stepson was taken from her, by due process of law, and bound out to him until the boy should be of age, to work without wages, of course. When Mrs. Cleaver protested, I suppose in rather a frantic way, she was driven from the courthouse, with a horsewhip, by the sheriff.

Not all the old-time stories were so serious. There is the story of the green country boy who never had seen a carpeted floor. A new family moved in from the North somewhere, and this boy went to the house one day. As he started to enter the door, he saw the carpet on the floor. Standing in the door, he swung his long arms and jumped clear across the small room, landing on the hearth before the fireplace. Turning to the astonished woman of the house, he exclaimed: "Who Mam! I mighty nigh stepped on your kiverled!" (coverlet or bedspread). Our friend in telling this story always ended with: "I never could make out whether that boy was as big a fool as he pretended to be or not. He made a mighty smart businessman when he was older and made the businessmen of Kansas City and St. Louis hustle to keep up with him," which is a way the hill boys have.

One old lady, who has lived here since the war, says that when she came, the "old settlers" told her of the time when a band of Spanish adventurers came up the Mississippi River and wandered through the Ozarks. Somewhere among the hills they hid their treasure in a cave, and it never has been discovered to this day.

But how old must a settler be to be an "old settler"? Or if you prefer the famous question, "How old is Ann?"*

---

*Slang for "Who knows?"

The March of Progress
February 1911

There is a movement in the United States today, widespread and very far-reaching in its consequences. People are seeking after a freer, healthier, happier life.

A great many of these people are discouraged by the amount of capital required to buy a farm and hesitate at the thought of undertaking a new business. But there is no need to buy a large farm. A small farm will bring in a good living with less work and worry, and the business is not hard to learn.

In a settlement of small farms the social life can be much pleasanter than on large farms where the distance to the nearest neighbor is so great. Fifteen or twenty families on five-acre farms will be near enough together to have pleasant social gatherings in the evenings. The women can have their embroidery clubs, their reading clubs, and even the children can have their little parties without much trouble or loss of time. This could not be done if each family lived on a 100- or 200-acre farm. There is less hired help required on the small farm also, and this makes the work in the house lighter.

---

*Our ideal home should be made by a
man and a woman together.*

I am an advocate of the small farm, and I want to tell you how an ideal home can be made on, and a good living made from, five acres of land.

Whenever a woman's homemaking is spoken of, the man in the case is presupposed, and the woman's homemaking is expected to consist in keeping the house clean and in serving good meals on time, etc. In short, all of her homemaking should be inside the house. It takes more than the inside of the house to make a pleasant home, and women are capable of making the whole home, outside and in, if necessary. She can do so to perfection on a five-acre farm by hiring some of the outside work done.

However, our ideal home should be made by a man and a woman together. First, I want to say that a five-acre farm is large enough for the support of a family.* From $75 to $150 a month, besides a great part of the living, can be made on that size farm from poultry or fruit or a combination of poultry, fruit, and dairy.

---

*Actually, their own farm was 100 acres at this time.

This has been proved by actual experience so that the financial part of this small home is provided for.

Conditions have changed so much in the country within the last few years that we country women have no need to envy our sisters in the city. We women on the farm no longer expect to work as our grandmothers did.

With the high prices to be had for all kinds of timber and wood, we now do not have to burn wood to save the expense of fuel, but can have our oil stove, which makes the work so much cooler in the summer, so much lighter and cleaner. There need be no carrying in of wood and carrying out of ashes, with the attendant dirt, dust, and disorder.

Our cream separator saves us hours formerly spent in setting and skimming milk and washing pans, besides saving the large amount of cream that was lost in the old way.

Then there is the gasoline engine. Bless it! Besides doing the work of a hired man outside, it can be made to do the pumping of the water and the churning, turn the washing machine, and even run the sewing machine.*

On many farms, running water can be supplied in the house from springs by means of rams or air pumps, and I know of two places where water is piped into and through the house from springs farther up on the hills. This water is brought down by gravity alone, and the only expense is the piping. There are many such places in the Ozark hills of which to take advantage.

This, you see, supplies water works for the kitchen and bathroom simply for the initial cost of putting in the pipes. In one farm home I know, where there are no springs from which to pipe the water, there is a deep well and a pump just outside the kitchen door. From this, a pipe runs into a tank in the kitchen and from this tank there are two pipes. One runs into the cellar and the other underground to a tank in the barnyard, which is of course much lower than the one in the kitchen.

When water is wanted down cellar to keep the cream and butter cool, a cork is pulled from the cellar pipe by means of a little chain and, by simply pumping the pump outdoors, cold water runs into the vat in the cellar. The water already there rises and runs out at the overflow pipe through the cellar and out at the cellar drain.

When the stock at the barn need watering, the cork is pulled from the other pipe, and the water flows from the tank in the kitchen into the tank in the yard. And always the tank in the kitchen is full of fresh, cold water, because this other water all runs through it. This is a simple, inexpensive contrivance for use on a place where there is no running water.

---

*Gas fumes and the possibility of fire seemed of less concern during the era of newly developed labor-saving devices than did any problems they might solve.

It used to be that the woman on a farm was isolated and behind the times. A weekly paper was what the farmer read, and he had to go to town to get that. All this is changed. Now the rural delivery brings us our daily papers, and we keep up on the news of the world as well as or better than those who live in the city. The telephone gives us connection with the outside world at all times, and we know what is going on in our nearest town by many a pleasant chat with our friends there.

Circulating libraries, thanks to our state university, are scattered throughout the rural districts, and we are eagerly taking advantage of them.

The interurban trolly lines being built throughout our country will make it increasingly easy for us to run into town for an afternoon's shopping or any other pleasure. These trolly lines are, and more will be, operated by electricity furnished by our swift running streams; and in a few years our country homes will be lighted by this same electric power.

Yes, indeed, things have changed in the country, and we have the advantages of city life if we care to take them. Besides, we have what it is impossible for the woman in the city to have. We have a whole five acres for our backyard and all outdoors for our conservatory, filled not only with beautiful flowers, but with grand old trees as well, with running water and beautiful birds, with sunshine and fresh air and all wild, free, beautiful things.

The children, instead of playing with other children in some street or alley, can go make friends with the birds on their nests in the bushes, as my little girl used to, until the birds are so tame they will not fly at their approach. They can gather berries in the garden and nuts in the woods and grow strong and healthy, with rosy cheeks and bright eyes. This little farm home is a delightful place for friends to come for afternoon tea under the trees. There is room for a tennis court for the young people. There are skating parties in the winter; and the sewing and reading clubs of the nearby towns, as well as the neighbor women, are always anxious for an invitation to hold their meetings there.

In conclusion, I must say if there are any country women who are wasting their time envying their sisters in the city—don't do it. Such an attitude is out of date. Wake up to your opportunities. Look your place over, and if you have not kept up with the modern improvements and conveniences in your home, bring yourself up to date. Then take the time saved from bringing water from the spring, setting the milk in the old way, and churning by hand to build yourself a better social life. If you don't take a daily paper, subscribe to one. They are not expensive and are well worth the price in the brightening they will give your mind, and in the pleasant evenings you can have reading and discussing the news of the world.

Take advantage of the circulating library. Make your little farm home noted for its hospitality and the social times you have there. Keep up with the march of progress, for the time is coming when the cities will be the workshops of the world and abandoned to the workers, while real cultural, social, and intellectual life will be in the country.

My Dream House
March 1920

When the days are growing longer and the sun shines warm on the south slopes with the promise of golden hours to come, my thoughts persist in arranging building plans; for always in the springtime I want to build a house.

The desire for changing the surroundings may be inherited from our wandering forefathers, who always moved their tents to fresh hunting grounds with the coming of summer; or perhaps mankind, in common with the birds, has an instinct to build nests when the spring comes. But whatever the reason, I think most persons share with me the longing to plan and to build at this season of the year.

When flimsy, short-lived materials are used in construction, the joy of the creation is soon swallowed up in dismay at the quick process of deterioration and decay.

But of late, stronger even than my love of planning has been my dissatisfaction with the usual manner of building, for when flimsy, short-lived materials are used in construction, the joy of the creation is soon swallowed up in dismay at the quick process of deterioration and decay.

Wooden buildings need a great deal of repairing, and their demand for paint is never satisfied. A short time ago a "paint up" campaign was put out in the papers of the country to promote the preservation of farm buildings.

I would like to take part in a build-up campaign to encourage the use of building materials that would be more lasting. I would like to see our farm homes built, not for the present generation only but for our children and our children's children.

Sometimes I wonder if the home ties would not be stronger if our homes were built with more of an idea of permanency.

I have a fancy that the farm home should seem to be a product of the soil where it is reared, a permanent growth, as it were, of conditions surrounding it wherever this is possible; and nothing gives this effect more than a house built from rocks from the fields. Such a house, well built, will last for generations. Cement is another material of which lasting and beautiful buildings may be made. Even the common earth, the soil beneath our feet, can be used as building material and will last for hundreds of years. Tamped earth is one of the very oldest of building materials. In New Mexico and Arizona are walls made of it that are 4,000 years old, and it is still being used in various parts of the world.

This tamped earth is not adobe but is a mixture of either sand or clay with loam. It is used dry and must be tamped down in the forms until it rings. Treated in this way, it becomes harder with the passing years.

Because of the excessive cost of the usual building materials, the use of earth in this manner has been revived in England and is proving very successful. In various localities in our own country some experimenting would be necessary to determine the best mixture of the loam.

A house planned with loving thought and carefully built of any of these lasting materials would be a much better monument to one's memory than a costly stone in a cemetery, because it would be their embodied idea and the work of their hands, an expression of the mind and soul of the builder.

I never shall forget a drive through a beautiful residence section of a Missouri town. The gentleman who accompanied me was a stonemason and builder. House after house that we passed, he told me he had built. Stone fences with beautiful gateways were the work of his hands. Calling my attention to a fine house, he said, "I built that house twenty years ago and see how well and true it stands."

Some of the fences had been built for twenty, some for fifteen and some for ten years and were still perfect, not a stone loosened nor settled. He was very proud of his good work, as he had every reason to be. "There," said he, "are my monuments. They will last long, long after I am gone."

How to Furnish a Home
November 1917

As someone has said, "Thoughts are things," and the atmosphere of every home depends on the kind of thoughts each member of that home is thinking.

I spent an afternoon a short time ago with a friend in her new home. The house was beautiful and well-furnished with new furniture, but it seemed bare and empty to me. I wondered why this was until I remembered my experience with my new house. I could not make the living room seem homelike. I would move the chairs here and there and change the pictures on the wall, but something was lacking. Nothing seemed to change the feeling of coldness and vacancy that displeased me whenever I entered the room.

---

*If the members of a home are
ill-tempered and quarrelsome, how
quickly you feel it when you enter the
house.*

Then, as I stood in the middle of the room one day wondering what I could possibly do to improve it, it came to me that all that was needed was for someone to live in it and furnish it with the everyday, pleasant thoughts of friendship and cheerfulness and hospitality.

We all know there is a spirit in every home, a sort of composite spirit composed of the thoughts and feelings of the members of the family as a composite photograph is formed of the features of different individuals. This spirit meets us at the door as we enter the home. Sometimes it is a friendly, hospitable spirit, and sometimes it is cold and forbidding.

If the members of a home are ill-tempered and quarrelsome, how quickly you feel it when you enter the house. You may not know just what is wrong, but you wish to make your visit short. If they are kindly, generous, good-tempered people, you will have a feeling of warmth and welcome that will make you wish to stay. Sometimes you feel that you must be very prim and dignified, and at another place you feel a rollicking good humor and a readiness to laugh and be merry. Poverty or riches, old style housekeeping or modern conveniences do not affect your feelings. It is the characters and personalities of the persons who live there.

Each individual has a share in making this atmosphere of the home what it is, but the mother can mold it more to her wishes.

I read a piece of poetry several years ago that was supposed to be a man speaking of his wife, and this was the refrain of the little story:

I love my wife because she laughs,
Because she laughs and doesn't care.

I'm sure that would have been a delightful home to visit, for a good laugh overcomes more difficulties and dissipates more dark clouds than any other one thing. And this woman was the embodied spirit of cheerfulness and good temper.

Let's be cheerful! We have no more right to steal the brightness out of the day for our own family than we have to steal the purse of a stranger. Let us be as careful that our homes are furnished with pleasant and happy thoughts as we are that the rugs are the right color and texture and the furniture comfortable and beautiful!

Rocky Ridge Farm
July 1911
by [Mrs.] A. J. Wilder*

To appreciate fully the reason why we named our place Rocky Ridge Farm, it should have been seen at the time of the christening. To begin with, it was not bottom land nor by any stretch of the imagination could it have been called second bottom. It was, and is, uncompromisingly ridge land, on the very tip-top of the ridge at that, within a very few miles of the highest point in the Ozarks. And rocky—it certainly was rocky when it was named, although strangers coming to the place now say, "but why do you call it Rocky Ridge?"

I had been ordered south because those prairies had robbed me of my health, and I was glad to leave them, for they had also robbed me of nearly everything I owned.

The place looked unpromising enough when we first saw it, not only one but several ridges rolling in every direction and covered with rocks and brush and timber. Perhaps it looked worse to me because I had just left the prairies of South Dakota where the land is easily farmed. I had been ordered south because those prairies had robbed me of my health,** and I was glad to leave them, for they had also robbed me of nearly everything I owned by continual crop failures. Still, coming from such a smooth country, the place looked so rough to me that I hesitated to buy it. But wife had taken a violent fancy to this particular piece of land, saying if she could not have it, she did not want any because it could be made into such a pretty place. It needed the eye of faith, however, to see that in time it could be made very beautiful.

So we bought Rocky Ridge Farm and went to work. We had to put a mortgage on it of $200, and had very little except our bare hands with which to pay it off, improve the farm, and make our living while we did it. It speaks well for the farm, rough and rocky as it was, that my wife and myself with my broken health were able to do all this.

---

*Although by-lined simply A. J. Wilder, what existing manuscript evidence there is of Almanzo's writing strongly suggests to scholars that Laura did all of the for-publication work in her household.

**Almanzo suffered a stroke after a bout with diphtheria. He was left with a lifelong limp.

A flock of hens—by the way, there is no better place in the country for raising poultry than right here—a flock of hens and the wood we cleared from the land bought our groceries and clothing. The timber on the place also made rails to fence it and furnished the materials for a large log barn.

At the time I bought it, there were on the place four acres cleared and a small log house with a fireplace and no windows. These were practically all the improvements, and there was not grass enough growing on the whole forty acres to keep a cow. The four acres cleared had been set out to apple trees, and enough trees to set twenty acres more were in nursery rows near the house. The land on which to set them was not even cleared of the timber. Luckily, I had bought the place before any serious damage had been done to the fine timber around the building site, although the start had been made to cut it down.

It was hard work and sometimes short rations at the first, but gradually the difficulties were overcome. Land was cleared and prepared by heroic effort in time to set out all the apple trees, and in a few years the orchard came into bearing. Fields were cleared and brought to a good state of fertility. The timber around the buildings was thinned out enough so that grass would grow between the trees, and each tree would grow in good shape, which has made a beautiful park of the grounds. The rocks have been picked up and grass seed sown so that the pastures and meadows are in fine condition and support quite a little herd of cows, for grass grows remarkably well on "Rocky Ridge" when the timber is cleared away to give it a chance. This good grass and clear spring water make it an ideal dairy farm.

Sixty acres more have been bought and paid for, which, added to the original forty, makes a farm of 100 acres. There is no wasted land on the farm except a wood lot which we have decided to leave permanently for the timber. Perhaps we have not made so much money as farmers in a more level country, but neither have we been obliged to spend so much for expenses; and as the net profit is what counts at the end of the year, I am not afraid to compare the results for a term of years with farms of the same size in a more level country.

Our little Rocky Ridge Farm has supplied everything necessary for a good living and given us good interest on all the money invested every year since the first two. No year has it fallen below ten percent, and one extra good year it paid 100 percent. Besides this, it has doubled in value, and $3,000 more since it was bought.

We are not by any means through with making improvements on Rocky Ridge Farm. There are on the place five springs of running water which never fail even in the dryest season. Some of these springs are so situated that by building a dam below them, a lake of three acres, twenty feet deep in places will be near the house. Another small lake can be made in the same way in the duck pasture, and these are planned for the near future. But the first thing on the improvement program is building a cement tank as a reservoir around a spring which is higher than the buildings. Water from this tank will be piped down and supply water in the house and the barn and the poultry yards.

When I look around the farm now and see the smooth, green, rolling meadows and pastures, the good fields of corn and wheat and oats, when I see the orchard and strawberry field like huge bouquets in the spring or full of fruit later in the season, when I see the grapevines hanging full of luscious grapes, I can hardly bring back to my mind the rough, rocky, brushy, ugly place that we first called Rocky Ridge Farm. The name given it then serves to remind us of the battles we have fought and won and gives a touch of sentiment and an added value to the place.

In conclusion, I am going to quote from a little gift book which my wife sent out to a few friends last Christmas:

> *Just come and visit Rocky Ridge,*
> *Please grant us our request;*
> *We'll give you all a jolly time—*
> *Welcome the coming; speed the parting guest.*

We Revel in Water!
April 1916

There once was a farmer, so the story goes, who hauled water in barrels from a distant creek. A neighbor remonstrated with him for not digging a well and having his water supply handier. The farmer contended that he did not have time.

"But," said the neighbor, "the time you would save by not having to haul water would be more than enough to do the work."

"Yes, I know," replied the farmer, "but you see, I am so busy hauling water that I can't get time to dig the well."

There is a story of another man who also had trouble in supplying his place with water. This man hauled water for half a mile.

"Why don't you dig a well," asked a stranger, "and not haul water so far?"
"Well," said the farmer, "it's about as fur to water one way as 'tis t'other."

I do not pretend to be the original discoverer of these stories, neither do I vouch for their truthfulness, but I do know that they correctly picture the fix we were in before we moved the spring.

"I am so busy hauling water that I can't get time to dig the well."

We "packed water from the spring" for years at Rocky Ridge Farm. Now and then, when we were tired or in a special hurry, we would declare that something must be done about it. We would dig a well or build a cistern or something, the something being rather vague. At last the "something" was what we did. Like the men in the stories, we were too busy "packing water" to dig a well, and anyway it was "about as fur to water one way as t'other," so we decided to make an extra effort and move a spring. There were several never-failing springs on the farm, but none of them were right at the house. We did not wish to move the house, and besides it is very easy to move a spring, if one knows how, much easier than to move a house.

Our trouble was to decide which spring. The one from which we carried water was nearest, but it would require a ram to raise the water up to the house as the spring was in a gulch much lower than the buildings. Then, too, although it never went dry, it did run a little low during a dry spell. There were the three springs in the "Little Pasture." They ran strong enough, but they also would require a ram to lift the water. We wished our water supply to be permanent and as little trouble to us as possible when once arranged, so we looked further. Up on a hill in the pasture about 1,400 feet from the buildings, was a spring which we had been watching for a year. The flow of water was steady, not seeming to be much affected by dry weather.

We found by using a level that this spring was enough higher than the hill where the buildings were situated to give the water a fall of sixty feet. We decided to move this spring, and the Man of the Place would do it with only common labor to help.

The spring was dug down to solid rock in the shape of a well, and a basin made in this a foot deep. In this well was built a cement reservoir eight feet in diameter, the walls of which were eleven feet high, extending three feet above the surface of the ground. It holds about thirty barrels of water. A heavy cement cover in the form of an arch was placed over the top. It takes two men to lift it so that no one will look in from curiosity and leave the cover displaced.

The cement was reinforced with heavy woven wire fence to make it strong. The walls and cover are so thick and the shade of the oaks, elms, and maples surrounding it so dense that the water does not freeze in winter and is kept cool in summer. A waste pipe was laid in the cement six inches from the top of the reservoir to allow the surplus water to flow off if the reservoir should become over full. It is in the nature of a water trap as the opening is beneath the surface of the water and both ends are covered with fine screen to prevent anything from entering the pipe.

The pipe that brings the water down to the buildings is in the lower side of the reservoir about a foot from the bottom. It was laid in the cement when the wall was built so that it is firmly embedded. The end which projects into the water was fitted with a drive well point, screened to keep out foreign substances and prevent sand and gravel from washing into the pipe.

The pipe is laid two feet underground all the way to the buildings, and grass grows thickly over it for the whole distance. Because of this, the water does not become heated while passing through in warm weather, and there is no danger of its freezing and bursting the pipe in winter. The screen in the drive well point is brass, and the pipes are heavily galvanized inside and out. There is, therefore, no taste of iron or rust added to the water. We have moved the spring so that it flows into a corner of the kitchen as pure as at its source.

We have multiplied our spring as well as moved it. We revel in water! There is a hydrant in the hen house, one in the barn, one in the calf lot, one in the garden, and one at the back of the house besides the faucets in the house. The supply of water is ample, for we tried it thoroughly during a dry season. By attaching a hose to a hydrant, we can throw water over the top of the house or barn in a steady stream with the full force of a sixty-foot fall and thirty barrels of water behind, so we feel we have protection in case of fire.

A man came out from town one day, and after seeing the water works and drinking some of the water, he exclaimed, "Why, this is better than living in town!"

We have saved more than time enough to dig a well; but now we do not need to dig it, so we find that time seems to run in doubles this way as well as the other.

We are told that "There is no great loss without some small gain." Even so, I think that there is no great gain without a little loss. We do not carry water from the spring anymore, which is a very great gain, but it was sometimes pleasant to loiter by the way and that we miss a little.

My Apple Orchard
June 1912
by [Mrs.] A. J. Wilder

When I bought my farm in the fall, some years ago, there were 800 apple trees on it growing in nursery rows. Two hundred had been set out the spring before, in an old worn-out field, where the land was so poor it would not raise a stalk of corn over four feet high. This field was all the land cleared on the place; the rest of the farm was covered with oak timber.

I have always thought it must have been a good agent who persuaded the man of whom I bought the place to mortgage it for 1,000 apple trees when the ground was not even cleared on which to set them. However, he unloaded his blunder onto me, and I knew nothing about an orchard; did not even know one apple from another. I did know though that apple trees, or indeed trees of any kind, could not be expected to thrive in land too poor to raise corn fodder, so whenever I made a trip to town, I brought back a load of wood ashes from the mill or a load of manure from the livery barn and put it around those trees that were already set out in the field.

The land was so poor it would not raise a stalk of corn over four feet high.

I cleared enough land that winter on which to set out the trees from the nursery, broke it the next spring, and put in the trees after I had worked it as smooth as I could. The trees already set out were 25 feet apart in the rows and 32 feet between the rows, so I set the others the same way. I dug the holes for the trees large and deep, making the dirt fine in the bottom and mixing some wood ashes with it.

I handled the trees very carefully so as not to injure the roots and spread the roots out as nearly as possible in a natural manner when setting the trees. Fine dirt was put over the roots at first and pressed down firmly, then the dirt was shoveled in to fill the hole. Some more wood ashes were mixed with the dirt when it was being shoveled in. I did not hill the dirt up around the tree but left it a little cupping for conserving moisture. All trash was raked away, leaving it clean and smooth, and again I used some wood ashes, scattering them around the tree, but being careful that none touched it to injure the bark. The ashes were used altogether with the idea of fertilizing the soil and with no idea of any other benefit, but I think they may have saved my orchard.

It is confessing to a colossal ignorance, but I found out later that I planted woolly aphis [aphids] on nearly every one of my apple tree roots. At the time, I thought that for some reason they were a little moldy. I read afterward in an orchard paper that the lye from wood ashes would destroy the woolly aphis and save the tree; and as the use of wood ashes around the trees was kept up for several years, I give them the credit for saving my trees.

As I never allowed hunting on the farm, the quail were thick in the orchard and used to wallow and dust themselves like chickens in this fine dirt close to the tree. I wish this fact to be particularly noted in connection with the other fact that I had no borers in my trees for years.

A near neighbor set out 2,000 trees about the same time and lost seven-eighths of them because of borers. He used every possible means to rid his trees of them except the simple one of letting the quail and other birds live in his orchard. Instead, he allowed his boys to kill every bird they saw.

My apples were sound and smooth, not wormy, which I also credit to the birds for catching insects of all kinds as I never sprayed the trees. Within the last few years, the hunters, both boys and men, have been so active that it has been impossible to save my quail; and so I have had to begin the eternal round of spraying and cutting the trees to get the borers out.

When I set the trees I trimmed them back a good deal. While I knew nothing of the science of trimming I knew that I did not want a forked tree, so I trimmed to one stem with a few little branches left at the top. I watched the trees as they grew and trimmed away, while they were very small, all the branches that would interlock or rub against another branch.

In the fall I always whitewashed the trees to keep the rabbits from gnawing the bark, and if the storms washed it off, I whitewashed them again. Every spring they were whitewashed in April as a sort of house-cleaning and to make the bark smooth so it would not harbor insects, for I found that if there was a rough place, that was where the eggs of insects were deposited.

Between the trees, I raised corn, potatoes, and garden until the trees were eight years old when I seeded that land down to timothy and clover. Of course, when I raised crops, I fertilized them enough to make them grow, and the trees always got their share. As a result, I get a good hay crop out of the orchard, making two good crops from the land.

I think that one thing that has made my orchard a success is that I took individual care of each tree. What that particular tree needed it got. Wife and I were so well acquainted with the trees that if I wished to mention one to her, I would say "that tree with the large branch to the south," or "the tree that leans to the north," etc. The tree that leaned was gently taught to stand straight so that the sun would not burn the bark. This was done by tying it to a stake firmly driven into the ground on the south side of the tree and from time to time shortening the string which held it.

The trees came into bearing at seven years old, and the apples were extra well colored and smooth skinned. I have had apple buyers and nursery men tell me that my orchard was the prettiest they ever saw, and my Ben Davis are different from any I have ever seen in being better colored and flavored and in the texture of the flesh. People even refuse to believe that they are Ben Davis at times. My orchard is mostly Ben Davis, and the rest is Missouri Pippin.

If I were to start another orchard, I would plow and cultivate the land for several seasons to prepare it for the trees. The wildness and roughness should be worked out in order to give the little trees a fair chance. Then I should plant apple seed where I wanted the trees to stand, and then bud onto the sprout the variety I wished to raise. In this way the taproot would not be disturbed, as it is by moving the tree, but would run straight down. This makes a longer-lived, stronger tree.

Heirs of the Ages
November 1923

While driving one day, I passed a worn-out farm. Deep gullies were cut through the fields where the dirt had been washed away by the rains. The creek had been allowed to change its course in the bottom of the field and had cut out a new channel, ruining the good land in its way. Tall weeds and brambles were taking more strength from the soil already so poor that grass would scarcely grow.

---

*We inherit the earth, the great round
world which is God's footstool.*

A Stranger's Opinion

With me as I viewed the place was a friend from Switzerland, and as he looked over the neglected farm, he exclaimed, "Oh, it is a crime! It is a crime to treat good land like that!"

The more I think about it, the more sure I am that he used the exact word to suit the case. It is a crime to wear out and ruin a farm, and the farmer who does so is a thief stealing from posterity.

We are the heirs of the ages; but the estate is entailed, as large estates frequently are, so that while we inherit the earth, the great round world which is God's footstool, we have only the use of it while we live and must pass it on to those who come after us. We hold the property in trust and have no right to injure it or to lessen its value. To do so is dishonest, stealing from our heirs their inheritance.

The world is the beautiful estate of the human family passing down from generation to generation, marked by each holder while in his possession according to his character.

Did you ever think how a bit of land shows the character of the owner? A dishonest greed is shown by robbing the soil; the traits of a spendthrift are shown in wasting the resources of the farm by destroying its woods and waters, while carelessness and laziness are plainly to be seen in deep scars on the hillsides and washes in the lower fields.

It should be a matter of pride to keep our own farm, that little bit of the earth's surface for which we are responsible, in good condition, passing it on to our successor better than we found it. Trees should be growing where otherwise would be waste places, with the waters protected as much as possible from the hot sun and drying winds, with fields free from gullies and the soil fertile.

CHAPTER 2

Nothing new under the sun

Sweet Williams
July 1917

The Man of the Place brought me a bouquet of wildflowers this morning. It has been a habit of his for years. He never brings me cultivated flowers but always the wild blossoms of field and woodland, and I think them much more beautiful.

In my bouquet this morning was a purple flag. Do you remember gathering them down on the flats and in the creek bottoms when you were a barefoot child? There was one marshy corner of the pasture down by the creek where the grass grew lush and green; where the cows loved to feed and could always be found when it was time to drive them up at night.

We heap up around us things that we do not need as the crow makes piles of glittering pebbles.

All through the tall grass were scattered purple and white flag blossoms, and I have stood in that peaceful grassland corner, with the red cow and the spotted cow and the roan, taking their good-night mouthfuls of the sweet grass, and watched the sun setting behind the hilltops and loved the purple flags and the rippling brook and wondered at the beauty of the world while I wriggled my bare toes down into the soft grass.

The wild sweet Williams in my bouquet brought a far different picture to my mind. A window had been broken in the schoolhouse at the country crossroads, and the pieces of glass lay scattered where they had fallen. Several little girls going to school for their first term had picked handfuls of sweet Williams and were gathered near the window. Someone discovered that the blossoms could be pulled from the stem and, by wetting their faces, could be stuck to the pieces of glass in whatever fashion they were arranged. They dried on the glass and would stay that way for hours and, looked at through the glass, were very pretty.

I was one of those little girls, and though I have forgotten what it was I tried to learn out of the book that summer, I never have forgotten the beautiful wreaths and stars and other figures we made on the glass with the sweet Williams. The delicate fragrance of their blossoms this morning made me feel like a little girl again.

The little white daisies with their hearts of gold grew thickly along the path where we walked to Sunday school. Father and sister and I used to walk the two and a half miles every Sunday morning. The horses had worked hard all the week and must rest this one day, and Mother would rather stay at home with baby brother,* so with Father and sister Mary I walked to the church through the beauties of the sunny spring Sundays.

I have forgotten what I was taught on those days also. I was only a little girl, you know. But I can still plainly see the grass and the trees and the path winding ahead, flecked with sunshine and shadow and the beautiful golden-hearted daisies scattered all along the way.

Ah well! That was years ago, and there have been so many changes since then that it would seem such simple things should be forgotten; but at the long last, I am beginning to learn that it is the sweet, simple things of life which are the real ones after all.

We heap up around us things that we do not need as the crow makes piles of glittering pebbles. We gabble words like parrots until we lose the sense of their meaning; we chase after this new idea and that; we take an old thought and dress it out in so many words that the thought itself is lost in its clothing, like a slim woman in a barrel skirt, and then we exclaim, "Lo, the wonderful new thought I have found!"

"There is nothing new under the sun," says the proverb. I think the meaning is that there are just so many truths or laws of life, and no matter how far we may think we have advanced, we cannot get beyond those laws. However complex a structure we build of living, we must come back to those truths, and so we find we have traveled in a circle.

. . . .

I believe we would be happier to have a personal revolution in our individual lives and go back to simpler living and more direct thinking. It is the simple things of life that make living worthwhile, the sweet fundamental things such as love and duty, work and rest, and living close to nature. There are no hot-house blossoms that can compare in beauty and fragrance with my bouquet of wildflowers.

*Charles Frederick Ingalls, born November 1, 1875, died August 27, 1876.

The Findleys Strive for an Education
August 1922

"We are putting what we earn into our children's minds, instead of into houses and clothes," said little Mrs. Findley as she smoothed the hair of small Ben, who leaned against her knee. "We think it a better investment.

"Oh yes, my husband agrees with me! He didn't at first. He said we couldn't educate the children because we were poor, but now he is as ambitious for them as I am."

"Tell me about it," I said, and this is the story she told me as we sat on the shady porch one pleasant afternoon.

"When I was a child we lived back in the woods, and father was poor. My own mother was dead, and while my stepmother did the best she could for me, there were smaller children to take care of and always so much to do. Father wanted me to go to school, but when I was needed at home to help, he could never see any other way but that I must stay and work. Then, too, he hadn't money to buy my school books.

"When I was twelve years old, my brother and I chopped a load of wood, hauled it to town, and sold it for money to buy a grammar and history."

It Was an Uphill Pull

"When I was twelve years old, my brother and I chopped a load of wood, hauled it to town, and sold it for money to buy a grammar and history. We hacked the wood up some, but we got it into sticks and we got the books.

"It was that way when I needed the first book for my children, Glen and Joette; there was no money to buy the book, so I took in a washing and got the money. I've always been ashamed of that work. It was not well done, because I was in such poor health that I had to hold myself up by the tub while I scrubbed; but that book just had to come and it came.

"You see, after I married, we lived in Joplin and my husband worked in the mines. Jess had been earning $4.50 a day, but it took it all to live; so when we came back to the hills, we had only our bare hands.

"Well, I started the children to work in their new book, and every day we had lessons. I taught them first a word, then the letters in it; and they had them ready for use in another word. When they learned a name, I showed

---

them the object; when they learned an action word, we acted it. For instance, when they read the word 'jump,' we jumped; and how they did enjoy saying their lessons to daddy in the evening, especially when he'd let them beat him.

Starting the Children at Home

"When Glen was seven years old and Joette six, I started them to school ready for the fourth grade work. The superintendent could not think it possible and insisted that they begin in the third grade; but after only one day there, they were promoted to the fourth.

"The first year they went to school only two months, then finished their grades at home. The next year they went two months and finished at home. The following year they went four months and were obliged to stop because of sickness, but again they finished the grades at home. Since then they have gone regularly, and at thirteen and fourteen years old have finished the first year in high school and the fifth set in bookkeeping.

"Violet and Ben have had the same training at home that the older children had and now, at six and eight years old, are ready to start to school in the fourth grade.

"Violet has been more difficult to teach than the others, because she likes to sew and play with her dolls better than to study. People said she was stupid and that I never would be able to push her as I had the others; but she was only different and just as smart, if not smarter. She just would not keep her mind on her books until she found she must and would be punished if she didn't. I know what her talent is, but she has to have her books, too; and she will sew all the better for having 'book learning.'

"Besides, I had made up my mind that through my children I would raise the standard of the family. It couldn't be bettered morally, but it could be raised educationally; and so Violet, as well as the rest, must study her books. I knew her well and gave her special attention so she is going right along with the others.

> *"I believe it would be much better for everyone if children were given their start in education at home."*

"I believe it would be much better for everyone if children were given their start in education at home. No one understands a child as well as his mother, and children are so different that they need individual training and study. A teacher with a roomful of pupils cannot do this. At home, too, they are in their mother's care. She can keep them from learning immoral things from other children. At home the expense is much less, for in school there are a great many expenses that are difficult for poor people to meet.

· ·

"The children are well started in getting their education. None of the family has ever graduated from high school, but my children will, and some of them will go to college too.

"Jess says I aim too high, but I tell him I'll shoot straight; for when a thing has to be done, it's done. And if people say the Jess Findley family were poor, they'll say, too, that the children were well educated; for that is where we are putting our life's work—into their heads.

"We are doing something worthwhile, for in raising the standard of our children's lives we are raising the standard of four homes of the future, and our work goes on and on, raising the standard of the community and of future generations."

When Mrs. Findley had finished her story, I mentally took note of one thought which has escaped so many of us. It was not the old story of an education always being within the grasp of those who really seek it; but that in raising the standard of the Findley home, the standard of four homes of the future had been elevated to the point which we like to think of as a representative "American Home." Here, mother love had combined with the vision of future usefulness in the country's citizenship, resulting in the finest service to which any parent can aspire.

"A Spirit of Sadness Over It All"
September 1919

We all, at times, have had the longing that Robert Burns so well expressed when he said, "Oh, wad some power the giftie gie us, to see oursel's as ithers see us." And lately I have had a glimpse of how we, as a class, appear to strangers, not merely strangers so far as acquaintance goes, but strangers to our life and customs.

Friends from Switzerland, motoring through from San Francisco to New York, broke the journey by a visit to Rocky Ridge Farm. Their account of the trip was very interesting, but a part of it has given me a picture of farm folks which is not at all pleasant to look upon.

> *"You all seem to take your pleasures so sadly. You appear to be quite happy and contented, but very sad."*

"So many farm people from adjoining states were camping at Colorado Springs," said Mme. Marquis. "And they brought so much of their work with them that I do not see how the vacation could do them any good. They brought such quantities of luggage, everything from their washboards and tubs to their talking machines. The women did the washing on those glorious mornings, rubbing away on the wrinkle-boards, and they spent the most of the time left sitting around in camp talking to one another. I heard one woman say, 'No, I haven't been up on Pike's Peak. It costs $2 to go up, and that's too much money.' And so, having come all the way to the foot of the Peak, they missed the climax of the whole trip, because it would cost a couple of dollars more.

"It seemed to me that they had worked hard all their lives, and at last they had reached the point where they were able to leave all their cares behind them, to get into their own motor cars and take a trip for pleasure and adventure. And then, at the last moment, they let their lifelong habits of pinching the pennies spoil it all. And, oh! Those farm women looked so worn and tired."

✳✳

The Man of the Place and I once went on a picnic fishing trip with a family who were friends of ours. And listening to Mme. Marquis tell of these women on their camping trip to Colorado Springs brought back to me the feeling of disillusion and utter weariness I experienced then.

I had expected relaxation and rest; but instead there was the cooking, the care of the children, the washing of many dishes and the making of beds, all to be done in the most difficult manner possible. If we had stayed long enough so that I had been obliged to do a washing I believe I would have wished to feed myself to the fishes. Once was enough. It was never again for me.

M. and Mme. Marquis were making the journey across the United States in a car for the sake of becoming acquainted with the people at home, and we took them with us to camp-meeting and to an all-day singing, to picnics and on short trips here and there.

"What do you think of us?" I asked M. Marquis. "How do we impress you?"

"Well, if I can explain," he answered with his delightful accent. "You are a very nice people. I have studied the faces in the crowd, and they are good faces, fine and beautiful, some of them. But you all seem to take your pleasures so sadly. You appear to be quite happy and contented, but very sad. There seems to be a spirit of sadness over it all. Do you not feel it?"

I was obliged to admit that I did, even within myself. Do we always carry our work and our sorrows with us, I wonder, as we did on the fishing party, and as the tired farm women did at Colorado Springs? Is it the constant, unrelieved carrying-about of our burdens that has caused our lives to be permeated with sadness so that it is felt by a sensitive person seeing us for the first time?

Another thing was revealed to us about ourselves during the visit of these strangers. That is that we have grown careless in our manners. They had time always for an exquisite courtesy, being never too tired or hurried to show their appreciation of a favor or to do a kindness when the chance came. Their courtesy never failed, even when the machine broke down on rough roads, or in the rush of farm work in which they eagerly took a part.

"We are all so careless about those things," said the Man of the Place to me. "I think we ought to try to do better."

"Yes," I replied. "Let's take time to be at least as nice as we know how to be. And after this, when I go on a vacation, I am going to leave my 'wrinkle-board' behind."

After all, a vacation is not a matter of place or time. We can take a wonderful vacation in spirit, even though we are obliged to stay at home, if we will only drop our burdens from our minds for a while. But no amount of travel will give us rest and recreation if we carry our work and worries with us.

Classed As Illiterates
May 1919

Among all the beautiful sights and sounds of spring, there is an ugly blot on the landscape here and there, a sight that is unpleasantly out of harmony and shows as little promise for the future as a blighted fruit tree. It is the presence of children at work in the fields when they should be in school.

. . . .

All the instruction in the farm papers, the wealth of knowledge, of new ideas and methods, of mutual help and the getting together spirit that all good farm papers are working to spread, does not reach the farmers who cannot read an article in a paper and understand it.

> *All the instruction in the farm papers . . . does not reach the farmers who cannot read.*

Besides the loss of all this, they are at the mercy of any unfounded report that may be circulated. As for instance, in regard to the League of Nations, which is now so much discussed, there is a report circulating in the back places to the effect that if the United States enters the League, we shall become subject to a foreign king. And it is believed literally by farmers who cannot read understandingly. Still, they would not be classed as illiterate, and there are no statistics from which we may learn how many such there are.

But below them is the ignorant mass of the rural population who have not attended school for even the two years necessary to pass the literacy test and who are classed as illiterate by the Federal Bureau of Education, which has compiled the statistics from the facts gathered. These illiterate persons amount to 10 percent of the rural population.*

Of the 37 million country people, 2,700,000 cannot read a farm paper nor an agricultural bulletin and must learn the news as well as trade market condi-

---

*There are "lies, damned lies, and statistics." The 1990 *World Almanac and Book of Facts* lists U.S. literacy at 99 percent; the *Information Please Almanac* lists literacy at 96 percent. In 1983 the U.S. Department of Education listed 23 million Americans as totally illiterate, about 10 percent of the population and forty-ninth in rank among one hundred and fifty-eight member nations of the United Nations in its literacy levels (see Jonathan Kozol, *Illiterate American*).

tions from some rumor, perhaps deliberately untrue, perhaps only a mistake through much passing from one to another.

"We shall have to spend great sums of money in improving our school systems! We shall have to undertake a nationwide propaganda for the betterment of school buildings, for the replacement of unsanitary shacks with modern structures, for the adequate compensation of competent teachers," says one editor writing on this subject. But of what use will all this be to the farmer boy who, in schooltime, is driving old Bill and Kate, with the heavy lines around his shoulders while with his hands he guides the plow, making the long furrows around and around the field which, later, he will help to plant to corn?

Will it mean that he must begin his work earlier in the morning and keep at it later in the evening to help his father earn the added taxes to pay for these improvements that more fortunate children may have the advantage of them?

"Pap needed me to help him," said one such boy now a grown man. "Pap needed me to help him. I know, and it's all right; but it's no use for me to take a farm paper, for I can't read it so I can understand it."

Our Next President
April 1920

Politics looks "mighty curious" as the time draws near for women all over the country to take part in it for the first time.

Do you suppose that our ideas of housekeeping have been all wrong, and we should have learned the milliner's trade in order to be a good cook and taught school in order that we may do the family washing properly? This seems to be the manner in which candidates for the managership of the biggest business in the world are being chosen.

Our next president, who will be our business manager for four years, should be chosen for his fitness for the place as though we were hiring him to attend to our own private business.

The biggest business in the world? Why that's the United States of America! The expenses of the business run into billions of dollars a year.

The income is furnished by you and me and others like us in many ways: by the taxes we pay directly, and goodness knows, they are coming high these days; by the tax on toilet articles; by the tax on legal papers; by duties on imports, which we pay in higher prices of the goods we buy; by an income tax if we are fortunate enough to have so much income. And all that not being enough, there is a bill now before Congress to put an excess profits tax on farm lands.

Besides the managing of these huge amounts of income and expense, there is a vast volume of trade at home and with foreign countries that must be looked after and regulated in such a way as to be fair to us all or as near as may be to that desired state.

Surely a man should be chosen as manager of such a business for his business ability, his qualities as an executive, his broad, comprehensive knowledge of world conditions and people, as well as of the home problems of our own country; for in our buying and selling, even of our eggs and butterfat, in our taxes and our wars, our peace and our prosperity, even our health and our lives, we are closely united with the rest of the world, for better or worse, until death parts us.

Our next president, who will be our business manager for four years, should be chosen for his fitness for the place as though we were hiring him to attend to our own private business; for a lack of knowledge or disposition on his part will be felt in our homes, from the front door to the kitchen. It will make a difference in the amount of our egg money and the prices of our new dresses.

In our own affairs we do not hire a person to take charge of an important work who has been carefully trained for something altogether different.

Our Brains—and Providence
May 1924

The Man of the Place was worried about the weather. He said the indications were for a dry season, and ever since I have been remembering droughts. There were dry years in the Dakotas when we were beginning our life together.* How heartbreaking it was to watch the grain we had sown with such high hopes wither and turn yellow in the hot winds! And it was backbreaking as well as heartbreaking to carry water from the well to my garden and see it dry up despite all my efforts.

I said at that time that thereafter I would sow the seed, but the Lord would give the increase if there was any, for I could not do my work and that of Providence also by sending the rain on the gardens of the just or the unjust.

---

*I would sow the seed, but the Lord
would give the increase
if there was any.*

But still I suppose our brains were given us to use by the same Providence that created the laws of nature, and what we accomplish by the use of them is, in a certain sense, Its work. Just as all good is for us if we but reach out our hand to take it, so in the higher atmosphere around our earth there is a great supply of moisture. It is there for our use if, with the brains which God has given us, we can find a way to tap it. This is what a California man claims to have done.

Hatfield, the rainmaker, lives in Glendale, California, near Los Angeles. He claims to be able to make rain by projecting into the atmosphere, from a high scaffolding, certain chemicals that attract and precipitate moisture. There are always storms in movement, and storm formations pass high over a country without ever condensing and causing rain. The way he operates, he'll make that storm give up its water as it comes along.

In 1915 there was a very severe drought in Southern California, especially in San Diego County where the water situation became critical. As a last resort, the San Diego Chamber of Commerce decided to try out this man Hatfield. A contract was made by which he was to receive $10,000 if he brought down water enough to fill the great irrigation reservoir. Shortly after he began

---

*See *The First Four Years*, published by Harper & Row, New York.

operations, the rain began to fall in such quantities that the reservoir not only filled but burst its dam, and the Chamber of Commerce, instead of paying him $10,000, brought suit against him for damages in destroying the dam.

. . . .

Home
August 1923

Out in the meadow, I picked a wild sunflower, and as I looked into its golden heart, such a wave of homesickness came over me that I almost wept. I wanted Mother, with her gentle voice and quiet firmness; I longed to hear Father's jolly songs and to see his twinkling blue eyes; I was lonesome for the sister with whom I used to play in the meadow picking daisies and wild sunflowers.

> *I wanted Mother, with her gentle voice*
> *and quiet firmness; I longed to hear*
> *Father's jolly songs and to see his*
> *twinkling blue eyes.*

Across the years, the old home and its love called to me, and memories of sweet words of counsel came flooding back. I realize that all my life the teachings of those early days have influenced me, and the example set by Father and Mother has been something I have tried to follow, with failures here and there, with rebellion at times; but always coming back to it as the compass needle to the star.

So much depends upon the homemakers. I sometimes wonder if they are so busy now with other things that they are forgetting the importance of this special work. Especially did I wonder when reading recently that there were a great many child suicides in the United States during the last year. Not long ago we had never heard of such a thing in our own country, and I am sure that there must be something wrong with the home of a child who commits suicide.

Because of their importance, we must not neglect our homes in the rapid changes of the present day. For when tests of character come in later years, strength to the good will not come from the modern improvements or amusements few may have enjoyed but from the quiet moments and the "still small voices" of the old home.

Nothing ever can take the place of this early home influence; and as it does not depend upon externals, it may be the possession of the poor as well as of the rich, a heritage from all fathers and mothers to their children.

The real things of life that are the common possession of us all are of the greatest value—worth far more than motor cars or radios, more than lands or money—and our whole store of these wonderful riches may be revealed to us by such a common, beautiful thing as a wild sunflower.

The Man of the Place
January 1920

The Man of the Place and I were sitting cozily by the fire. The evening lamp was lighted and the day's papers and the late magazines were scattered over the table. But though we each held in our hands our favorite publications, we were not reading. We were grumbling about the work we had to do and saying all the things usually said at such times.

"People used to have time to live and enjoy themselves, but there is no time anymore for anything but work, work, work."

"People used to have time to live and enjoy themselves, but there is no time anymore for anything but work, work, work."

Oh, we threshed it all over as everyone does when they get that kind of grouch, and then we sat in silence. I was wishing I had lived altogether in those good old days when people had time for things they wanted to do.

What the Man of the Place was thinking, I do not know; but I was quite surprised at the point at which he had arrived, when he remarked out of the silence, in rather a meek voice, "I never realized how much work my father did. Why, one winter he sorted 500 bushels of potatoes after supper by lantern light. He sold them for $1.50 a bushel in the spring, too, but he must have got blamed tired of sorting potatoes down cellar every night until he had handled more than 500 bushel of them."

"What did your mother do while your father was sorting potatoes?" I asked.

"Oh, she sewed and knit," said the Man of the Place. She made all our clothes, coats and pants, undergarments for Father and us boys as well as everything she and the girls wore, and she knit all our socks and mittens— shag mittens for the men folks, do you remember, all fuzzy on the outside? She didn't have time enough in the day to do all the work and so she sewed and knit at night."

I looked down at the magazine in my hand and remembered how my mother was always sewing or knitting by the evening lamp. I realized that I never had done so except now and then in cases of emergency.

But the Man of the Place was still talking. "Mother did all her sewing by hand then," he said, "and she spun her own yarn and wove her own cloth. Father harvested his grain by hand with a sickle and cut his hay with a scythe. I do wonder how he ever got it done."

Again we were silent, each busy with our own thoughts. I was counting up the time I give to club work and lodge work and—yes, I'll admit it—politics. My mother and my mother-in-law had none of these, and they do use up a good many hours. Instead of all this, they took time once in a while from their day and night working to go visit a neighbor for the day.

"Time to enjoy life!" Well, they did enjoy it, but it couldn't have been because they had more time.

Why should we need extra time in which to enjoy ourselves? If we expect to enjoy our life, we will have to learn to be joyful in all of it, not just at stated intervals when we can get time or when we have nothing else to do.

It may well be that it is not our work that is so hard for us as the dread of it and our often expressed hatred of it. Perhaps it is our spirit and attitude toward life, and its conditions that are giving us trouble instead of a shortage of time. Surely the days and nights are as long as they ever were.

A feeling of pleasure in a task seems to shorten it wonderfully, and it makes a great difference with the day's work if we get enjoyment from it instead of looking for all our pleasure altogether apart from it, as seems to be the habit of mind we are more and more growing into.

We find in the goods we buy, from farm implements to clothing, that the work of making them is carelessly and slightingly done. Many carpenters, blacksmiths, shoemakers, garment makers and farm hands do not care how their work is done just so quitting time and the paycheck comes. Farmers are no different except that they must give more attention to how a thing is done because it is the result only that brings them any return.

It seems that many workmen take no pride or pleasure in their work. It is perhaps partly a result of machine-made goods, but it would be much better for us all if we could be more interested in the work of our hands, if we could get back more of the attitude of our mothers toward their handmade garments and of our fathers' pride in their own workmanship.

There is an old maxim which I have not heard for years nor thought of in a long time. "To sweep a room as to God's laws, makes that, and the action fine." We need more of that spirit toward our work.

As I thought of my neighbors and myself, it seemed to me that we were all slighting our work to get time for a joyride of one kind or another.

Not that I object to joyriding! The more the merrier, but I'm hoping for a change of mind that will carry the joy into the work as well as the play.

"All work and no play makes Jack a dull boy," surely, and it makes Jill also very dull indeed; but all play and no work would make hoboes of us. So let's enjoy the work we must do to be respectable.

The Man of the Place had evidently kept right on thinking of the work his father used to do. "Oh, well," he said as he rose and lighted the lantern preparatory to making his late round to see that everything was all right at the barns, "I guess we're not having such a hard time after all. It depends a good deal on how you look at it."

"Yes," said I, "Oh yes, indeed! It depends a good deal on how you look at it."

Kind Hearts
March 1922

Officially, winter is over and spring is here. For most of us, it has been a hard winter despite the fact that the weather has been pleasant the greater part of the time. There are things other than zero weather and heavy snow falls that make hard winters.

*I often have thought that we are a little
old-fashioned here in the Ozark hills;
now I know we are.*

But we know all about those things, and so I'll tell you of something else—something as warming to the heart as a good fire on the hearth is to a chilled body on a cold day.

I often have thought that we are a little old-fashioned here in the Ozark hills; now I know we are, because we had a "working" in our neighborhood this winter. That is a blessed, old-fashioned way of helping out a neighbor.

While the winter was warm, still it has been much too cold to be without firewood; and this neighbor, badly crippled with rheumatism, was not able to get up his winter's wood. With what little wood he could manage to chop, the family scarcely kept comfortable.

So the men of the neighborhood gathered together one morning and dropped in on him. With cross-cut saws and axes, they took possession of his wood lot. At noon a wood saw was brought in, and it sawed briskly all the afternoon. By night there was enough wood ready for the stove to last the rest of the winter.

The women did their part, too. All morning they kept arriving with well-filled baskets, and at noon a long table was filled with a country neighborhood dinner.

After the hungry men had eaten and gone back to work, the women and children gathered at the second table, fully as well supplied as the first, and chatted pleasant neighborhood gossip while they leisurely enjoyed the good things. Then when the dishes were washed, they sewed, knit, crocheted and talked for the rest of the afternoon.

It was a regular old-fashioned good time, and we all went home with the feeling expressed by a newcomer when he said, "Don't you know I'm proud to live in a neighborhood like this where they turn out and help one another when it's needed."

"Sweet are the uses of adversity" when it shows us the kindness in our neighbors' hearts.

The Wanton Destruction of Trees
October 1919

The American Forestry Association has sent out a plea to make a great national road of memory of the Lincoln Highway* by planting trees in memory of our national heroes all along its 3,000 miles.

Besides using our native trees, it is planned to bring over and plant Lombardy Poplars from France, chestnut and oak from England, and cherry and plum from Japan.

This plan for making a living memorial to American heroes has been endorsed by councils of Daughters of the Confederacy; and the Department of the Interior and the Forestry Department are aiding in the work.

Such a great, national, tree-bordered highway might help us to realize the unnecessary ugliness of most of our country roads.

For sentimental reasons alone such a memorial would be most wonderful, for while in life our heroes stood between us and danger, their memory would in this way still hover over us and give us comfort and pleasure, linked ever more closely to us by our loving thought in the planting and care of the living, breathing monument, which will reach across our common country from coast to coast.

As an example, such a great national tree-bordered highway might help us to realize the unnecessary ugliness of most of our country roads, and perhaps in time, they also may be tree-embowered and beautiful.

Motoring on the Ozark highway the other day, I passed over a long stretch of the road where the large, beautiful native oak and walnut trees had been cleared away from beside it, leaving the roadway unshaded, bare, and ugly. A little farther on, I came to a place where the farmers on each side had set out young walnut trees in even spaces along the road in an attempt to put back the beauty and usefulness which had been destroyed by cutting down the forest trees.

It seems such a pity that we can learn to value what we have only through the loss of it. Truly "we never miss the water 'till the well runs dry.'"

People painstakingly raised shade trees on the bare prairies; but where we already had the shade and beauty of the forest we have carelessly failed to pre-

---

*In 1925 it became U.S. Highway 30.

serve it, and now in many places must carefully rebuild what we have destroyed, taking years to replace what was removed in only a few days.

While a drive along a shady roadway is much more pleasant than one on a hot and dusty road, still pleasure and beauty are not all that are to be considered. There is also a utility side to the idea of trees along the way, for they help to keep the roadbed in good condition by retaining moisture and preventing washing away of the soil.

In many parts of Europe the fruit and nut trees along the roads bring enough of an income to keep up the roads so that the people pay no road tax. Rather staggering, that idea of self-supporting roads to a people who spend so much for poor roads as we do. Another curious little fact in regard to trees in Europe is that anyone in Switzerland who cuts down a forest tree must plant another to take its place.

Of course, in the clearing of our great new country, we could not do that; but we have destroyed trees when it was not necessary, seemingly through a spirit of wantonness, and so we have a double task before us: to plant trees where they did not grow and to replant in some places where they have been cut down. The work has been well started in some prairie states. Six thousand trees have been set out by the United States balloon school at Ft. Omaha.

. . . .

People of wooded districts can save themselves much trouble and expense later by preserving the trees along the roadways, for I am sure the Lincoln Highway will set the fashion which all our country's roads will follow in time.

Be True to Yourself
July 1923

At a gathering of women the other day, a subject came up for discussion on which I knew the opinions held by several present, as they had expressed them to me privately.

It happened that a woman who held the opposite opinion to theirs led off in the talk and a number followed her lead; then these women who differed fell in with what they thought was the popular side and by a few words let it be understood that they were in accord with the opinion stated, and so what might have been an interesting and profitable discussion became merely a tiresome reiteration of the same idea.

I knew those women had been false to themselves, but I was not surprised, for I have been observing along that line recently.

I knew those women had been false to themselves, but I was not surprised, for I have been observing along that line recently and have seen so much of the same thing. As people are pretty much the same everywhere, I do not think that this spirit is shown in one community alone.

For fear of giving offense, many persons agree to anything that is proposed when they have no intention of doing it and will find an excuse later. They join in with what they think is popular opinion until it is almost impossible to tell where anyone stands on any subject or to do anything, because one cannot tell upon whom to depend. This disposition is found everywhere, from social affairs to the man who agrees to come and work.

Have you not found it so? Of course, it is easier, for a time, to go with the current; but how much more can be accomplished if we would all be honest in our talk. And how much wasted effort would be saved! We all despise a coward, but we sometimes forget that there is a moral as well as a physical cowardice, and that it is just as contemptible.

I am sure that moral cowardice is responsible for a great deal of the trouble and confusion in the world. It gives unprincipled persons an opportunity to "put things over" that they would not have if others had the courage of their convictions. Besides, it is weakness to one's personality and moral fiber to deny one's opinions or falsify one's self, while it throws broadcast into the world just that much more cowardice and untruth.

We all know who is the father of lies, and a lie can be acted as well as spoken, while an untruth is often expressed by silence. It is not necessary to be unpleasant if we disagree; an opinion supported by a good reason, kindly stated, should not offend, neither should a pleasant refusal to join in anything proposed. We may be friendly and courteous and still hold frankly to our honest convictions. But—

> *This above all, to thine own self be true*
> *And it will follow as the night the day,*
> *Thou canst not then be false to any man.* *

---

*From *Hamlet,* I, iii, by William Shakespeare.

Love of Home
April 1923

Just how much does home mean to you? Of what do you think when it is mentioned? Is it only the four walls and the roof within the shelter of which you eat and sleep or does it include the locality also—the shade trees around the house, the forest trees in the wood lot, the little brook that wanders through the pasture where the grass grows lush and green in spring and summer, the hills and valleys, and the level fields of the farm lands over which the sun rises to greet you in the early morning and sets in glorious waves of color as you go about your evening tasks?

Where the home is eliminated an important part of our social structure is missing.

When I think of home, the picture includes all these things and even the farm animals that are our daily care, our vexation, and our pride, and so I know I can never be a "Tin Can Tourist"; for a shelter on wheels moving from place to place cannot furnish all I require of a home.

But if home to you is only a shelter, then you might be happy with this modern Gipsy band. According to *World Traveler* magazine, the "Tin Can Tourists of the World" was organized in 1917 at Tampa, Florida, of a few tourists who made traveling in motor cars their principal business. In 1922 there were 200,000 of them.

These people live in their motor cars and tents, spending the summer in the north and going south for the winter.

No Responsibility or Care

"Labor—physical or mental—if it is not taboo in their creed, is reduced to the smallest possible proportions; likewise it follows that expenditures are put upon their most economical basis. Care, responsibility, and ambition—these things have no longer a place in the life of a Tin Can Tourist," says Norman Borchardt.

At first these tourists went back to farms and work when winter was over, but now at least 30 percent of them live in their cars the year around, and the number who do this is increasing fast.

There are families of children being raised in these traveling homes, and since reading the article, I have been wondering just what this all will mean to us in the future.

A Danger to Customs

It seems to me that such a class of careless, unresponsible drifters will be a danger to our customs and our country, for where the home is eliminated an important part of our social structure is missing. No shelter on four wheels, continually on the move, can really be a home, though children reared to know no better would not understand the difference.

I am jealous for the farm home and fearful of anything that seems to threaten it, so I hope we will do what we can to counteract the effect of so many choosing a homeless life by letting our love of home grow into a strong and beautiful sentiment, embracing the whole of the farm lands and all that goes to make life possible and pleasant upon them.

The Love of Home

We can teach this love of home to the children, and it will help to hold them steady when their time comes. They may need such help more than you think, for the greater number of the "Tin Can Tourists" are from farms of the Middle West.

Far in the Future
June 1922

Gnawing away at the mountains of shale near Denver is a machine that eats rocks, transforming them into oil, paraffin, perfumes, dyes, synthetic rubber—in all, 155 different products, including gasoline and lubricating oils. The separating of the shale rock into these elements is done with heat generated by oil burners; and there is absolutely no waste, for the refuse, dumped out at the back of the machine, is made up of hydrocarbons of great commercial value.

*That which is the wonder of one age
and hardly believable is the
commonplace of the next.*

The story of this rock-eating monster is worthy of a place with the tales brought to Europe by travelers in India who first saw cotton and sugar cane. They told that in that strange land were "plants that bore wool without sheep and reeds that bore honey without bees."

The first cotton cloth brought to Europe came from Calicut and was called "calico." Only kings and queens could afford to wear it.

Arabs brought the lumps of sweet stuff, like gravel, that they called "sukkar." This was so scarce and precious in Europe that it was prescribed as medicine for kings and queens when they were ill.

From the days when sugar and cotton were such wonders to the time when a machine crushes rocks and from them distills delicate perfumes and beautiful colors has not been so very long when measured by years; but measured by the advance of science and invention, it has been a long, long way.

Looking forward, we stand in awe of the future, wondering if the prophecy of Berthelot, the great French chemist, will be fulfilled. He says the time will come when man, by the aid of chemistry, will take his food from the air, the water, and the earth without the necessity of growing crops or killing living creatures; when the earth will be covered with grass, flowers, and woods among which mankind will live in abundance and joy.

This is far in the future and almost impossible of belief, but that which is the wonder of one age and hardly believable is the commonplace of the next. We go from achievement to achievement, and no one knows the ultimate heights the human race may reach.

The Great Woods Have Been Destroyed
September 1919

What a frightful thing it would be if we were to wake some morning and find there was no fuel of any kind in the United States with which to cook our breakfast. Yet this astounding thing may happen to our grandchildren, our children, or even in our own lifetime if our days should be "long in the land."

Men have usually supplied the family fuel in a large offhand manner, but women have always seen that the woodbox or coal hod was filled at night to be on hand for the morning's work.

Yet this astounding thing may happen to our grandchildren, our children, or even in our own lifetime.

If we do not intend that the stove shall remain cold and the family be breakfastless on that surprising morning in the future, it is time we were looking after the supply of fuel, for "John has been careless" and the woodpile is too small.

Too many of the forests of the United States have been made into lumber even though there never has seemed to be lumber enough, and the waste of timber has been great. The great woods of the East and the North of our country have been destroyed.

Three thousand saw mills are now busily at work in the South, and the timber is fast disappearing before them. Within five years they will have cut out all the timber and disappeared from the South. Then only the forests of the Pacific coast will remain, and they will not last long. In less than seventy years the supply of timber in the United States will be used up.

When the time comes, those of us who have permitted this destruction, if there are any of us left, will wish to hide our faces from the generations we have robbed; but we will be unable to "take to the tall timber" as certain politicians are said to have done in the past.

There will be no lumber to build the houses and no wood to cook breakfast. I fear that even the dim mists of the past will be no refuge for the people who have permitted such a condition to come about, and that we will be held up to scorn and reproach.

People then will not be able to use coal in place of wood for the supply of coal is fast disappearing. The end of hard coal is in sight. Soft coal therefore must be the basis of the country's industrial life as well as its fuel. There is, to be sure, a great deal of soft coal left; but it is of poor quality and must be especially prepared for use to be satisfactory.

Dr. Garfield, former fuel administrator, does not favor government ownership, but says there should be cooperation between the government and all basic industries to eliminate waste and all needless expense. The greater difficulties and more costly equipment in mining inferior coal and also the higher wages make prices higher.

But cost alone is not the greatest problem. There is danger of a power shortage which will stop all manufacturing unless a way is found to furnish a national power supply. Two-thirds of all our coal mined goes into the production of power. Eleven million persons are working in our manufacturing plants and more than double the power was used last year than was used in 1900.

The expense of the power is from 2 percent to 20 percent of the cost of an article, and when we buy $50 worth of goods, we can figure that about $2 goes for the coal that supplied the power to manufacture them. Quite a tax!

Electricity is the only thing that can save the situation. One ton of coal used in generating electricity will furnish power equal to four tons.

Secretary Lane* has a plan for furnishing electric power through a large central station. He urges a power survey of the whole United States, the locating of central stations and smaller supply stations.

It is known that in the territory between Boston and Richmond is situated one-fourth of the power-generating capacity of the country, and as an illustration of the plan, I quote Floyd W. Parsons in the *Saturday Evening Post*: "The logical development is a multiple-transmission line of high voltage extending all the way from Boston to Washington and on to Richmond. Energy could be delivered into this unified system by power stations located near the mine mouths and by hydro-electric plants located at the 20 or more water power sites tributary to this area."

Thus might be created rivers of power flowing through the country and furnishing energy and power to our manufactories at much less than half of what it costs now.

They have one such great power line in California and another, 500 miles long, reaching from Tonopah, Nevada, to Yuma, Arizona.

There is water power enough in the Ozark Hills to furnish power and light for that section of country and, if included in the national system with the coal of Kansas and Illinois, would do its part in caring for the whole. The railroads could be electrified also, and by the careful handling of our natural power and fuel, by a responsible head, that cold and dreary breakfastless morning might never arrive. It need never arrive if we see to it that our water power and what is left of our fuel supply is handled carefully and intelligently. It is time to get busy with the woodbox.

*Franklin K. Lane, Secretary of the Interior.

Income and Expenses
October 1920

When there is so much talk of extravagance and mismanagement, both public and private, it is very encouraging to know that our present state government has been so well managed that there is to be a lessening of the taxes because the state does not need so much income. On May 2 the balance in the state treasury was $11,006,898.94 and there were no outstanding debts.

. . . .

Interest on the balance in the treasury is now bringing to the state $1,000 a day, which goes into the general revenue fund. As this is the fund that is used for the running expenses of the state government, the amount that must be collected by taxes is lessened by just that $1,000 a day.

---

*Everyone these days has a try at
telling what is wrong with
business conditions.*

The budget system, bringing expenses within the income, with a margin over for savings, is quite as good for private use. It helps amazingly to keep down expenses as I know from experience.

We all try to save and would be inclined to resent it if anyone should say we were not careful in our spending, but we are too much like the town woman who boycotted eggs because they were too high and then, without a protest, paid $36 for a pair of low shoes. Unless we figure carefully on both income and expenses, it is so easy to throw away with one hand what we save with the other.

The other day I sent to town for a toilet preparation, the price of which has always been 50 cents. When the Man of the Place brought it home, he said the price was $1; and the reason was plain when I had examined the goods. They were done up in a new style and very fancy package.

Now it was the preparation I needed, not a fancy package, but that sporty container had doubled the price.

Everyone these days has a try at telling what is wrong with business conditions. I am sure that one thing causing us a great deal of trouble and making much higher the high cost of living is the extra price we pay for fancy packages.

Compensations
November 1919

"One gains a lot by going out into the world, by traveling and living in different places," Rose said to me one day, "but one loses a great deal, too. After all, I'm not sure but the loss is greater than the gain."

A friend writes me of New York,
"I like it and I hate it."

"Just how do you mean?" I asked.

"I mean this," said Rose. "The best anyone can get out of this world is happiness and contentment, and people here in the country seem so happy and contented, so different from the restless people of the cities who are out in the rush of things."

So after all, there are compensations. Though we do not have the advantages of travel, we stay-at-homes may acquire a culture of the heart which is almost impossible in the rush and roar of cities.

I think there are always compensations. The trouble is we do not recognize them. We usually are so busily longing for things we can't have that we overlook what we have in their place that is even more worthwhile. Sometimes we realize our happiness only by comparison after we have lost it. It really appears to be true that:

> *To appreciate Heaven well*
> *A man must have some 15 minutes of Hell.*

Talking with another friend from the city gave me still more of an understanding of this difference between country and city.

"My friends in town always are going somewhere. They never are quiet a minute if they can help it," he said. "Always they are looking for something to pass the time away quickly as though they were afraid to be left by themselves. The other evening one of the fellows was all broken up because there was nothing doing. 'There isn't a thing on for tonight,' he said. 'Not a thing!' He seemed to think it was something terrible that there was nothing special on hand for excitement, and he couldn't bear to think of spending a quiet evening at home."

What an uncomfortable condition to be in—depending altogether on things outside of one's self for happiness and a false happiness at that, for the true must come from within.

If we are such bad company that we can't live with ourselves, something is seriously wrong and should be attended to, for sooner or later we shall have to face ourselves alone.

There seems to be a madness in the cities, a frenzy in the struggling crowds. A friend writes me of New York, "I like it and I hate it. There's something you've got to love, it's so big—a people hurrying everywhere, all trying to live and be someone or something—and then when you see the poverty and hatefulness, the uselessness of it all, you wonder why people live here at all. It does not seem possible that there are any peaceful farms on the earth."

And so more than ever I am thankful for the peacefulness and comparative isolation of country life. This is a happiness which we ought to realize and enjoy.

We who live in the quiet places have the opportunity to become acquainted with ourselves, to think our own thoughts, and live our own lives in a way that is not possible for those who are keeping up with the crowd, where there is always something "on for tonight," and who have become so accustomed to crowds that they are dependent upon them for comfort.

In thine own cheerful spirit live,
Nor seek the calm that others give;
For thou, thyself, alone must stand
Not held upright by other's hand.

CHAPTER 3

The garden
of our lives

I Don't Know What the World Is Coming To
June 1921

Did you ever hear anyone say, "I don't know what the world is coming to; people didn't used to do it that way; things were different when I was young," or words to that effect?

Is it possible you ever said anything of the kind yourself? If so, don't be deluded into thinking it is because of your knowledge of life or that the idea is at all original with you. That remark has become a habit with the human race, having been made at least 900 years ago, and I suspect it has been repeated by every generation.

Not long ago, I caught myself saying, "When I was a child, children were more respectful to their parents."

An interesting article in *Asia* tells of a book of old Japan that is being translated by the great Japanese scholars, Mr. Aston and Mr. Sansome. The book was written by a lady of the court, during the reign of the Japanese Emperor Ichijo nearly a thousand years ago.

Among other interesting things in the article, I found this quotation from the old book: "'In olden times,' said one of her Majesty's ladies, 'even the common people had elegant tastes. You never hear of such things nowadays.'"

Doesn't that have a familiar sound? One's mind grows dizzy trying to imagine what things would have been like in the times that were "olden times" a thousand years ago, but evidently things were "going from bad to worse" even then.

"Distance lends enchantment to the view," looking in one direction as well as in another, and that is why, I think, events of olden times and of our childhood and youth are enveloped in such a rosy cloud, just as at the time the future glowed with bright colors. It all depends on which way we're looking. Youth ever gazes forward while age is inclined to look back. And so older persons think things were better when they were young.

"When I Was a Child—"

Not long ago, I caught myself saying, "When I was a child, children were more respectful to their parents"; when as a matter of fact, I can remember children who were not so obedient as some who are with us today; and I know, when I am truthful with myself, that it always, as now, has taken all kinds of children to make the world.

Sometimes we are inclined to wish our childhood days might come again, but I am always rescued from such folly by remembering a remark I once heard a man make: "Wish I were a boy again!" he exclaimed, "I do not! When I was a boy I had to hoe my row in the cornfield with father and the hired man; I must keep up too, and then while they rested in the shade I had to run and get the drinking water."

And so quite often the rather morbid longing for the past will be dispelled by facing the plain facts.

There are abuses in the world, today, surely; there have always been. Our job is to face those of our day and correct them.

We have been doing a great deal of howling over the high prices we have to pay and the comparatively low value we get, and we should do more than cry aloud about it; but we would have suffered worse in those good old times after the Civil War when the coarsest of muslin and calico cost 50 cents a yard, and banks failed overnight leaving their worthless money in circulation.

Prices have not been so high after this much greater war, and our money has been good. It is a frightful thing that our civilization should be disgraced by the conditions of the world today, but in the former Dark Ages of history there was no Red Cross organization working to help and save.

Abuses there are, to be sure, wrongs to be righted, sorrows to be comforted; these are obstacles to be met and overcome. But as far back as I can remember, the old times were good times; they have been good all down through the years, full of love and service, of ideals and achievement—the future is in our hands to make it what we will.

Love and service, with a belief in the future and expectation of better things in the tomorrow of the world is a good working philosophy; much better than, "in olden times—things were so much better when I was young." For there is no turning back nor standing still; we must go forward, into the future, generation after generation toward the accomplishment of the ends that have been set for the human race.

The notes of the great bell over a Buddhist temple in Japan are said to announce the transience of life and to say as it tolls—

> *All things are transient.*
> *They, being born, must die,*
> *And being born, are dead,*
> *And being dead, are glad to be at rest.*

But however fleeting and changeable life may appear to be on the surface, we know that the great underlying values of life are always the same; no different today than they were a thousand years ago.

Make Your Garden!
February 1918

Now is the time to make your garden! Anyone can be a successful gardener at this time of year, and I know of no pleasanter occupation these cold, snowy days than to sit warm and snug by the fire, making garden with a pencil—in a seed catalog. What perfect vegetables we do raise in that way and so many of them! Our radishes are crisp and sweet, our lettuce tender, and our tomatoes smooth and beautifully colored. Best of all, there is not a bug or worm in the whole garden, and the work is so easily done.

He figured that I would be a millionaire within five years.

In imagination we see the plants in our spring garden, all in straight, thrifty rows with the fruits of each plant and vine numerous and beautiful as the pictures before us. How near the real garden of next summer approaches the ideal garden of our winter fancies depends upon how practically we dream and how we work.

It is so much easier to plan than it is to accomplish. When I started my small flock of Leghorns a few years ago, a friend inquired as to the profits of the flock and, taking my accounts as a basis, he figured I would be a millionaire within five years. The five years are past, but, alas, I am still obliged to be economical. There was nothing wrong with my friend's figuring except that he left out the word "if," and that made all the difference between profits figured out on paper and those worked out by actual experience.

My Leghorns would have made me a millionaire—if the hens had performed according to schedule; if the hawks had loved field mice better than spring chickens; if I had been so constituted that I never became weary; if prices—but why enumerate? Because allowance for that word "if" was not made in the figuring, the whole result was wrong.

It is necessary that we dream now and then. No one ever achieved anything from the smallest object to the greatest unless the dream was dreamed first. Those who stop at dreaming never accomplish anything.

We must first see the vision in order to realize it; we must have the ideal or we cannot approach it; but when once the dream is dreamed, it is time to wake up and "get busy." We must "do great deeds, not dream them all day long."

The dream is only the beginning. We'd starve to death if we went no further with that garden than making it by the fire in the seed catalog. It takes judgment to plant the seeds at the right time, in the right place, and hard digging to make them grow, whether in the vegetable garden or in the garden of our lives.

We can work our dreams out into realities if we try, but we must be willing to make the effort. Things that seem easy of accomplishment in dreams require a lot of good common sense to put on a working basis and a great deal of energy to put through to a successful end. When we make our dream gardens, we must take into account the hot sun and the blisters on our hands; we must make allowance for and guard against the "ifs" so that when the time to work has come, they will not be of so much importance.

We may dream those dreams of our own, of a comfortable home, of that education we are going to have and those still more excellent dreams of the brotherhood of man and liberty and justice for all; then let us work to make this "the land where dreams come true."

Parable of Wild Fruit
July 1920

Out in the berry patch, the bluejays scolded me for trespassing. They talked of a food shortage and threatened terrible things to profiteers who took more than their share of the necessaries of life. But I was used to their clamor and not alarmed even when one swooped down and struck my bonnet. I knew they would not harm me and kept right on picking berries. This is a parable. I give it to you for what it is worth, trusting you to draw your own comparisons.

When we came to the Ozarks, we reveled in the wild fruit, for as yet there was no tame fruit on the place.

When the Man of the Place and I, with the small daughter, came to Missouri some years ago, we tried to save all the wild fruit in the woods. Coming from the plains of Dakota where the only wild fruit was the few chokecherries growing on the banks of the small lakes, we could not bear to see go to waste the perfectly delicious wild huckleberries, strawberries, and blackberries which grew so abundantly everywhere on the hills.

By the way, did you ever eat chokecherries? At first taste they are very good, and the first time I tried them I ate quite a few before my throat began to tighten with a fuzzy, choking feeling. A green persimmon has nothing on a ripe chokecherry, as I know. I have tried both. So when we came to the Ozarks, we reveled in the wild fruit, for as yet there was no tame fruit on the place.

Huckleberries came first, and we were impatiently waiting for them to ripen when somebody told me that the green ones made good pies. Immediately, I went out into the little cleared space in the woods where the low huckleberry bushes grew and gathered a bucket of berries. Company was coming to dinner next day, and I took special pains to make a good pie of the berries; for I did want my new neighbors to enjoy the visit. And the crust of the pie was deliciously crisp and flaky, but after one taste, the visitors seemed to hesitate.

I took a mouthful of my piece and found it bitter as gall. I never tasted gall, but that is the bitterest expression I know and nothing could be more bitter than that pie.

"Oh!" I exclaimed. "They told me green huckleberries were good!"

"These can't be huckleberries," said Mrs. X, "for green huckleberries do make good pies."

Mr. X was examining the berries in his portion. "These are buckberries," he said. "They grow on a bush about the size of a huckleberry bush, and you must have made a mistake when you gathered them."

And so I added to my knowledge the difference between huckleberries and buckberries, and we have enjoyed many a green huckleberry pie since then. Used when quite small, the berries not only taste delicious but give a bouquet of perfume to the pie that adds wonderfully to the pleasure of eating it.

When blackberries came on, chiggers were ripe also, and there is nothing a chigger enjoys so much as feasting on a "foreigner." The blackberry patches are their home, and we made many a chigger happy that season. We gathered the berries by bucketsful; we filled the pans and pots and all the available dishes in the house, then hastily we bathed in strong soapsuds and applied remedies to the worst bitten spots. Then I put up the berries and cleared the decks for the next day's picking, for gather them we would, no matter how the chigger bit.

I was thinking of these experiences while the bluejays screamed at me in the berry patch—tame berries now. We never pick the wild ones these days because there are large tame ones in the plenty.

The apple trees that were little switches when we picked the wild fruit have supplied us with carloads of apples. Even the chiggers never bother us anymore.

We are so accustomed to an abundance of fruit that we do not appreciate the fine cultivated sorts as we did the wild kinds that we gathered at the cost of so much labor and discomfort.

There is a moral here somewhere, too, I am sure, and again I will leave it for you to discover.

Are You Your Children's Confidant?
September 1921

A letter from my mother, who is seventy-six years old, lies on my desk beside a letter from my daughter far away in Europe. Reading the message from my mother, I am a child again and a longing unutterable fills my heart for Mother's counsel, for the safe haven of her protection and the relief from responsibility which trusting in her judgment always gave me.

But when I turn to the letter written by my daughter, who will always be a little girl to me no matter how old she grows, then I understand and appreciate my mother's position and her feelings toward me.

Many of us have the blessed privilege of being at the same time mother and child, able to let the one interpret the other to us until our understanding of both is full and rich. What is there in the attitude of your children toward yourself that you wish were different? Search your heart and learn if your ways toward your own mother could be improved.

I am a child again and a longing unutterable fills my heart for Mother's counsel.

In the light of experience and the test of the years, can you see how your mother might have been more to you, could have guided you better? Then be sure you are making the most of your privileges with the children who are looking to you for love and guidance. For there is, after all, no great difference between the generations; the problems of today and tomorrow must be met in much the same way as those of yesterday.

During the years since my mother was a girl to the time when my daughter was a woman, there have been many slight, external changes in the fashions and ways of living, some change in the thought of the world, and much more freedom in expressing those thoughts. But the love of mother and child is the same, with the responsibility of controlling and guiding on the one side and the obligation of obedience and respect on the other.

The most universal sentiment in the world is that of mother-love. From the highest to the lowest in the scale of humanity, and all through the animal kingdom, it is the strongest force in creation, the conserver of life, the safeguard of evolution. It holds within its sheltering care the fulfillment of the purpose of creation itself. In all ages, in all countries it is the same—a boundless, all-enveloping love; if necessary, a sacrifice of self for the offspring.

Think of the number of children in the world, each the joy of some mother's heart, each a link connecting one generation with another, each a hope for the future. . . .

It stuns the mind to contemplate their number and their possibilities, for these are the coming rulers of the world: the makers of destiny, not only for their own generation but for the generations to come. And they are being trained for their part in the procession of time by the women of today. Surely, "The hand that rocks the cradle is the hand that rules the world."

Kinfolks or Mere Relations?
August 1916

"I do like to have you say kinfolks. It seems to mean so much more than relations or relatives," writes my sister from the North. They do not say kinfolks in the North. It is a Southern expression.

This remark was enough to start me on a line of thought that led me far afield. Kinfolks! It is such a homey sounding word and strong, too, and sweet. Folks who are akin—why they need not even be relatives or "blood kin!" What a vista that opens up! They are scattered all over the world, these kinfolks of ours, and we will find them wherever we go, folks who are akin to us in thought and belief, in aspirations and ideas, though our relatives may be far away. Those of our own family may be akin to us also, though sometimes they are not.

There was trouble, serious trouble and disagreement. The surprising thing was in the form it took.

Old Mr. Weeks died last winter. His will left the fine farm to his youngest son, subject to providing a home for his mother so long as she lived. A comparatively small sum of money was left each of the seven other children who were scattered in other states. And now a strange thing happened! We always expect to hear of trouble and quarreling among the heirs over a will and an estate, and in this case we were not disappointed. There was trouble, serious trouble and disagreement. The surprising thing was in the form it took. The youngest son refused flatly to abide by his father's will. He would not take that whole farm for himself! "It was not fair to the others!"

His brothers and sisters refused absolutely to take any share of the farm. "It would not be right," they said when their brother had made the farm what it was by staying at home and working on it while they had gone away on their own affairs. Lawyers were even called into the case, not to fight for a larger share for their clients, but to persuade the other party to take more of the property than he wished to take. There is nothing new under the sun, we are told, but if anything like this ever happened before, it has not been my good fortune to hear of it. The members of this family were surely kinfolks as well as relatives.

Two sisters, Mabel and Kate, were left orphans when eighteen and twenty years old. There was very little for their support, so as they would be obliged to

---

add to their income in some way, they went into a little business of ladies' furnishing goods. All the responsibility was left with Mabel, although they were equal partners, and she also did most of the work. Kate seemed to have no sense of honor in business nor of the difference between right and wrong in her dealings with her sister. At last Mabel had a nervous breakdown under the strain and the shock of the sudden death of her fiance. While Mabel was thus out of the way, Kate sold the business, married and left town, and when Mabel recovered, she found that the business and her sister were gone, that the account at the bank was overdrawn and a note was about due which had been given by the firm and to which her own name had been forged. Because of the confidence which her honor and honesty had inspired, Mabel was able to get credit and make a fresh start. She has paid the debts and is becoming prosperous once more.

Were Mabel and Kate kinfolks? Oh no! Merely relatives!

Troubles Grow As We Talk About Them
January 1920

The snow was falling fast and a cold wind blowing the other morning. I had just come in from feeding the chickens and was warming my chilled self when the telephone rang.

"Hello!" said I and a voice full of laughter came over a wire. "Good morning!" it said. "I suppose you are busy making a garden today."

"Making a garden?" I asked wonderingly.

"Yes," replied the voice, "you said some time ago that you enjoyed making a garden in the wintertime beside a good fire, so I thought you'd be busily at it this morning."

"Well," I replied defensively, "the vegetables one raises in the seed catalogs are so perfectly beautiful." And with a good laugh, we began the day right merrily in spite of the storm outside.

If we want vegetables, we must make them grow, not leave the ground barren where we have destroyed the weeds.

So after many days my words came back to me and the thoughts that followed them were altogether different from those connected with them before.

We do grow beautiful gardens beside the fire on cold winter days as we talk over the seed catalogs; and our summer gardens are much more of a success because of these gardens in our minds. We grow many other things in the same way. It is truly surprising how anything grows and grows by talking about it.

We have a slight headache and we mention the fact. As an excuse to ourselves for inflicting it upon our friends, we make it as bad as possible in the telling. "Oh, I have such a dreadful headache," we say and immediately we feel much worse. Our pain has grown by talking of it.

If there is a disagreement between friends and the neighbors begin talking about it, the difficulty grows like a jimson weed, and the more it is talked about the faster it grows.

When there is a disagreement between workmen and their employers, the agitators immediately begin their work of talking and the trouble grows and grows until strikes and lockouts and riots are ripened and harvested and the agitators grow fat on the fruits thereof.

The same law seems to work in both human nature and in the vegetable

---

kingdom and in the world of ideas with the changes caused just by talk, either positive or negative. Even peas and cabbages grow by cultivation, by keeping the soil "stirred" about them.

Now it isn't enough in any garden to cut down the weeds. The cutting out of weeds is important, but cultivating the garden plants is just as necessary. If we want vegetables, we must make them grow, not leave the ground barren where we have destroyed the weeds. Just so, we must give much of our attention to the improvements we want, not all to the abuses we would like to correct. If we hope to improve conditions, any conditions, anywhere, we must do a great deal of talking about the better things.

If we have a headache we will forget it sooner if we talk of pleasant things. If there is misunderstanding and bad feeling between neighbors, we can cultivate their friendliness by telling each of the other's kind words before the trouble began. Perhaps a crust has formed around the plant of their friendship, and it only needs that the soil should be stirred in order to keep on growing.

We Keep Right on Eating
January 1922

With the holidays safely past, it is a good time to make resolutions not to overeat. It is easy to do so just after eating too much of too many good things.

We do eat too much! Everyone says so! But we keep right on eating. I remember a neighborhood dinner I attended recently. You who have been to such dinners know how the table was loaded. There were breads and meats; vegetables and salads; pies of every kind, with flaky crusts and sweet, juicy fillings; cakes—loaf, layer, cup, white, yellow, pink, chocolate, iced and plain; pickles, preserves and canned fruit and such quantities of it all! We ate all we could and then some.

We ate all we could and then some.

Then I learned of a dinner prepared for guests in the mountains of Albania* to which the neighbors were bidden. The food was coarse cornbread made without leavening, sweet and nutty, and so precious that the tiniest crumb, if dropped on the floor or table, must be picked up, kissed, and the sign of the cross made over it. Lean pork, stripped of every scrap of fat, was broiled on sticks over the fire.

In Albania it is etiquette to leave a great deal of the food, and it was sent away while the guests were still hungry. Then a wooden bowl filled with cubes of fat pork fried crisp was brought. This was also removed before hunger was satisfied, and water was brought for washing the hands. The strangers who were guests ate first, then the neighbors ate, and, after them, the family who entertained.

"In Albania it is not good manners to show eagerness for food," said the guide. "Albanians are not greedy."

---

*Her daughter, Rose Wilder Lane, wrote of Albania in *The Peaks of Shala.*

Keep Journeying On
March 1918

Youth longs and manhood strives, but age remembers,
Sits by the raked-up ashes of the past
And spreads its thin hands above the glowing embers
That warm its shivering life-blood till the last.*

Those lines troubled me a great deal when I first read them. I was very young then, and I thought that everything I read in print was the truth. I didn't like it a little bit that the chief end of my life and the sole amusement of my old age should be remembering. Already there were some things in my memory that were not particularly pleasant to think about. I have since learned that few persons have such happy and successful lives that they would wish to spend yeas in just remembering.

No one can really welcome the first
gray hair or look upon the first
wrinkles as beautiful.

One thing is certain, this melancholy old age will not come upon those who refuse to spend their time indulging in such dreams of the past. Men and women may keep their life's blood warm by healthy exercise as long as they keep journeying on instead of sitting by the way trying to warm themselves over the ashes of remembrance.

Neither is it a good plan for people to keep telling themselves they are growing old. There is such a thing as a law of mental suggestion that makes the continual affirmation of a thing work toward its becoming an accomplished fact. Why keep suggesting old age until we take on its characteristics as a matter of course? There are things much more interesting to do than keeping tally of the years and watching for infirmities.

I know a woman who, when she saw her first gray hair, began to bewail the fact that she was growing old, and began to change her ways to suit her ideas of old age. She couldn't "wear bright colors any more"; she was "too old." She must be more quiet now: "It was not becoming in an old person to be so merry." She had not "been feeling well lately," but she supposed she was "as well as could be expected of a person growing old," and so on and on.

---

*From "The Iron Gate," by Oliver Wendell Holmes.

I never lost the feeling that the years were passing swiftly and that old age was lying in wait for the youngest of us when in her company.

Of course, no one can really welcome the first gray hair or look upon the first wrinkles as beautiful, but even those things need not affect our happiness. There is no reason why we should not be merry as we grow older. If we learn to look on the bright side while we are young, those little wrinkles at the corners of the eyes will be "laughing wrinkles" instead of "crow's feet."

There is nothing in the passing of the years by itself to cause one to become melancholy. If they have been good years, then the more of them the better. If they have been bad years, be glad they are passed and expect the coming ones to be more to your liking.

. . . .

Perhaps, after all, the poet whose verse I have quoted meant it as a warning that if we did not wish to come to that unlovely old age, we must keep on striving for ourselves and for others. There was no age limit set by the great poet when he wrote:

Build thee more stately mansions, O my soul,
*As the swift seasons roll!**

It is certainly a pleasanter, more worthwhile occupation to keep on building than to be raking up the ashes of dead fires.

---

*From Oliver Wendell Holmes's "The Chambered Nautilus."

Getting the Worst of It
March 1917

Whenever two or three women were gathered together during the winter, sooner or later someone would ask, "Are your hens laying?"

In one such small crowd where town and country women mingled, I was very much interested and also amused by a conversation which took place between a country woman and a woman who lives in town. Of course, the inevitable question was asked, and the country woman answered that her hens were doing their duty. Then a town woman inquired, "What are you getting for eggs?"

"Thirty cents," replied the country woman.

"They make us pay 33 cents when we get them at the store," said the town woman. "Why can't you bring me my eggs?"

"I can," said the country woman. "How many would you want?"

"Oh! Bring me three dozen. Might as well save 9 cents," replied the town woman.

Perhaps I imagined it, but I certainly thought that the country woman's left eyelid dropped for an instant as she looked up at me, but her glance was so quick I could not be sure. Her reply was quick too.

"Why! I thought you were offering me the 3 cents a dozen more," she said. The town woman disclaimed this in a tone of surprise, and the country woman asked, "How about dividing it?"

"Oh! I wouldn't bother with it for that," said the other in a tone of disgust.

"It is less bother for me to deliver our eggs all in one place. We sell them by the case, you know," said the country woman, and again I thought her eyelid dropped as she glanced once more in my direction. I wish I could be sure about that wink. It would make such a difference in the conclusions one might draw.

There, I said to myself, is the producer and consumer question in a nutshell with the real reason why that terrible bogey, "the middleman" gets such a chance at us. Too much bother, unwillingness to cooperate and compromise, or in other words just plain selfishness is the cause at the bottom of all the trouble. The consumer wants something done about the high cost of living, but he wants all the benefit to accrue to himself. The producer wants something done to lessen the difference between the price at which he sells and what the consumer pays, but he also desires what is thus saved to come his way, while the speculator standing between smiles to himself, secure in his position because of this weakness of human nature. For the rest of us, the punishment fits the crime, and I am inclined to think that we get no more than we deserve.

After all, it is through some fault or weakness of our own that most of the evils of life come to us. It is as if our strength of character and virtues formed a guard around us, but a fault or weakness of character makes an opening through which our punishment comes.

✳✳

There was once a small boy with a quarrelsome disposition and a great unwillingness to obey the rules his mother made. At school he would seek a quarrel and get the thrashing he deserved; then he would come home, disobey his mother and be punished; then he would sit down and wail, "O-o-h! I always get the worst of it! I don't know why, but at school and everywhere I always get the worst of it!"

It was tragic for the child, but to me there was always something irresistibly comic about it also, because it reminded me so strongly of grown-ups I knew. We have all seen such persons. There are those who persistently disobey the laws of health, which, being nature's laws, are also God's laws, and then when ill health comes, wonder why they should be compelled to suffer.

Others by their bad temper and exacting dispositions estrange their relatives and repel friendly advances. Then they bewail the fact that their friends are so few.

From these, clear on down to the man who carelessly picked up the lid lifter from the hot part of the stove and then turned impatiently upon his wife exclaiming, "Why didn't you tell me that was hot!" we are all alike eager to lay upon someone else the blame for the troubles that come from our own faults, and all remind me of the boy who wailed, "I always get the worst of it! I don't know why—but I always get the worst of it!"

The Source of Improvement
February 1917

"I cannot stand still in my work. If I do not keep studying and going ahead, I slip back," said a friend the other day.

"Well, neither can I in my work," I thought. My mind kept dwelling on the idea. Was there a work that one could learn to do with a certain degree of excellence, and then keep that perfection without a ceaseless effort to advance?

How easy and delightful life might be if we could do this, if when we had attained the position we wished, we might rest on our oars and watch the ripples on the stream of life.

---

*Our friends and neighbors are either
better friends and neighbors today
than they were several years ago or
they are not so good.*

Turning my mind resolutely from the picture of what would happen to the person who rested on his oars, expecting to hold his position where the tide was rippling, I began looking around for that place in life where one could stand still, without troubling to advance and without losing what already had been gained.

My friend who plays the piano so beautifully was a fair performer years ago but has improved greatly as time has gone by. She spends several hours every day at the instrument practicing. "I have to practice," she says, "or I shall lose my power of execution," and because she does practice to keep what she already has, she goes on improving from day to day and from year to year.

In contrast to this is the other friend who used to sing so much and who had such a lovely voice. She hardly ever sings now and told me the other day that she thought she was losing her voice. She also said that she was so busy she had no time to practice.

There is also the woman who "completed her education" some years ago. She thought there was no need for further effort along that line and that she had her education for all time, so she settled down to the housework and the poultry. She had read very little of anything that would help her to keep abreast of the times and does not now give the impression of being an educated, cultured person, but quite the reverse. No doubt she has forgotten more than I ever knew, but the point is that she has lost it. Refusing to go ahead, she has dropped back.

Even a housekeeper who is a good housekeeper and stays such becomes a better and more capable one from the practice and exercise of her art and profession. If she does not, you may be sure she is slipping back, and instead of being proficient will soon be careless, a woman who will say, "I used to be a good housekeeper, but—"

The same rule applies to character. Our friends and neighbors are either better friends and neighbors today than they were several years ago or they are not so good. We are either broader minded, more tolerant and sympathetic now than we used to be or the reverse is true. The person who is selfish, or mean or miserly—does he not grow more so as the years pass, unless he makes a special effort to go in the other direction?

Our graces are either growing or shrinking. It seems to be a law of nature that everything and every person must move along. There is no standing still. The moment that growth stops, decay sets in.

One of the greatest safeguards against becoming old is that of continuing to grow mentally, you know.

If we do not strive to gain, we lose what we already have, for just so surely as "practice makes perfect," the want of practice or the lack of exercise of talents and knowledge makes for the opposite condition.

We must advance or we slip back and few of us are bright enough to turn a slip to good account as did the school boy of long ago. This particular boy was late at school one icy winter morning, and the teacher reproved him and asked the reason for his tardiness.

"I started early enough," answered Tom, "but it was so slippery that every time I took one step ahead I slipped back two steps."

There was a hush of astonishment, and then the teacher asked, "But if that is true, how did you ever get here?"

"Oh, that's easy," replied Tom. "I was afraid I was going to be late and so I just turned around and came backwards."

A Man's Word Is All He Has
September 1922

It is said that "money is the root of all evil," but money that is at the root of any evil in itself represents selfishness. . . .

It would be nearer the truth to say that selfishness is the root of evil and the overvaluation of money only one manifestation of it.

Money hasn't any value of its own; it represents the stored up energy of men and women and is really just someone's promise to pay a certain amount of that energy.

If there were only one thing of any value in this world and it were in our possession, how precious it would be to us.

It is the promise that has the real value. If no dependence can be put on the promises of a nation, then the currency of that nation, which is its promise to pay, is worthless. Bank notes depend for their value on the credit of the bank that issues them, and a man's note is good or not according to whether his promise to pay can be relied on.

So it comes to this: that as the business of the world is done on credit, a man's word, backed by his character, is the unit of value; and that character is the root of good or evil, making his word, good or worthless.

If there were only one thing of any value in this world and it were in our possession, how precious it would be to us. How carefully we would guard it from all smirching or damaging, defending it with our lives if necessary! There would be no carelessness in the keeping of it, no reckless giving of it here and there as though it amounted to nothing.

Listen then to this Eastern proverb: "In this world, a man's word is all he has that is of real value; it is at the bottom of all other values."

The Helping Hand of Helpfulness
December 1916

I know a little band of friends that calls itself a woman's club. The avowed purpose of this club is study, but there is an undercurrent of deeper, truer things than even culture and self-improvement. There is no obligation, and there are no promises; but in forming the club and in selecting new members, only those are chosen who are kind-hearted and dependable as well as the possessors of a certain degree of intelligence and a small amount of that genius which is the capacity for careful work. In short, those who are taken into membership are those who will make good friends, and so they are a little band who are each for all and all for each.

Cooperation, helpfulness, and fair dealing are so badly needed in the world, and if they are not learned as children at home, it is difficult for grownups to have a working knowledge of them.

If one needs the helping hand of comradeship, not one but all are eager and willing to help, with financial aid if needed, but more often with a good word or a small act of kindness. They are getting so in the habit of speaking good words that I expect to see them all develop into Golden Gossips.

Ever hear of golden gossip? I read of it some years ago. A woman who was always talking about her friends and neighbors made it her *business* to talk of them, in fact, never said anything but *good* of them. She was a gossip, but it was "golden gossip." This woman's club seems to be working in the same way and associations of friendship and mutual helpfulness are being built up which will last for life. It is a beautiful thing, and more than ever one is impressed with the idea that it is a pity there are—

So many gods, so many creeds,
So many paths that wind and wind
When just the art of being kind
*Is all the sad world needs.**

*From "The World's Need," by Ella Wheeler Wilcox.

* *

"Money is the root of all evil," says the proverb, but I think that proverb maker only dug down part way around the plant of evil. If he had really gotten to the root of the matter, I am sure he would have found that root to be selfishness—just selfishness pure and simple. Why all the mad scramble for money? Why are we all "money-mad Americans"? It is just for our selfish gratification with things that money can buy, from world dominion to a stick of striped candy—selfishness, just selfishness.

Not long ago, I was visiting in a family where there were several children. The father lost his memorandum book and was inquiring for it. No one had seen it. "I wish," he said, "that you children would find it for me before I come back at noon." There was silence for a minute, and then one of the children said: "Why don't you put up a quarter? That'll find it!"

"Well, I will," his father answered and at once the children were all eagerness to search. It seemed to me such a pity to appeal to a selfish interest in the home where there should be loving service freely given.

In the blacksmith shop, one hot day last summer, the blacksmith was sweating over his hot irons when two idle boys sauntered in and over to the water bucket. It was empty. "Ain't yuh got no water?" asked one of the boys.

"Not if the bucket is empty," answered the blacksmith.

Then the man for whom the blacksmith was working spoke up. "Why don't you go get a bucket of water?" he asked.

"I will for a nickel," said the boy.

"Yes, we'll go for a nickel," agreed the other boy.

"Were you going to pay for your drink?" asked the man innocently, and the boys looked at him surprised and then slunk away without filling the bucket. Just an example of selfishness made more contemptible by being so plainly unfair.

Cooperation, helpfulness, and fair dealing are so badly needed in the world, and if they are not learned as children at home, it is difficult for grownups to have a working knowledge of them.

So much depends on starting the children right!

Growing Older
January 1923

With the coming of another new year we are all . . . a year older. Just what does it mean to us—this growing older? Are we coming to a cheerful, beautiful old age, or are we being beaten and cowed by the years as they pass?

A friend said to me, "Growing old is the saddest thing in the world."

Bruised we must be now and then, but beaten, never, unless we lack courage.

Not long since a friend said to me, "Growing old is the saddest thing in the world." Since then I have been thinking about growing old, trying to decide if I thought her right. But I cannot agree with her. True, we lose some things that we prize as time passes and acquire a few that we would prefer to be without. But we may gain infinitely more with the years than we lose in wisdom, character, and the sweetness of life.

As to the ills of old age, it may be that those of the past were as bad but are dimmed by the distance. Though old age has gray hair and twinges of rheumatism, remember that childhood has freckles, tonsils, and the measles.

The stream of passing years is like a river with people being carried along in the current. Some are swept along, protesting, fighting all the way, trying to swim back up the stream, longing for the shores that they have past, clutching at anything to retard their progress, frightened by the onward rush of the strong current and in danger of being overwhelmed by the waters.

Moving with Faith

Others go with the current freely, trusting themselves to the buoyancy of the waters, knowing they will bear them up. And so with very little effort, they go floating safely along, gaining more courage and strength from their experience with the waves.

As New Year after New Year comes, these waves upon the river of life bear us farther along toward the ocean of Eternity, either protesting the inevitable and looking longingly back toward years that are gone or with calmness and faith facing the future serene in the knowledge that the power behind life's currents is strong and good.

And thinking of these things, I have concluded that whether it is sad to grow old depends on how we face it, whether we are looking forward with confidence or backward with regret. Still, in any case, it takes courage to live long successfully, and they are brave who grow old with smiling faces.

CHAPTER 4

Have you seen
any fairies lately?

Fairies Still Appear to Those with Seeing Eyes
April 1916

Have you seen any fairies lately? I asked the question of a little girl not long ago. "Huh! There's no such thing as fairies," she replied. In some way the answer hurt me, and I have been vaguely disquieted when I have thought of it ever since. By the way, have you seen any fairies lately? Please do not answer as the little girl did, for I'm sure there are fairies and that you at least have seen their work.

In the long, long ago days, when the farmers gathered their crops, they always used to leave a part of whatever crop they were harvesting in or on the ground for the use of the "Little People." This was only fair, for the "Little People" worked hard in the ground to help the farmer grow his crops, and if a share were not left for them, they became angry and the crops would not be good the next year. You may laugh at this as an old superstition, but I leave it to you if it has not been proved true that where the "Little People" of the soil are not fed the crops are poor.

A primrose by the river's brim
A yellow primrose was to him
and nothing more.

We call them different names now—nitrogen and humus and all the rest of it—but I always have preferred to think of them as fairy folk who must be treated right.

Our agricultural schools and farm papers spend much time and energy telling us to put back into the soil the elements of which we rob it. Only another way of saying, "Don't rob the 'Little People'; feed them!"

Dryads used to live in the trees, you know—beautiful, fairy creatures who now and then were glimpsed beside the tree into which they vanished. There have been long years during which we have heard nothing of them, but now scientists have discovered that the leaves of trees have eyes, actual eyes that mirror surrounding objects. Of what use are eyes to a tree, I wonder? Would it not be fine if the men of science gave us back all our fairies under different names?

Then there is the old myth of Santa Claus! What child in these deadly, matter-of-fact times believes in Santa Claus? Yet who can deny that at Christmastime there is a spirit, bringing gifts, abroad in the world, who can come down the chimney, or through the keyhole for that matter, and travel in the same night from the North Pole to the South? Why not let the children believe in Santa Claus? Later they will understand that it is only a beautiful imagery. It is surely no harm to idealize things and make them more real by investing them with personalities, and it might do away with some of the sordid estimating of the price of gifts, which children learn so surprisingly young.

I have a feeling that childhood has been robbed of a great deal of its joys by taking away its belief in wonderful, mystic things, in fairies and all their kin. It is not surprising that when children are grown, they have so little idealism or imagination nor that so many of them are like the infidel who asserted that he would not believe anything that he could not see. It was a good retort the Quaker made, "Friend! Does thee believe thee has any brains?"

※※※

A young friend with whom I talked the other day said that life was so "much more interesting" to her since she "began to look below the surface of things and see what was beneath." There are deeps beyond deeps in the life of this wonderful world of ours. Let's help the children to see them instead of letting them grow up like the man of whom the poet wrote,

> *A primrose by the river's brim*
> *A yellow primrose was to him and nothing more.*

Let's train them, instead, to find "books in the running brooks, sermons in stones and good in everything."*

But have you seen any fairies lately, or have you allowed the harsher facts of life to dull your "seeing eye"?

Where Sunshine Fairies Go

> *The sunshine fairies cannot rest*
> *When evening bells are rung;*
> *Nor can they sleep in flowers*
> *When bedtime songs are sung.*
>
> *They are such busy fairies,*
> *Their work is never done,*
> *For all around and round the world*
> *They travel with the sun.*

---

*From *As You Like It*, II, i, by William Shakespeare.

And while you're soundly sleeping,
They do the best they can
A-painting cherry blossoms
In far away Japan.

The poppy fields of China,
With blossoms bright and gay,
They color on their journey—
And then pass on their way.

And all the happy children,
In islands of the sea,
Know little Ray O'Sunshine,
Who plays with you and me.

EDITOR'S NOTE: The following poems about fairies were written by Mrs. Wilder for the *San Francisco Bulletin* when she was visiting her daughter, Rose, in 1915.

Naughty Four O'Clocks
April 1915

There were some naughty flowers once,
Who were careless in their play;
They got their petals torn and soiled
As they swung in the dust all day.

Then went to bed at four o'clock,
With faces covered tight,
To keep the fairy Drop O'Dew
From washing them at night.

Poor Drop O'Dew! What could she do?
She said to the Fairy Queen,
"I cannot get those Four O'Clocks
To keep their faces clean."

The mighty Storm King heard the tale;
"My winds and rain," roared he,
"Shall wash those naughty flowers well,
As flowers all should be."

So raindrops came and caught them all
Before they went to bed,
And washed those little Four O'clocks
At three o'clock instead.

The Fairy Dew Drop
February 1915

Down by the spring one morning
Where the shadows still lay deep,
I found in the heart of a flower
A tiny fairy asleep.

Her flower couch was perfumed,
Leaf curtains drawn with care,
And there she sweetly slumbered,
With a jewel in her hair.

But a sunbeam entered softly
And touched her, as she lay,
Whispering that 'twas morning
And fairies must away.

All colors of the rainbow
Were in her robe so bright
As she danced away with the sunbeam
And vanished from my sight.

'Twas while I watched them dancing,
The sunshine told me true
That my sparkling little fairy
Was lovely Drop O'Dew.

When Sunshine Fairies Rest
March 1915

The fairies in the sunshine
Have many things to do.
They are busy night and day,
But have their rest time too.

For always in the sunlight
They do their very best,

But when the day is cloudy
The sunshine fairies rest.

They go to sleep on soft clouds
A-float around the sun
And tuck their toes in cloudlets,
Until their nap is done.

So when the day is rainy,
The dull sky overhead
Is just the soft gray curtain,
Around their downy bed.

Then when their rest is over,
Just as the clouds go by,
They all come out together—
The rainbow in the sky!

The Fairies in the Sunshine
March 1915

The little sunshine fairies
Are out on sunny days.
They gaily go a-dancing
Along the country ways.

They paint the flower faces,
The leaves of forest trees,
And tint the little grasses
All waving in the breeze.

(One painting tiger lilies,
Who runs away and goes
To play awhile with baby,
Puts speckles on his nose!!)

They color all the apples
And work for days and weeks
To make the grapes bloom purple
And paint the peaches' cheeks.

Ah! There's a tiny fairy!
She's in the garden bed!
It's little Ray O'Sunshine
Who makes the roses red.

Lesson from an Irish Fable
November 1922

Some time ago I read an Irish fairy story which told how a mortal, on a fairy steed, went hunting with the fairies. He had his choice of whether the fairy horse should become large enough to carry a man-sized man or be small enough to ride the horse as it was.

He chose to become of fairy size and, after the magic was worked, rode gayly with the fairy king until he came to a wall so high he feared his tiny horse could not carry him over; but the fairy king said to him, "Throw your heart over the wall, then follow it!" So he rode fearlessly at the wall, with his heart already bravely past it, and went safely over.

"Throw your heart over the wall,
then follow it!"

I have forgotten most of the story and do not remember the name of the author, though I wish I did; but often I think of the fairy's advice. Anyone who has ridden horses much understands how the heart of the rider going over fairly lifts the horse up and across an obstacle. And I have been told, by good drivers, that it holds true in taking a motor car up a difficult hill.

But the uplift of a fearless heart will help us over other sorts of barriers. In any undertaking, to falter at a crisis means defeat. No one ever overcomes difficulties by going at them in a hesitant, doubtful way.

If we would win success in anything, when we come to a wall that bars our way, we must throw our hearts over and then follow confidently. It is fairy advice, you know, and savors of magic, so following it we will ride with the fairies of good fortune and go safely over.

CHAPTER 5

The rush of work

Tired to Death with Work
March 1920

"You are tired to death with work," I read. "Work with a little 'w' is killing the soul out of you. Work with a little 'w' always does that to men if they give it the whole chance. If you don't mix some big 'W' work in with it, then indeed your life will be disastrous, and your days will be dead."

"What is it you mean by big 'W' work?" he asked. "Of course, that's the work you love for the work's sake. It's the work you do because you love the thing itself you're working for."

I closed the book. "That is plenty enough to think about for a while," I said to myself. "I don't want any more ideas mixed with that until I thresh it out well."

We are all doing a great deal of little "w" work, and it is necessary and right that we should. We must work for the pay or the profit that comes from it whether or not we love what we are working for, because we must live and lay by something for old age.

But it is sadly true that giving all our time and thought and effort to personal gain will cause us to become selfish and small and mean. If instead we devote ourselves, a part of our time, to work we love for itself, for what we are accomplishing, we grow stronger and more beautiful of soul.

No one is excessively fond of the work
he is, or has been, doing.

Perhaps we all have been too intent on our own financial gain. From first-hand experience as well as the printed news, it would appear that no one is excessively fond of the work he is, or has been, doing. Everyone is insisting on more money and less work or more profit and less return for it—little "w" work, all of it.

But there are encouraging signs in these somewhat discouraging times of grafters and grafting, of profits and profiteering, of distrust and suspicion, jealousy and strife. Sounds ugly, does it not? But those are the things to which our attention is called daily.

However, as I have said, there are hopeful signs. Only the other day a county officer refused a $900 raise in his salary because, he said, knowing the condition of the country as he did, he knew that the money was needed so much worse for other things.

Although it was a stormy day when I read of this man, it seemed as though the sunshine was streaming over the world. A public official placing the welfare of the community before his private gain so far as to refuse more pay for his services is wonderfully encouraging to our hopes for our country. If there were enough of such public-spirited men, the difficulties which we are facing as a nation would soon disappear.

To work for the good of the community without full reward in money but because we love our fellows and long for the common betterment is work with a big "W," work that will keep our souls alive.

Then there is the owner of the apartment house in New York who did not raise the rent! When at last his tenants had a meeting and voted to pay more rent, he refused to accept it; but when they insisted, he took it and spent it all on improvements which made the tenants more comfortable.

. . . .

There is also the young woman with the musical talent and the lovely singing voice, who uses it so freely for the pleasure and benefit of others; and the one who grows beautiful flowers because she loves them and delights in giving them away.

There is, after all, a great deal of work being done in the world for the love of the thing worked for, with no thought of selfishness, and the lives of such workers are fuller and richer for it.

Going After the Cows
April 1923

With the birds singing, the trees budding, and "the green grass growing all around," as we used to sing in school, who would not love the country and prefer farm life to any other? We are glad that so much time can be spent out-of-doors while going about the regular affairs of the day, thus combining pleasure with work and adding good health for full measure.

---

*I have never lost my childhood delight
in going after the cows.*

I have a favorite way of doing this, for I have never lost my childhood delight in going after the cows. I still slip away from other things for the sake of the walk through the pastures, down along the creek, and over the hill to the farthest corner where the cows are usually found, as you can all bear witness.

Bringing home the cows is the childhood memory that oftenest recurs to me. I think it is because the mind of a child is peculiarly attuned to the beauties of nature, and the voices of the wildwood, and the impression they made was deep.

"To him who, in the love of nature, holds community with her visible forms, she speaks a various language,"* you know. And I am sure old Mother Nature talked to me in all the languages she knew when, as a child, I loitered along the cow paths, forgetful of milking time and stern parents waiting, while I gathered wildflowers, waded in the creek, watched the squirrels hastening to their homes in treetops, and listened to the sleepy twitterings of birds.

Wild strawberries grew in grassy nooks in springtime. The wild plum thickets along the creek yielded their fruit about the time of the first frost in the fall. And all the time between, there were ever varied, never failing delights along the cow paths of the old pasture. Many a time, instead of me finding the cows, they, on their journey home unurged, found me and took me home with them.

The voices of nature do not speak so plainly to us as we grow older, but I think it is because, in our busy lives, we neglect her until we grow out of sympathy. Our ears and eyes grow dull, and beauties are lost to us that we should still enjoy.

Life was not intended to be simply a round of work, no matter how interesting and important that work may be. A moment's pause to watch the glory of a sunrise or a sunset is soul satisfying, while a bird's song will set the steps to music all day long.

---

*From "Thanatopsis," by William Cullen Bryant.

Mrs. Jones Takes the Rest Cure
February 1919

The telephone rang sharply in Mrs. Jones's dining room early one morning, and Billy answered it, for his mother was busy.

"This is Uncle John," said the voice on the phone. "We are thinking of coming out to your place for a week; it's so awfully hot in town, and the children wish to play around in the country. Tell your mother."

"Wait a minute," said careful Billy and, laying the receiver down, he turned to his mother, who was clearing the breakfast table, and repeated the message.

Mrs. Jones was tired that morning. It was hot in the country, too, especially over the cook stove, and there was so much work ahead that she could not see her way through it.

"Mother is sick. She is sick to death of this endless work, and if you will clear away the breakfast things, I believe I'll go lie down."

She threw up her hands with a gesture of dismay. "Oh, I'm just sick!" she exclaimed.

Billy turned slowly to the telephone, but there was a twinkle in his eye. Though slow of movement, he was not slow mentally; and he was his mother's right-hand man.

"Hullo," he said and then, "I'm afraid it won't do. Mother's ill," and hung up the receiver.

Mrs. Jones gasped. "Oh, Billy!" she said, and then she thought, "Well, why not?" If John and his wife and the two boys came to be fed and waited on, she would get none of the week's work done and would be exhausted when the end of the week came. If she were ill (?), the work planned for the week would not be done either, but at the end of the week, she might be rested.

"Well, Billy," she said, "Mother is sick. She is sick to death of this endless work, and if you will clear away the breakfast things, I believe I'll go lie down."

This was the way Mrs. Jones came to take the rest cure for a week, lending the children a helping hand only now and then when they got into serious difficulty and consoling herself for her desertion of them by planning a vacation for them later.

Everyone seems to be so overburdened these days; let's be considerate about our visiting.

I had company myself one day last summer. Mr. and Mrs. P and their three children drove up in their car at just eleven o'clock one morning. I welcomed them as prettily as I knew how, made them comfortable in the cool living room, and said: "If you will please excuse me now, I shall get us all some dinner."

"Oh! We can't stay for dinner," said Mrs. P; we shall stay only a few minutes." After that I could not leave them to get dinner for the Man of the Place and his hired help, so I sat with them trying to be entertaining, though wondering frantically how I could hasten the dinner when I was free to get it.

They stayed on and on. At half past eleven, I again urged them to stay and tried to excuse myself from the room. They only refused again, saying they must go. But they didn't. At a quarter to twelve, I felt that in some way, if I should ask them again, they would stay to dinner and let me get it; but I had become angry and resolved that if they should stay all day, I would not again ask them to eat with us. They left at a few minutes past twelve, just as the men appeared in the barn door coming to dinner.

We do enjoy company, all of us, but we are all tired. We have been working unusually hard for two years and have been under a nervous strain besides.* We have each adjusted our burden so that we are more or less able to carry it, but a little addition to it makes it, in some cases, unbearable. It was the last straw in the camel's load that broke his back, you know.

Company we must have! Visiting should be more frequent that we may exchange ideas and learn to know and love one another, and there are ways that this may be made easy for us all instead of burdening one another by being inconsiderate.

One of the pleasantest times I remember last summer was a surprise visit from a family of five persons. In the middle of the morning, a team drove up and the five were unloaded at my door.

"Daddy was coming on business," cried one of the grown daughters, "and we desired to visit with you so we just came along."

"Don't be scared," said the soft-voiced mother. "We took you by surprise so we brought a picnic dinner, and we won't let you even build a fire. Just bring out what you have cooked and let's all picnic together."

They proposed eating out under the trees, but we decided it would be pleasanter to spread the dinner on the long table on the screened north porch. How simple and easy, with nobody overworked or tired, and we did have such a good visit.

---

*The strain of World War I.

Let's Not Depend on Experts
September 1916

"Clothes are much more sanitary if not ironed after washing," said a physician in an article on fresh air and sunshine which I read the other day. Isn't that delightful news and especially so in hot weather? I have not ironed knit underwear, stockings, sheets or towels for years but; although I knew there was a very good reason for not doing so, I have always felt rather apologetic about it.

I should like to know who designed our furniture as we use it today. It must have been a man.

Science is surely helping the housewife! Now instead of fearing that the neighbors will say I am lazy or a poor housekeeper when they find out that I slight my ironing, I can say: "Oh no! I never do much ironing, except the outside clothes. We must not iron out the fresh air and sunshine, you know. It is much more healthful not to, the doctors say."

Seriously, there is something very refreshing about sheets and pillow slips just fresh from the line after being washed and dried in the sun and air. Just try them that way and see if your sleep is not sweeter.

Our inability to see things that are right before our eyes until they are pointed out to us would be amusing if it were not at times so serious. We are coming, I think, to depend too much on being told and shown and taught instead of using our own eyes and brains and inventive faculties, which are likely to be just as good as any other person's.

I should like to know who designed our furniture as we use it today. It must have been a man. No woman, I am sure, at least no woman who has the care of a house would ever have made it as it is. Perhaps, if some physician or some domestic science teacher would point out to us the unnecessary dirt and the extra work caused by the height of our furniture, we would insist on having it different. Otherwise, it is quite likely we shall keep on in the same old way, breaking our backs and overworking tired muscles, or we shall become careless and let the dirt accumulate.

Most furniture, and especially that in the bedroom where of all places cleanliness should be most observed, is just high enough from the floor to permit dust and dirt to gather underneath but not high enough to be cleaned easily. It is more than likely, also, not to fit back smoothly against the wall but to sit out just far enough to make another hiding place for dust. The only way to clean under and behind such articles is to move them bodily from their place, clean the wall and floor, and then move them back. This should be done every few days. However, dragging heavy dressers and wardrobes from their places and then putting them back again is hard work, and it is a great deal worse than time wasted to do it.

Built-in furniture does away with a great deal of heavy work. A little built-in cupboard and a light dressing table may take the place of the heavy dresser. One does not have to clean under, behind, or on top of closets and wardrobes that reach smoothly from floor to ceiling, nor do sideboards and china closets built into the walls need to be moved when cleaning the dining room.

When Proverbs Quarrel
September 1918

It had been a busy day, and I was very tired when, just as I was dropping off to sleep, I remembered that bit of mending I should have done for the Man of the Place. Then I must have dreamed, for in my fancy, I saw that rent in the garment enlarge and stretch into startlingly large proportions.

At the same time a familiar voice sounded in my ear, "A stitch in time saves nine," it said.

I felt very discouraged indeed at the size of the task before me and very much annoyed that my neglect should have caused it to increase to nine times its original size when, on the other side of me, a cheerful voice insinuated, "It is never too late to mend."

> *I had not realized that there were so many wise proverbs and that they might fall out among themselves.*

Ah! There was that dear old friend of my grandmother's, who used to encourage her to work until all hours of the night to keep the family clothes in order. I felt impelled to begin at once to mend that lengthened rent, but paused as a voice came to me from a dark corner saying, "A chain is no stronger than its weakest link."

"Shall a man put new wine into old bottles," chimed in another. "Of course not," I thought, "then why put new cloth—"

But now the voices seemed to come from all about me. They appeared to be disputing and quarreling or at least disagreeing among themselves.

"Oh, what a tangled web we weave when first we practice to deceive," said a smug, oily voice.

"But practice makes perfect," piped a younger voice sweetly, though with an impudent expression.

"And if at first you don't succeed, try, try again," chirped a small voice with a snicker, and it seemed to me that the room was filled with soft laughter.

Evidently thinking that something should be done to put the younger folks in their place, a proverb with a very stern voice spoke from a far corner. "Children should be seen and not heard," he said, and a demure little voice at once answered, "Out of the mouth of babes cometh wisdom."

This was really growing interesting. I had not realized that there were so many wise proverbs and that they might fall out among themselves.

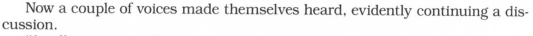

Now a couple of voices made themselves heard, evidently continuing a discussion.

"A rolling stone gathers no moss," said a rather disagreeable voice, and I caught a shadowy glimpse of a hoary old proverb with a long, gray beard.

"But a setting hen never grows fat," retorted his companion in a sprightly tone.

"An honest man is the noblest work of God," came a high, nasal voice with a self-righteous undertone.

"Ah, yes! Honesty is the best policy, you know," came the answer in a brisk business-like tone, just a little cutting.

"A fool and his money are soon parted," said a thin, tight-lipped voice with a puckering quality that I felt sure would draw the purse strings tight.

"Oh, well, money is the root of all evil, why not be rid of it?" answered a jolly, rollicking voice with a hint of laughter in it.

But now there seemed to be danger of a really violent altercation for I heard the words "sowing wild oats," spoken in a cold, sneering tone, while an angry voice retorted hotly, "There is no fool like an old fool," and an admonitory voice added, "It is never too late to mend." Ah! Grandmother's old friend with a different meaning in the words.

Then at my very elbow, spoken for my benefit alone, I heard again the words, "It is never too late to mend." Again, I had a glimpse of that neglected garment with the rent in it grown to unbelievable size. Must I? At this time of night! But a soft voice whispered in my ear, "Sufficient unto the day is the evil thereof," and with a smile at grandmother's friend, I drifted into dreamless sleep.

Farmers—Need More Wives?
July 1916

One of the neighbors needed some help in the hay harvest. Being too busy to go himself, he called a town friend by telephone and asked him, if possible, to send out someone to work through haying. Mansfield has made a beautiful shady park of the public square in the center of the town, and it is the gathering place for those who have idle time on their hands. Everyone enjoys it, the busy man with just a few idle minutes as well as the town loafers who, perhaps, have a few busy minutes now and then. It seemed like a good place to look for a man to help in the hay field, so here the obliging friend went.

*I ran away from a thousand things
waiting to be done and stole a little
visit with a friend.*

"Any of you fellows want a job?" he asked of a group resting in the shade. "Yes," said one man. "I do." "Work on a farm?" asked the friend. "Yes, for I need a job," was the reply. "Can you go out in the morning?" was the next question. "How far out is it?" asked the man who needed a job. "Two miles and a half," he was told. "Can't do it!" he exclaimed, dropping back into the restful position from which he had been disturbed. "I wouldn't go that far from town to work for anybody."

The Man of the Place, inquiring in town for help, was told that it was not much use to look for it. "Jack was in the other day and begged with tears in his eyes for someone to come help him get in his hay, and he couldn't get anyone." Jack's place is only half a mile from town, so surely it could not be too far out; but to be sure the sun was shining rather warm in the hay field and the shade in the park was pleasanter. All of which reminds one of the tramp of whom Rose Wilder Lane tells in her *Soldiers of the Soil*. She met him, one of many, while on her walking tour through the state of California. After listening to his tale of woe, she asked him why he did not look for work on a farm. She was sure there must be a chance to find a job there, for the farmers were very short of help. To her suggestion, the tramp replied, "Who wants to work like a farmer anyway!"

No one seems to want to "work like a farmer," except the farmer's wife. Well! Perhaps she does not exactly want to, but from the way she goes about it, no one would suspect that she did not. In our neighborhood we are taking over more of the chores to give the men longer days in the field. We are milking the cows, turning the separator, feeding the calves and the pigs, and doing what-ever else is possible, even going into the fields at times. Farmers are being urged to raise more food for world consumption, to till more acres, and also produce more to the acre. Their hands are quite full now, and it seems that about the only way they could procure more help would be to marry more wives.

A few days ago, I ran away from a thousand things waiting to be done and stole a little visit with a friend. And so I learned another way to cut across a corner and save work. Here it is, the way Mrs. Craig makes plum jelly. Cook the plums and strain out the juice; then to 3 cups of the boiling juice add 4 cups of sugar and stir until dissolved. Fill jelly glasses at once and set to one side. If the juice is fresh, it will be jelled in the morning; but if the juice is from canned plums, it takes longer and may have to set over until the next day, but it jells beautifully in the end.

Does It Pay to Be Idle?
February 1916

A stranger once went to a small inland town in the Ozarks to look over the country. As he left the little hotel in the morning for his day's wandering among the hills, he noticed several men sitting comfortably in the shade of the "gallery," gazing out into the street.

When the stranger returned late in the afternoon, the "gallery" was still occupied by the same men looking as though they had not stirred from their places since he left them there in the early morning.

This happened for three days, and then as the stranger was coming in from his day's jaunt in the evening, he stopped and spoke to one of the men. "Say," he asked, "how do you fellows pass the time here all day? What do you do to amuse yourselves?"

---

*Vices are simply overworked virtues
anyway.*

A man emptied his mouth of its accumulation of tobacco juice and replied in a lazy drawl, "Oh, we jest set and—think—and—sometimes—we—jest—set."

I have laughed many times over this story, which I know to be true, with never a thought except for the humor of the tale beyond the hackneyed ones on the value of wasted time—the vice of idleness.

We are told continually by everyone interested in our welfare or in "making the wheels go round" how to employ our spare moments to the best advantage, until, if we followed their advice, there would be no spare moments.

It is rank heresy, I know, to detract from these precepts, but lately I have been wondering whether perhaps it is not as great a fault to be too energetic as it is to be too idle.

Perhaps it would be better all around if we were to "jest set and think" a little more, or even sometimes "jest set."

Vices are simply overworked virtues anyway. Economy and frugality are to be commended, but follow them on in an increasing ratio and what do we find at the other end? A miser! If we overdo the using of spare moments, we may find an invalid at the end, while perhaps, if we allowed ourselves more idle time, we would conserve our nervous strength and health to more than the value of the work we could accomplish by emulating at all times the little busy bee.

I once knew a woman, not very strong, who, to the wonder of her friends,

went through a time of extraordinary hard work without any ill effects.

I asked her for her secret, and she told me that she was able to keep her health, under the strain, because she took twenty minutes of each day in which to absolutely relax both mind and body. She did not even "set and think." She lay at full length, every muscle and nerve relaxed, and her mind as quiet as her body. This always relieved the strain and renewed her strength.

I spent a delightful day not long ago, visiting in a home where there are several children and the little mother not over strong. She is doing nothing to add to the family income, has no special work of her own to earn some pin money, but the way she has that little family organized would be a lesson in efficiency to many a businessman. The training she is giving the children, and the work she is doing in preparing them to meet the problems of life and become self-supporting, self-respecting citizens could not be paid for in money.

The children all help and the work for the day goes forward with no confusion. There is nothing left undone because one person thought another was to do it. There are no whines such as "I did that yesterday; let sister (or brother) do it this time." Each child has a particular part of the work to do. Each knows what his work is and that he is responsible for that work being done as it should be.

"I don't know what to do with Edith.
I've no idea where she learned it, but
she is a regular little liar."

One of the girls does the upstairs work; another has the care of the parlor, dining room, and library. The two smaller girls must keep their playthings in order and not leave their belongings scattered around the house. The mother does the cooking and the washing of the dishes. The places of each are changed from time to time that there may be no unfairness and that each may learn to do the different kinds of work. One boy keeps water in the house, milks the cow, and keeps the motor car clean. Another boy brings in the wood and runs errands.

Each receives for the work done a few cents a week, and this is their spending money to do with as they please. When it is spent, there is no teasing for a few cents to spend for this and that. They know the amount of their income and plan and spend accordingly. In this way they are learning the value of money: to work for what they want instead of begging for it and to live within their income. If their work is not well done, a fine of a few cents is a better punishment than a scolding or a whipping, leaving both parties with their self-respect uninjured while the child can see the punishment fits the crime.

****

"I don't know what to do with Edith," said a mother to me. "I've no idea where she learned it, but she is a regular little liar. I can't depend on a thing she says."

Edith was a very bright, attractive child about three years old. Just then she started to go into another room. "Oh! Don't go in there!" her mother exclaimed. "It's dark in there and there is a big dog behind the door." The child opened the door a crack, peeped around it, smiled a knowing smile, and went on in. Evidently, she knew her mother and that she "could not depend on a thing she said," that she was "a regular little—" Sounds ugly, doesn't it? Perhaps I'd better not quote it at all, but where do you suppose Edith learned to be untruthful?

****

When I went to San Francisco last summer, I left the Man of the Place and his hired man to "batch it." There were no women relatives near, no near neighbors with whom they could board, and, of course, it was out of the question to hire a girl to stay with two lone men.

I was sorry for them, but our only child lives in San Francisco, and I had not seen her for four years. Besides, there was the fair [the San Francisco Exhibition], so I left them and went.

Now the Man of the Place says, "If any man thinks housekeeping is easy work and not all a woman ought to do, just let him roll up his sleeves and tackle the job."

More than any other business, that of farming depends upon the home, and it is almost impossible for any farmer to succeed without the help of the house. In the country the home is still depended upon to furnish bed and board and the comforts of life.

It is a good idea sometimes to think of the importance and dignity of our everyday duties. It keeps them from being so tiresome; besides, others are apt to take us at our own valuation.

Join 'Don't Worry' Club
March 1916

"Eliminate—To thrust out." Did you ever hear of the science of elimination? Didn't know there was such a science? Well, just try to eliminate, or to thrust out from your everyday life the unnecessary, hindering things; and if you do not decide that it takes a great deal of knowledge to do so successfully, then I will admit that it was my mistake.

The spring rush is almost upon us. The little chickens, the garden, the spring sewing and house-cleaning will be on our hands soon, and the worst of it is, they will all come together unless we have been very wise in our planning.

I found that I was becoming like the man who did "wish Saturday would hurry and come" so that he could take a bath.

It almost makes one feel like the farmer's wife who called up the stairs to awaken the hired girl on a Monday morning. "Liza Jane," she called, "come hurry and get up and get the breakfast. This is wash day, and here it is almost 6 o'clock and the washing not done yet. Tomorrow is ironing day and the ironing not touched; next day is churning day and it's not begun, and here the week is half gone and nothing done yet."

You'd hardly believe it, but it's true. And it's funny, of course, but one can just feel the worry and strain under which the woman was suffering. All without reason, too, as the greater parts of our worry usually are.

It seems to me that the first thing that should be "thrust out" from our household arrangements is that same worry and feeling of hurry. I do not mean to eliminate haste, for sometimes, usually in fact, that is necessary; but there is a wide difference between haste and hurry. We may make haste with our hands and feet and still keep our minds unhurried. If our minds are cool and collected, our "heads" will be able to "save our heels" a great deal.

An engineer friend once remarked of the housekeeping of a capable woman, "There is no lost motion there." She never worried over her work. She appeared to have no feeling of hurry. Her mind, calm and quiet, directed the work of her hands and there was no bungling, no fruitless running here and there. Every motion and every step counted so that there was "no lost motion."

Household help is so very hard to get, especially on the farm, that with the housekeeper it has become a question of what to leave undone or cut out altogether from her scheme of things as well as how to do in an easier manner what must be done.

****

The Man of the Place loved good things to eat. Does yet for that matter, as, indeed, I think the men of all other places do. Trying to make him think I was a wonder of a wife, I gratified this appetite until, at last, when planning the dinner for a feast day, I discovered to my horror that there was nothing extra I could cook to mark the day as being distinct and better than any other day. Pies, the best I could make, were common everyday affairs. Cakes, ditto. Puddings, preserves, and jellies were ordinary things. Fried, roasted, broiled, and boiled poultry of all kinds was no treat, we had so much of it as well as other kinds of meat raised on the farm. By canning and pickling and preserving all kinds of vegetables and fruits, we had each and every kind the year around. In fact, we were surfeited with good things to eat all the time.

As I studied the subject, it was impressed upon me that in order to thoroughly enjoy anything, one must feel the absence of it at times, and I acted upon that theory. We have fresh fruit the year around—our apples bridging the gap from blackberries and plums in the summer to the first strawberries in the spring—and these fresh fruits are usually our desserts. Fresh fruits are better, more healthful, more economical, and so much less work to serve than pies, puddings, and preserves. These things we have on our feast days, for Sunday treats, and for company. They are relished so much more because they are something different.

I stopped canning vegetables altogether. There is enough variety in winter vegetables, if rightly used, and we enjoy the green garden truck all the more for having been without it for a few months. The family is just as well if not better satisfied under this treatment, and a great deal of hard work is left out.

Some time ago the semiannual house-cleaning was dropped from my program, very much to everyone's advantage. If a room needed cleaning out of season, I used to think "Oh well, it will soon be house-cleaning time" and let it wait until then. I found that I was becoming like the man who did "wish Saturday would hurry and come" so that he could take a bath. Then I decided I would have no more house-cleaning in the accepted meaning of that word.

The first step in the new order of things was to dispense with carpets and use rugs instead. When a rug needs shaking and airing, it gets it then, or as soon as possible, instead of waiting until house-cleaning time. If the windows need washing, they are washed the first day I feel energetic enough. The house is gone over in this way a little at a time when it is needed and as suits my convenience, and about all that is left of the bugaboo of house-cleaning is the putting up of the heater in the spring and the taking it out in the fall.

Never do I have the house in a turmoil and myself exhausted as it used to be when I house-cleaned twice a year.

To be sure there are limits to the lessening of work. I could hardly go so far as a friend who said, "Why sweep? If I let it go today and tomorrow and the next day, there will be just so much gained, for the floor will be just as clean when I do sweep, as it would be if I swept every day from now until then." Still, after all, there is something to be said for that viewpoint. The applied science of the elimination of work can best be studied by each housekeeper for herself, but believe me, it is well worth studying.

✳✳

During the first years of his married life, a man of my acquaintance used to complain bitterly to his wife because she did not make enough slop in the kitchen to keep a hog. "At home," he said, "they always kept a couple of hogs, and they did not cost a cent, for there was always enough waste and slop from the kitchen to feed them." How ridiculous we all are at times! This man actually thought that something was wrong instead of being thankful that there was no waste from his kitchen. The young wife was grieved, but said she did not "like to cook well enough to cook things and throw them to the hogs for the sake of cooking more."

The food on her table was always good, even if some of it was made over dishes; and after a time, her husband realized that he had a treasure in the kitchen, and that it was much cheaper to feed the hogs their proper food than to give them what had been prepared for human consumption.

There are so many little heedless ways in which a few cents are wasted here and a few more there. The total would be truly surprising if we should sum them up. I illustrated this to myself in an odd way lately. While looking over the pages of a catalog advertising articles from 2 cents to 10 cents, the Man of the Place said, "There are a good many little tricks you'd like to have. Get what you want; they will only cost a few cents." So, I made out a list of what I wanted, things I decided I could not get along without as I found them, one by one, on those alluring pages. I was surprised when I added up the cost to find that it amounted to $5. I put the list away intending to go over it and cut out some things to make the total less. That was several months ago, and I have not yet missed any of the things I would have ordered. I have decided to let the list wait until I do.

A Fool and His Son Are Soon Parted
January 1923

Heartache, rather than contentment and happiness, has been the lot of a friend of ours who failed to recognize the inalienable right of a child to have something of his very own.

Grudgingly was the money given;
always was there the insistent demand
for an accounting of every cent.

Reared on one of the best farms in Missouri, the son of the house, as he grew into manhood, resented the fact that no matter how hard he labored or how prosperous the season, the day never came when he could call a dime his own. Always it was, "Dad, can I have money for a pair of shoes," or "Dad, I'd like to go to the picnic tomorrow. Can I have 50 cents to spend?" Grudgingly was the money given; always was there the insistent demand for an accounting of every cent. "Someday, son," he'd say, "I'm going to give you a farm. Got to count the pennies and work hard."

Came the day when the boy was a man and demands were made for a fixed sum. "Give me even 50 cents a day, Dad," he said, "when you pay the hired men $2.50, and I'll be satisfied." But the father turned a deaf ear and a stony heart to the appeal, and so the boy left home to win his way among strangers.

Embittered is the father, sorrowful the mother, and only He who looks down into the hearts of men may know the hunger that fills each heart as they go their separate ways. How is it with you, friend?

A Day Off Now and Then
February 1914

Distances are long in the country, and although it is very pleasant to go and spend the day with a friend, it takes a good while to see many people in that way. Women who have been rather isolated all summer need to be enlivened by seeing people, the more the better. There is something brightening to the wits and cheering to the spirits in congenial crowds that is found in nothing else. Why not form a neighborhood club and combine the pleasure of going "a visiting" with the excitement of a little crowd and the joy of entertaining our friends all together when our turn comes? It is less trouble to entertain several at once

The long, bright days of summer, when we all long to go picnicking and fishing, offer simply a different form of entertainment and social life and should be enjoyed to the full.

than to entertain several times; besides, there is a great saving of time, and as the club meets at first one house and then another, the neighborhood visiting is done with less of work and worry and more of pleasure than in any other way.

Needed by Country Women

It used to be that only the women in town could have the advantages of women's clubs, but now the woman in the country can be just as cultured a club woman as though she lived in town. The neighborhood club can take up any line of work or study the members wish. Courses of reading can be obtained from the state university or the International Congress of Farm Women, and either organization will be glad to help with plans, advice, and instruction. Bits of fancy work or sewing may be taken to the meetings, and the latest stitch or the shortcut in plain sewing can be learned by all. Recipes may be exchanged, good stories told, songs sung, and jokes enjoyed.

The serving of some dainty refreshments would add to the pleasure of the afternoon and keep the social graces in good practice. Women in the country, as well as those in town, need these occasions to show what charming hostesses and pleasant guests they can be. If the men folks want to go along, by all means, let them do so. They might gather by themselves and discuss farm matters. They might even organize and have a little farmers' club of their own, if they have not done so already; then they would be even more willing to hitch up and drive to the meeting place.

No Tiresome Meetings

There are so many ways to vary the meetings and programs they need never become tiresome or dull. Now and then the meeting may be held in the evening and an entertainment given by home talent. Sometimes the club might go in a body to a lecture or some amusement in town or for a little excursion to the nearest city. A regular organization with the proper officers, a motto, and membership badges will add to the interest, as will also being an auxiliary of some larger organization such as the International Congress of Farm Women.

Although the fall with its greater amount of leisure may be the best time to start a club of this kind, it need not be given up at the coming of spring. The long, bright days of summer, when we all long to go picnicking and fishing, offer simply a different form of entertainment and social life and should be enjoyed to the full. Perhaps the meetings might best be further apart while the rush of work is on, but a day off now and then will never be noticed in the work and will do the workers a world of good.

About Work
February 1919

There is good in everything, we are told, if we will only look for it; and I have at last found the good in a hard spell of illness. It is the same good the Irishman found in whipping himself.

"Why in the world are you doing that?" exclaimed the unexpected and astonished spectator.

> *"I eat all right and sleep all right," said he. "I even feel all right, but just the sight of a piece of work makes me tremble."*

"Because it feels so good when I stop," replied the Irishman with a grin. And this thing of being ill certainly does feel good when it stops. Why, even work looks good to a person who has been through such an enforced idleness, at least when strength is returning. Though I'll confess, if work crowds on me too soon, I am like the friend who was recovering from influenza rather more slowly than is usually the case.

"I eat all right and sleep all right," said he. "I even feel all right, but just the sight of a piece of work makes me tremble."

"That," said I, "is a terrible affliction, but I have known persons who suffer from it who never had the influenza."

But I'm sure we will all acknowledge that there is an advantage in having been ill if it makes us eager for work once more. Sometimes, I fancy we do not always appreciate the value of work, and how dry and flavorless life would be without it.

If work were taken from us, we would lose rest also, for how could we rest unless we first became tired from working? Leisure would mean nothing to us for it would not be a prize to be won by effort and so would be valueless. Even play would lose its attraction for, if we played all the time, play would become tiresome; it would be nothing but work after all.

In that case, we would be at work again and perhaps a piece of actual work would become play to us. How topsy-turvy! But there is no cause for alarm. None of us is liable to be denied the pleasure of working, and that is good for us no one will deny. Man realized it soon after he was sentenced to "earn his bread by the sweat of his brow," and with his usual generosity he lost no time in letting his womankind in on a good thing.

When the Blues Descend
August 1920

The whole world was a deep, dark blue, for I had waked with a grouch that morning. While blue is without doubt a heavenly color, it is better in skies than in one's mind; for when the blues descend upon a poor mortal on earth, life seems far from being worth the living.

I didn't want to help with the chores; I hated to get breakfast; and the prospect of doing up the morning's work afterward was positively revolting.

I didn't want to help with the chores; I hated to get breakfast; and the prospect of doing up the morning's work afterward was positively revolting. Beginning the usual round of duties—under protest—I had a great many thoughts about work and none of them was complimentary to the habit. But presently my mind took a wider range and became less personal as applied to the day just beginning.

First, I remembered the old, old labor law, "Six days shalt thou labor and do all thy work: But the seventh day is the sabbath of the Lord thy God: in it thou shalt not do any work."*

It used to be impressed upon us as most important that we must rest on the seventh day. This doesn't seem to be necessary any longer. We may not, "Remember the sabbath day to keep it holy,"** but we'll not forget to stop working. With our present attitude toward work, the emphasis should be put upon "Six days thou shalt labor," and if we stick it out to work the six days, we will rest on the seventh without any urging. Given half a chance, we will take Saturday off also and any other day or part of a day we can manage to sneak, besides which the length of a work day is shrinking and shrinking for everyone except farmers, and they are hoping to shorten theirs.

But really the old way was best, for it takes about six days of work to give just the right flavor to a day off. As I thought of all these things, insensibly, my ideas about work changed. I remembered the times of enforced idleness when recovering from an illness and how I longed to be busily at work again. Also I

---

*Exodus 20:9–10.
**Exodus 20:8.

recollected a week of vacation that I once devoted to pleasure during which I suffered more than the weariness of working while I had none of its satisfaction. For there is a great satisfaction in work well done, the thrill of success in a task accomplished.

I got the thrill at the moment that my mind reached the climax. The separator was washed. It is a job that I especially dislike, but while my mind had been busy far afield, my hands had performed their accustomed task with none of the usual sense of unpleasantness, showing that, after all, it is not so much the work we do with our bodies that makes us tired and dissatisfied as the work we do with our minds.

We have been, for so long, thinking of labor as a curse upon man that, because of our persistently thinking of it as such, it has very nearly become so.

There always has been a great deal of misplaced pity for Adam because of his sentence to hard labor for life when really that was all that saved him after he was deported from paradise, and it is the only thing that has kept his descendents as safe and sane even as they are.

There is nothing wrong with God's plan that man should earn his bread by the sweat of his brow. The wrong is in our own position only. In trying to shirk while we "let George do it," we bring upon ourselves our own punishment; for in the attitude we take toward our work, we make of it a burden instead of the blessing it might be.

Work is like other good things in that it should not be indulged in to excess, but a reasonable amount that is of value to one's self and to the world, as is any honest, well-directed labor, need never descend into drudgery.

It is a tonic and an inspiration and a reward unto itself. For the sweetness of life lies in usefulness like honey deep in the heart of a clover bloom.

Life Is an Adventure
March 1916

As I was passing through the Missouri building, at the exposition last summer, I overheard a scrap of conversation between two women. Said the first woman, "How do you like San Francisco?" The other replied, "I don't like San Francisco at all! Everywhere I go there is a Chinaman on one side, a Jap on the other and a n——r behind."

These women were missing a great deal, for the foreign life of San Francisco is very interesting; and the strange vari-colored peoples on the streets give a touch of color and picturesqueness that adds much to the charm of the city. A morning's walk from the top of Russian Hill, where I lived when there, would take me through "Little Italy" where one hears Italian spoken on all sides; where the people are black-eyed and handsome with a foreign beauty and where, I am sure, the children are the most beautiful in the world.

To me it is a joy that "no man knoweth
what a day may bring forth."

From there I passed directly into "Chinatown" where the quaint babies look exactly like Chinese dolls, and the older people look exactly as if they had stepped out of a Chinese picture. The women, in their comfortable loose garments made of black or soft colored silks, with their shiny, smoothly combed black hair full of bright ornaments, were, some of them, very pretty. Only the older men seemed to be wearing the Chinese dress. The younger men were dressed like any American businessman.

It is a curious fact that the second generation of Chinese born in San Francisco are much larger than their parents and look a great deal more like our own people, while the third generation can scarcely be distinguished from Americans. And oh, the shops of Chinatown! I do not understand how any woman could resist their fascination. Such quaint and beautiful jewelry, such wonderful pieces of carved ivory, such fine pottery, and such silks and embroideries as one finds there!

Wandering on from Chinatown, I would soon be at Market Street, which is the main business street of San Francisco; and everywhere, as the women in the Missouri building had said, there was "a Chinaman on one side, a Jap on the other and a n——r behind."

It gives a stay-at-home Middle Westerner something of a shock to meet a group of turbaned Hindus on the street or a Samoan or a Filipino or even a

Mexican. People in happier times spent hundreds of dollars and months of time in traveling to see these foreign people and their manner of living. It is all to be seen, on a smaller scale, in this city of our own country.

Walking on the Zone one day at the fair, Daughter and I noticed ahead of us five sailormen. They were walking along discussing which one of the attractions they should visit. They were evidently on shore for a frolic. Tired of "rocking in the cradle of the deep," they were going to enjoy something different on shore. Should they see the wonderful educated horse? "No! Who cared anything about an old horse?" Should they see Creation, the marvelous electrical display? "No! Not that! We're here for a good time, aren't we?"

Perhaps by now you suspect that Daughter and I had become so interested, we determined to know which of the attractions they decided was worthwhile. We followed with the crowd at their heels. The sailors passed the places of amusement one after another until they came to a mimic river, with a wharf and row boats, oars and all. Immediately, they made a rush for the wharf, and the last we saw of them they were tumbling hilariously into one of the boats for a good old row on the pleasant, familiar water.

Do you know, they reminded me in some way of the women in the Missouri building who did not like San Francisco.

A friend of mine used to sympathize with a woman for being "tied down" to a farm with no opportunity to travel or to study and with none of the advantages of town or city life. To her surprise she found that her sympathy was not needed. "My body may be tied here," her friend said, "but my mind is free. Books and papers are cheap and what I cannot buy, I can borrow. I have traveled all over the world."

The daughter of this woman was raised with a varied assortment of these same books and papers, pictures and magazines. When later she traveled over the United States, becoming familiar with the larger cities as well as the country, from Canada to the Gulf and from San Francisco to New York City, she said there was a great disappointment to her in traveling. She seemed to have seen it all before and thus had no "thrills" from viewing strange things. "I have read about foreign countries just as much," she said, "and I don't suppose I'll find anything in the world that will be entirely new to me." Which shows that a very good travel education can be had from books and papers and also proves once more the old saying that, "As the twig is bent the tree inclines."

✳✳✳

Over at a neighbor's the other day, I learned something new as, by the way, quite often happens. She has little soft homemade mattresses, as thick as a good comforter, to lay over the top of the large mattresses on her beds. Over these small mattresses she slips a cover as one does a case on a pillow. They are easily removed for washing and protect the mattress from soil, making it a simple matter to keep the beds clean and sweet.

This neighbor also makes her sheets last twice as long by a little trick she has. When the sheets begin to wear thin in the middle, she tears them down the center and sews the outsides together. Then she hems the outer edges down the sides. This throws the thin part to the outside, and the center, where the wear comes, is as good as new. Of course, the sheet has a seam down the middle, but it is not so very many years ago that all our sheets were that way, before we had sheeting and pillow tubing.

* *

It is no use trying! I seem unable today to get away from the idea of travel, perhaps because I read the *National Geographic* magazine last night. A sentence in one of the articles keeps recurring to me, and I am going to quote it to you, for you may not have noticed it. "It is not a figure of speech to say that every American has it in his heart that he is in a small sense a discoverer; that he is joining in the revelation to the world of something that it was not before aware of and of which it may someday make use."

We have the right, you know, to take a thought and appropriate it to our own uses; and so I have been turning this one over and over in my mind with all sorts of strange ramifications. The greater number of us cannot be discoverers of the kind referred to in the article quoted, for like the woman before mentioned, our bodies are tied more or less securely to our home habitat; but I am sure we are all discoverers at heart.

Life is often called a journey, "the journey of life." Usually when referred to in these terms it is also understood that it is "a weary pilgrimage." Why not call it a voyage of discovery and take it in the spirit of happy adventure?

Adventurers and travelers worthy of the name always make nothing of the difficulties they meet, nor are they so intent on the goal that they do not make discoveries on the way. Has anyone ever said to you, as a warning, "No man knoweth what a day may bring forth?" I have heard it often, and it is always quoted with a melancholy droop at the corners of the mouth. But why! Suppose we do not know what will happen tomorrow. May it not just as well be a happy surprise as something unpleasant?

To me, it is a joy that "no man knoweth what a day may bring forth," and that life is a journey from one discovery to another. It makes of every day a real adventure; and if things are not to my liking today, why, "There's a whole day tomorrow that ain't tetched yet," as the old man said. "No man knoweth" what the day will be like. It is absolutely undiscovered country. I'll just travel along and find out for myself.

Did you ever take a little trip anywhere with your conscience easy about things at home, your mind free from worry, and with all care cast aside and, eyes wide open, give yourself to the joy of every passing incident, looking for interesting things which happen every moment? If you have, you will understand. If not, you should try it, and you will be surprised how much adventure can enter into ordinary things.

CHAPTER 6

A great many
interesting things

The Hard Winter
February 1917

In the late issue of a St. Louis paper, I find the following: "Experts in the office of home economics of the United States Department of Agriculture have found it is possible to grind whole wheat in an ordinary coffee mill fine enough for use as a breakfast cereal and even fine enough for use in breadmaking."

If the experts of the Department of Agriculture had asked anyone of the 200 people who spent the winter of 1880–81 in De Smet, South Dakota, they might have saved themselves the trouble of experimenting. I think, myself, that it is rather a joke on our experts at Washington to be thirty-six years behind times.

That winter, known still among the old residents as "the hard winter," we demonstrated that wheat could be ground in an ordinary coffee mill.

That winter, known still among the old residents as "the hard winter,"* we demonstrated that wheat could be ground in an ordinary coffee mill and used for breadmaking. Prepared in that way, it was the staff of life for the whole community. The grinding at home was not done to reduce the cost of living, but simply to make living possible.

De Smet was built as the railroad went through, out in the midst of the great Dakota prairies far ahead of the farming settlements, and this first winter of its existence it was isolated from the rest of the world from December 1 until May 10 by the fearful blizzards that piled the snow forty feet deep on the railroad tracks. It was at the risk of life that anyone went even a mile from shelter, for the storms came up so quickly and were so fierce it was literally impossible to see the hand before the face, and men had frozen to death within a few feet of shelter because they did not know they were near safety.

The small supply of provisions in town soon gave out. The last sack of flour sold for $50 and the last of the sugar at $1 a pound. There was some wheat on hand, brought in the fall before for seed in the spring [by Almanzo and his brother Royal], and two young men [Almanzo and Cap Garland] dared to drive fifteen miles to where a solitary settler had also laid in his supply of seed wheat. They brought it in on sleds. There were no mills in town or country so

---

*This whole winter is described in *The Long Winter*. Trains carrying food did not get through from late November to early May.

this wheat was all ground in the homes in coffee mills. Everybody ground wheat, even the children taking their turns, and the resultant whole-wheat flour made good bread. It was also a healthful food, and there was not a case of sickness in town that winter.

It may be that the generous supply of fresh air had something to do with the general good health. Air is certainly fresh when the thermometer registers all the way from 15 to 40 degrees below zero with the wind moving at blizzard speed. In the main street of the town, snowdrifts in one night were piled as high as the second stories of the houses and packed hard enough to drive over, and the next night the wind might sweep the spot bare. As the houses were new and unfinished so that the snow would blow in and drift across us as we slept, fresh air was not a luxury. The houses were not overheated in daytime either, for the fuel gave out early in the winter and all there was left with which to cook and keep warm was the long prairie hay. A handful of hay was twisted into a rope, then doubled and allowed to twist back on itself and the two ends tied together in a knot, making what we called "a stick of hay."

It was a busy job to keep a supply of these "sticks" ahead of a hungry stove when the storm winds were blowing, but everyone took his turn good naturedly. There is something in living close to the great elemental forces of nature that causes people to rise above small annoyances and discomforts.

A train got through May 10 and stopped at the station. All the men in town were down at the tracks to meet it, eager for supplies, for even the wheat had come to short rations. They found that what had been sent into the hungry town was a trainload of machinery. Luckily, there were also two immigrant cars well supplied with provisions which were taken out and divided among the people.

Our days of grinding wheat in the coffee mills were over, but we had learned without expert aid that it can be done and that the flour so ground will make good bread and mush.

We had all become experts and demonstrated the fact.

The Friday Night Literary
January 1919

The influenza epidemic has been particularly hard on farm folks, coming as it did just at the close of the season's work when country people were beginning to relax from the strain of raising the year's crops.* It is at this time we usually meet one another and become acquainted again. There has been so much depending on our work, especially for the last two years, that we have attended to our business even more strictly than usual, and we were really lonesome for some good times together. But, being advised by the doctors not to gather in crowds, we have stayed at home as much as possible. Let's hope it hasn't become a habit!

There is one social affair, which used to belong to country life, that I would like to see come back again. That is the old-fashioned Friday night literary at the schoolhouse.

Sometimes I wonder if telephones and motor cars are altogether blessings for country people. When my neighbor can call me up for a short visit over the phone, she is not so likely to make the necessary effort to come and spend the afternoon; and I get hungry for the sight of her face as well as the sound of her voice. When she gets into her motor car, it is almost sure to run for twelve to fifteen miles before she can stop it, and that takes her away down the road past me. I have no hope that my rather prosy conversation can rival the joy of a ride in the car, and we see less and less of each other.

I am not really prejudiced against the motor car and the telephone. It is the way they are used to which I am objecting. Now when my neighbor calls me up to say she is coming over, I think very highly of the telephone as an adjunct to country life, for it gives me time to dust the mantle shelf, jump into a clean dress, and shut the bedroom door. Then I can meet her serenely as though things were always that way. But I don't like to visit over the phone. I'd much rather be sitting in the same room with my neighbor so I can see how her new dress is made and if she has another gray hair.

There is one social affair, which used to belong to country life, that I would like to see come back again. That is the old-fashioned Friday night literary at

---

*An epidemic of flu swept over war-weakened Europe and North America following World War I. Millions died in this catastrophe that may have killed more people than the war itself.

the schoolhouse. You older people who used to attend them, did you ever enjoy yourselves better anywhere?

At early candle light, parents and pupils from all over the district gathered at the schoolhouse, bringing lanterns and candles and sometimes a glass lamp to give an added touch of dignity to the teacher's desk. The lighting was good enough, for eyes were stronger in the days before brilliant lights were so common. Do you remember how the schoolchildren spoke their pieces and dialogs? It gave one a touch of distinction to speak a part in a dialog.

Then came the debate. Sometimes the older pupils of the school, sometimes a few of the pupils and some of the grownups, or again just the grownups took part in the debate. The questions debated were certainly threshed out to a conclusion. I have been thinking lately what a forum for discussing the questions of the day, political and otherwise, the old-fashioned debate would be. I think that farmers do not discuss these things enough among themselves these days. They are more likely to talk them over with their banker or their merchant when they go to town; and their minds on the questions of the day take their color from town opinion.

We farmers are very slow to realize that we are a class by ourselves. The bankers are organized, even internationally, as a class; merchants, both wholesale and retail, are organized and working in a body for the interests of merchants; labor, except that of the farmer, his wife and children, is very much organized; and yet many farmers are still contending, single-handed, as individuals against these huge organizations. We are so slow to organize and to work together for our mutual interests. The old-fashioned debates at the country schoolhouse would be a place and time where farmers could discuss these things among themselves.

An understanding among farmers, of themselves and how their interests are affected by the questions of the hour, is seriously needed. We cannot take our opinions from our fathers nor even keep the opinions we formed for ourselves a few years ago. Times and things move too fast. We must learn to look at things, even politics, from a farmer's standpoint. The price of hogs is more important to us than whether one political party wins an election simply as a political party. I would like to hear such timely questions discussed in an old-time debate; and I really think that a training in public speaking and an understanding of public questions would be worth more to pupils of the schools than games of basketball, because by exercising their brains they might grow into intelligent, wide-awake citizens.

Well, the debate is finished, and it is time for the spelling-down match. How earnestly we used to line up for the struggle and valiantly contest for the honor of remaining longest on the floor, and how we used to laugh when some small schoolchild spelled down an outsider who had forgotten the lessons in the old spelling book.

On Chickens and Hawks
June 1917

"In the spring a young man's fancy lightly turns to thoughts of love," sings the poet, but in the spring the fancy of a hawk surely turns to spring chickens. Day after day, he dines on the plumpest and fairest of the flock. I may spend half the day watching and never catch a glimpse of him, then the moment my back is turned—swoop!—and he is gone with a chicken.

I should like to sentence the ex-governor who vetoed the state bounty on hawks to make his living raising chickens.

I should like to sentence the ex-governor who vetoed the state bounty on hawks to make his living raising chickens in the hills and not permit him to have a gun on the place just by way of fitting the punishment to the crime.

I know it is said that hawks are a benefit to the farmers because they catch field mice and other pests, but I am sure they would not look for a mouse if there were a flock of chickens near by.

Times and Things
July 1922

My neighbor, who came from a city where her husband worked for a salary, said to me, "It is difficult for anyone who has worked for wages to get used to farming. There is a great difference between having a good paycheck coming twice a month or having only the little cash one can take in on a small farm. Why we have scarcely any money at all to spend!"

---

*So we must mix our times and things,
but let's mix 'em with brains.*

"You spent the paycheck for your living expenses did you not," I asked?
"All of it," she answered. "Every bit! We never could save a cent of it."
"And you have your living now, off the farm," said I.
"Yes, and a good one," she replied, "with a little left over. But it was great fun spending the paycheck. If we'd had a little less fun, we might have had more left."

All of which brings us to the question the little girl asked: "Would you rather have times or things"—good times to remember or things to keep, like bank accounts, homes of our own, and such things?

Things alone are very unsatisfying. Happiness is not to be found in money or in houses and lands, not even in modern kitchens or a late model motor car. Such things add to our happiness only because of the pleasant times they bring us.

But times would be bad without some things. We cannot enjoy ourselves if we are worried over how we shall pay our bills or the taxes or buy what the children need.

And so we must mix our times and things, but let's mix 'em with brains, as the famous artist said he mixed his paints, using good judgment in the amount we take.

When Grandma Pioneered
August 1921

Grandma was minding the baby. "Oh, yes, she is sweet," she said, "but she is no rarity to me. You see there were ten of us at home, and I was the oldest save one and that a boy. Seems like I've always had a baby to take care of. There were the little ones at home, then when I was older, I used to go help the neighbors at times; and there was always a new baby, for women them days didn't hire help unless they were down sick. When I was married, I had eleven of my own; now it's the grandchildren. No, indeed! Babies are no rarity to me! I was just a child myself when father and mother drove an ox team into the Ozarks. Father stopped the wagon in the thick woods by the big road, cut down some trees, and made a rough log cabin. But mother never liked the house there; father was away so much, and she didn't like to stay alone with the young ones so near the road. The Ozarks was a wild, rough country then, and all kinds of persons were passing; so father built another house down by the spring out of sight, and we lived there.

Snakes were thick, too, and not so pleasant to meet; but none of us ever got bit, though we went barefoot all summer and until freezing weather.

"The woods were full of wild turkey and deer; when we children hunted the cows at night, we thought nothing of seeing droves of them. Snakes were thick, too, and not so pleasant to meet; but none of us ever got bit, though we went barefoot all summer and until freezing weather.

"Father used to tan the hides of deer and cattle and make our shoes, but later we had 'boughten' shoes. Then the men of the settlement would drive their ox teams south into the pineries in the fall and haul in logs to the mills. When they had hauled a certain number of loads, they were paid with a load of logs for themselves. These they had sawed into lumber and hauled the lumber to Springfield or Marshfield, seventy-five or one hundred miles, and sold it to get their tax money and shoes for the family.

"The men worked away a good deal and the mothers and children made the crops. Neighbors were few and far apart, but we were never lonely; didn't have time to be. We raised wheat and corn for our bread; hogs ran loose in the woods and, with venison and wild turkey, made our meat; we kept some sheep for the wool, and we raised cotton.

"After we had gathered the cotton from the fields, we handpicked it from the seeds. We carded the cotton and wool and then spun them into yarn and thread and wove them into cloth; we made our own blankets and coverlets and all the cloth we used, even our dresses.

"We worked long days. As soon as we could see in the morning, two of us would go into the woods and drive up the oxen for the day's work. Then we girls worked all day in the fields while mother worked both in the house and out. Soon as supper was over, we built a brush fire in the fireplace to make light; and while one tended the fire to keep it bright, the others spun and wove and knit and sewed until 10 or 11 o'clock. Passing a house after dark, anytime before midnight, you could always hear the wheel awhirring and the loom at work. We cooked in the fireplace, too, and I was sixteen years old before I ever saw a cookstove.

"When the crops were raised, mother and we children did the threshing. The wheat was spread on poles with an old blanket under them to catch the grain as it dropped through; and we flailed it out with hickory poles, then blew the dust out in the wind, and it was ready to take to mill.

"We were taught to be saving. The shoes bought in the fall must last a year, and we were careful with them. When they got calico into the country, it cost 25 cents a yard, and if we had a calico dress we wore it for very best. When we took it off, we brushed off all the dust, turned it, folded it, and laid it carefully away.

"I never got much schooling. There was three months school in the year beginning the first Monday in September, but that was molasses-making, potato-digging, corn-picking time, and we older children had to stay home and do the work. The little ones went, and by the time they were older, we had things in better shape so they got lots more learning. But it was too late for us.

"Now school comes before the work at home, and when children go to school, it takes all their time; they can't do anything else.

"I wish folks now had to live for a little while like we did when I was young, so they would know what work is and learn to appreciate what they have. They have so much they are spoiled, yet every cent they get they must spend for something more. They want cars and pianos and silk dresses. Why when I was married, all my wedding clothes were of my own spinning and weaving, but my husband was so proud he wouldn't let me wear my linsey dresses but bought me calico instead.

"Ah, well, times have changed! I'm an old woman and have worked hard all my life, but even now I can work down some of the young ones."

Make a New Beginning
January 1918

We should bring ourselves to an accounting at the beginning of the New Year and ask these questions: What have I accomplished? Where have I fallen short of what I desired and planned to do and be?

I never have been in favor of making good resolutions on New Year's Day just because it was the first day of the year. Any day may begin a new year for us in that way, but it does help some to have a set time to go over the year's efforts and see whether we are advancing or falling back.

I never have been in favor of making good resolutions on New Year's Day just because it was the first day of the year.

If we find that we are quicker of temper and sharper of tongue than we were a year ago, we are on the wrong road. If we have less sympathy and understanding for others and are more selfish than we used to be, it is time to take a new path.

I helped a farmer figure out the value of his crops raised during the last season recently, and he was a very astonished person. Then when we added to that figure the amount he had received for livestock during the same period, he said: "It doesn't seem as if a man who had taken in that much off his farm would need a loan."

This farmer friend had not kept any accounts and so was surprised at the money he had taken in and that it should all be spent. Besides the help in a business way, there are a great many interesting things that can be gotten out of farm accounts if they are rightly kept.

The Man of the Place and I usually find out something new and unexpected when we figure up the business at the end of the year. We discovered this year that the two of us, without any outside help, had produced enough in the last year to feed thirty persons for a year—all the bread, butter, meat, eggs, sweetening, and vegetables necessary—and this does not include the beef cattle sold off the place.

. . . .

So if you have not done so, just figure up for yourselves, and you will be surprised at how much you have accomplished.

Having a Family Motto
August 1922

Naming the home place is an old, old custom, but the people who lived at such places used to have a family motto, also. Families as well as farms have distinguishing traits of character, and there are always some of these on which a family prides itself. Only the other day I heard a man say, "My father's word was as good as his note, and he brought us children up that way."

"My father's word was as good as his note, and he brought us children up that way."

Why not have a family motto expressing something for which we, as a family, stand?

Such a motto would be a help in keeping the family up to standard by giving the members a cause for pride in it and what it represents; it might even be a help in raising the standard of family life and honor.

If the motto of a family were, "My word is my bond," do you not think the children of that family would be proud to keep their word and feel disgraced if they failed to do so?

Suppose the motto were, "Ever ready," would not the members of that family try to be on the alert for whatever came?

Perhaps it would be possible to cure a family weakness by choosing a motto representing its opposite as an ideal for the family to strive toward. We might keep our choice a family secret until we have proven ourselves and could face the world upon it.

Though in these days we would not put the motto upon our shield as did the knights of old, we could use it in many ways. If carried only in our hearts, it would draw the family closer together.

Let's have a family motto as well as a farm name!

The First Frost
October 1917

Did the first frost catch you unready? It would be quite unusual if it didn't because I never knew anyone to be ready for cold weather in the fall or for the first warm spell in the spring. It is like choosing the right time to be ill or like choosing an out-of-the-way place for a boil—it simply isn't done!

I know a man who had a little patch of corn. He was not quite ready to cut it and besides he said, "It is just a little green." He let it wait until the frost struck it, and now he says it is too dry and not worth cutting. The frost saved him a lot of hard work.

---

*I never knew anyone to be ready for
cold weather in the fall or for the first
warm spell in the spring.*

This man's disposition reminds me of that of a renter we once had who was unable to plow the corn in all summer. Before it rained the ground was so hard he could not keep the plow in, and besides, if it did not rain, there would be no corn anyway, and he believed it was going to be a dry season. When it did rain, it was too wet to plow, and never was he ready and able to catch that cornfield when the ground was right for plowing.

And that reminds me of the other renter who was always ready to take advantage of his opportunities. His horses would break into the cornfield at night, or were turned in (we never knew which), and in the fall when The Man of the Place wanted a share of what corn was left, he was told that the horses had eaten all his share.

These anecdotes are not intended as any reflection on renters. I could tell some in which the joke is on the other side if I had the space.

The tragedy of being unready is easy to find, for more often than not success or failure turn upon just that one thing. There was a time, perhaps long ago, when you were not ready for examinations and failed to pass; then there was the time you were not ready to make that good investment because you had been spending carelessly. We can all remember many times when we were not ready. While being ready for and equal to whatever comes may be in some sense a natural qualification, it is a characteristic that may be cultivated, especially if we learn easily by experience.

It was interesting to see the way different persons showed their character after the first frost. One man considered that the frost had done his work for him and so relieved him of further effort. Others went along at their usual gait and saved their fodder in a damaged condition. They had done the best they could, let Providence take the responsibility. Still others worked through the moonlight nights and saved their feed in good condition in spite of the frost. They figured that it "was up to them" and no little thing like the first frost should spoil their calculations.

It does not so much matter what happens. It is what one does when it happens that really counts.

Our Fair and Our Fancy
November 1916

The annual fair at Mansfield was a success in spite of the drought. Farmers surely are the most optimistic people in the world! Although badly punished in the conflict with the forces of nature this season, they were by no means defeated, as was proved by the agricultural exhibits; and everywhere could be overheard planning for next year's campaign.

Discouraged? Not a bit of it! "It's been a bad season, but we'll come out all right," said one man. "The old cows will take us through." One could understand his confidence after looking at the stock exhibited. Purebred Jerseys, Holsteins, and Polled Durhams were there, each so good in its way that one could not be partial to any.

. . . .

One amusement feature provided as a free show on the street was, to me, shocking. I knew, of course, that the thing is often done, but I never have watched while knives were thrown around a human target. The target, as usual, was a woman, and a man threw the knives.

---

*The target, as usual, was a woman,
and a man threw the knives.*

Effacing myself behind a convenient corner, which hid the spectacle, I watched the faces of the crowd. They reminded me strongly of the faces of the crowd watching a Mexican bullfight that I saw in a moving picture. There happened to be no bloodshed in the knife throwing; but judging by the expression of some of the faces, there was a tense expectancy and unconsciously almost a hope that there might be.

In the crowd were women and children as well as men and boys, all eager, alert, and watching—for what? A failure of nerve perhaps in one of the performers; an instant's dimming of vision or slight miscalculation on the part of the man. There is something thrilling and ennobling in seeing a person brave death in a good cause or for an ideal, but to watch anyone risk being butchered merely to make holiday sport savors too much of other things. We condemn the bullfight and the spectators, you know. Is it perhaps a case of the pot calling the kettle black?

* *

It is not alone "one touch of nature" which "makes the whole world kin," but every emotion which writes itself on the human countenance creates a family likeness with others of its kind, even between people of different races. I saw this plainly when present at a Chinese Salvation Army meeting on a street corner in San Francisco's Chinatown. The crowd was large, and all Chinese except myself and escort.

Although Chinese was the only language spoken, and I could not understand a word; I could follow the exhorter's meaning and by the expressions on the faces about me could tell the state of mind of his audience. It was one of my many curious experiences in the city, and when the leader started singing "Onward, Christian Soldiers," in Chinese and the crowd joined in, I felt as though my ears must be bewitched. It was quite as startling as it was to see the words "Methodist Episcopal Church" over the door of the beautiful building, built in Chinese style on another street corner in Chinatown. The words seemed no more to belong with the fanciful Chinese architecture than the Chinese words belonged with the good old American hymn tune sung by Oriental folks.

Chasing Thistledown
June 1917

Did you ever chase thistledown? Oh, of course, when you were a child, but I mean since you have been grown! Some of us should be chasing thistledown a good share of the time.

There is an old story, for the truth of which I cannot vouch, which is so good that I am going to take the risk of telling it; and if any of you have heard it before, it will do no harm to recall it to your minds. A woman once confessed to the priest that she had been gossiping. To her surprise, the priest instructed her to go gather a ripe head of the thistle and scatter the seed on the wind, then to return to him. This she did, wondering why she had been told to do so strange a thing; but her penance was only begun, for when she returned to the priest, instead of forgiving her fault, he said: "The thistledown is scattered as were your idle words. My daughter, go and gather up the thistledown!"

"Well, y-e-s," we reply, "I've known her a long time," and we leave the new acquaintance wondering what it is we know against Mrs. Smith.

It is so easy to be careless and one is so prone to be thoughtless in talking. I told only half of a story the other day heedlessly overlooking the fact that by telling only a part, I left the listeners with a wrong impression of some very kindly persons. Fortunately, I saw in time what I had done, and I pounced on that thistledown before the wind caught it or else I should have had a chase.

A newcomer in the neighborhood says, "I do like Mrs. Smith! She seems such a fine woman."

"Well, y-e-s," we reply, "I've known her a long time," and we leave the new acquaintance wondering what it is we know against Mrs. Smith. We have said nothing against her, but we have "damned her with faint praise" and a thistle seed is sown on the wind.

The noun "gossip" is not of the feminine gender. No, absolutely not! A man once complained to me of some things that had been said about his wife. "Damn these gossiping women!" he exclaimed. "They do nothing but talk about their neighbors who are better than they. Mrs. Cook spends her time running around gossiping when she should be taking care of her children. Poor things, they never have enough to eat by their looks. Her housework is never done, and as for her character, everybody knows about—" and he launched into a detailed account of an occurrence which certainly sounded very compromising as he told it. I repeated to myself his first remark with the word *men* in place of the word *women* just to see how it would sound.

And so we say harmful things carelessly; we say unkind things in a spirit of retaliation or in a measure of self-defense to prove that we are no worse than others, and the breeze of idle chatter from many tongues picks them up, blows them here and there, and scatters them to the four corners of the earth. What a crop of thistles they raise!

If we were obliged to go gather up the seed before it had time to grow as the woman in the story was told to do, I am afraid we would be even busier than we are.

What Became of the Time We Saved?
April 1917

A few days ago, with several others, I attended the meeting of a woman's club in a neighboring town. We went in a motor car, taking less than an hour for the trip on which we used to spend three hours before the days of motor cars; but we did not arrive at the time appointed nor were we the latest comers by any means. Nearly everyone was late, and all seemed in a hurry. We hurried through the proceedings; we hurried in our friendly exchanges of conversation; we hurried away; and we hurried all the way home where we arrived late as usual.

What became of the time the motor car
saved us? Why was everyone late
and in a hurry?

What became of the time the motor car saved us? Why was everyone late and in a hurry? I used to drive leisurely over to this town with a team, spend a pleasant afternoon, and reach home not much later than I did this time, and all with a sense of there being time enough, instead of a feeling of rush and hurry. We have so many machines and so many helps, in one way and another, to save time; and yet I wonder what we do with the time we save. Nobody seems to have any!

Neighbors and friends go less often to spend the day. Instead, they say, "We have been planning for so long to come and see you, but we haven't had time," and the answer will be: "Everyone makes the same complaint. People don't go visiting like they used to. There seems to be no time for anything." I have heard this conversation, with only slight variations, so many times that I should feel perfectly safe to wager that I should hear it anytime the subject might be started. We must have all the time there is, the same as always. We should have more, considering the timesaving, modern conveniences. What becomes of the time we save?

. . . .

If there were any way possible of adding a few hours to the day, they could be used handily right now; for this is surely the farm woman's busy time. The gardens, the spring sewing, the housecleaning more or less caused by the change from cold to warm weather, and all the young things on the place to be

---

cared for call for agility, to say the least, if a day's work is to be done in a day.

Some people complain that farm life is monotonous. They surely never had experience of the infinite variety of tasks that come to a farm woman in the merry springtime! Why, the ingenuity, the quickness of brain, and the sleight of hand required to prevent a young calf from spilling its bucket of milk at feeding time, and the patience necessary to teach it to drink are a liberal education in itself, while the vagaries of a foolish sitting hen will relieve the monotony for the entire day!

So much of the work of the farm that we take as a matter of course is strange and interesting to a person who is not used to it. A man who has been in business in town for over twenty years is moving his family to the farm this spring and expects to be a farmer. The old order, you see, is reversed. Instead of retiring from a farm to town, he is retiring from town to a farm. I was really surprised, in talking with him, to find how many things there are for a beginner to learn.

Just a Question of Tact
October 1916

"You have so much tact and can get along with people so well," said a friend to me once. Then, after a thoughtful pause, she added, "But I never could see any difference between tact and trickery." Upon my assuring her that there was no difference, she pursued the subject further.

"Now I have no tact whatever, but speak plainly," she said pridefully. "The Scotch people are, I think, the most tactful, and the Scotch, you know, are the trickiest nation in the world."

"I told you I had no tact."

As I am of Scotch descent, I could restrain my merriment no longer, and when I recovered enough to say, "You are right, I am Scotch," she smiled ruefully and said, "I told you I had no tact."

Tact does for life just what lubricating oil does for machinery. It makes the wheels run smoothly, and without it there is a great deal of friction and the possibility of a breakdown. Many a car on the way of life fails to make the trip as expected for lack of this lubricant.

Tact is a quality that may be acquired. It is only the other way of seeing and presenting a subject. There are always two sides to a thing, you know; and if one side is disagreeable, the reverse is quite apt to be very pleasant. The tactful person may see both sides but uses the pleasant one.

"Your teeth are so pretty when you keep them white," said Ida to Stella, which, of course, was equal to saying that Stella's teeth were ugly when she did not keep them clean, as frequently happened; but Stella left her friend with the feeling that she had been complimented and also with the shamed resolve that she would keep those pretty teeth white.

Tom's shoulders were becoming inclined to droop a little. To be sure, he was a little older than he used to be and sometimes very tired, but the droop was really caused more by carelessness than by anything else. When Jane came home from a visit to a friend whose husband was very round-shouldered indeed, she noticed more plainly than usual the beginning of the habit in Tom.

"Oh, Tom! I'm so glad you are tall and straight, not round-shouldered like Dick.

Choosing a moment when he straightened to his full height and squared his shoulders, she said: "Oh, Tom! I'm so glad you are tall and straight, not round-shouldered like Dick. He is growing worse every day until it is becoming a positive deformity with him." And Tom was glad she had not observed the tendency in his shoulders, and thereafter their straightness was noticeable.

Jane might have chosen a moment when Tom's shoulders were drooping and with perfect truthfulness have said: "Tom! You are getting to be round-shouldered and ugly like Dick. In a little while you will look like a hunchback."

Tom would have felt hurt and resentful and probably would have retorted, "Well, you're getting older and uglier too," or something like that; and his hurt pride and vanity would have been a hindrance instead of a help to improvement.

The children, of course, get their bad tempers from their fathers, but I think we get our vanity from Adam, for we all have it, men and women alike; and like most things, it is good when rightly used.

Tact may be trickery, but after all I think I prefer the dictionary definition—"nice discernment." To be tactful, one has only to discern or distinguish or, in other words, to see nicely and speak and act accordingly.

My sympathy just now, however, is very much with the persons who seem to be unable to say the right thing at the proper time. In spite of oneself, there are times when one's mental fingers seem to be all thumbs. At a little gathering not long ago, I differed with the hostess on a question which arose and disagreed with just a shade more warmth than I intended. I resolved to make it up by being a little extra sweet to her before I left.

The refreshments served were so dainty and delicious that I thought I would find some pleasant way to tell her so. But alas! As it was a very hot day, ice water was served after the little luncheon, and I found myself looking sweetly into my hostess's face and heard myself say, "Oh, wasn't that water good." What could one do after that, but murmur the conventional, "Such a pleasant afternoon," at leaving and depart feeling like a little girl who had blundered at her first party.

The Old Dash Churn
September 1916

"All the world is queer, except for thee and me," said the old Quaker to his wife, "and sometimes I think thee is a little queer."

The Man of the Place once bought me a patent churn. "Now," said he, "throw away that old dash churn. This churn will bring the butter in three minutes." It was very kind of him. He had bought the churn to please me and to lighten my work, but I looked upon it with a little suspicion.

I dropped it—just as far as I could.

There was only one handle to turn and opposite it was a place to attach the power from a small engine. We had no engine, so the churning needed to be done with one hand while the other steadied the churn and held it down. It was hard to do, but the butter did come quickly; and I would have used it anyway because the Man of the Place had been so kind.

The tin paddles which worked the cream were sharp on the edges, and they were attached to the shaft by a screw which was supposed to be loosened to remove the paddles for washing; but I could never loosen it and usually cut my hands on the sharp tin. However, I used the new churn, one hand holding it down to the floor with grim resolution, while the other turned the handle with the strength of despair as the cream thickened. Finally, it seemed that I could use it no longer. "I wish you would bring in my old dash churn," I said to the Man of the Place. "I believe it is easier to use than this after all."

"Oh!" said he, "you can churn in three minutes with this, and the old one takes half a day. Put one end of a board on the churn and the other on a chair and sit on the board, then you can hold the churn down easily!" And so when I churned I sat on a board in the correct mode for horseback riding and though the churn bucked some, I managed to hold my seat.

"I wish," said I to the Man of the Place, "you would bring in my old dash churn. (It was where I could not get to it.) I cut my hands on these paddles every time I wash them."

"Oh, pshaw!" said he, "you can churn with this churn in three minutes—"

One day when the churn had been particularly annoying and had cut my hand badly, I took the mechanism of the churn—handle, shaft, wheels, and paddles all attached—to the side door which is quite high from the ground and threw it as far as I could. It struck on the handle, rebounded, landed on the paddles, crumpled and lay still—and I went out and kicked it before I picked it up. The handle was broken off, the shaft was bent, and the paddles were a wreck.

"I wish," I remarked casually to the Man of the Place, "that you would bring in my old dash churn. I want to churn this morning."

"Oh, use the churn you have," said he. "You can churn in three minutes with it. What's the use to spend half a day—"

"I can't," I interrupted. "It's broken."

"Why, how did that happen?" he asked.

"I dropped it—just as far as I could," I answered in a small voice, and he replied regretfully, "I wish I had known that you did not want to use it. I would like to have the wheels and shaft, but they're ruined now."

. . . .

As the old Quaker remarked to his wife, "Sometimes I think thee is a little queer."

Christmas When I Was Sixteen
December 1924

The snow was scudding low over the drifts of the white world outside the little claim shanty. It was blowing through the cracks in its walls and forming little piles and miniature drifts on the floor, and even on the desks before which several children sat, trying to study; for this abandoned claim shanty, which had served as the summer home of a homesteader on the Dakota prairie, was being used as a schoolhouse during the winter.

The walls were made of one thickness of wide boards with cracks between, and the enormous stove that stood nearly in the center of the one room could scarcely keep out the frost, though its sides were a glowing red. The children were dressed warmly and had been allowed to gather closely around the stove following the advice of the county superintendent of schools who, on a recent visit, had said that the only thing he had to say to them was to keep their feet warm.*

I was only sixteen years old and twelve miles from home during a frontier winter.

This was my first school; I'll not say how many years ago, but I was only sixteen years old and twelve miles from home during a frontier winter. I walked a mile over the unbroken snow from my boarding place to school every morning and back at night. There were only a few pupils, and on this particular snowy afternoon, they were restless, for it was nearing 4 o'clock and tomorrow was Christmas. "Teacher" was restless too, though she tried not to show it, for she was wondering if she could get home for Christmas Day.

It was almost too cold to hope for Father to come, and a storm was hanging in the northwest which might mean a blizzard at any minute. Still, tomorrow was Christmas—and then there was a jingle of sleigh bells outside. A man in a huge fur coat in a sleigh full of robes passed the window. I was going home after all!

When one thinks of twelve miles now, it is in terms of motor cars and means only a few minutes. It was different then, and I'll never forget that ride. The bells made a merry jingle, and the fur robes were warm; but the weather

---

*Chapters eight and nine of *These Happy Golden Years* tell of this time.

was growing colder, and the snow was drifting so that the horses must break their way through the drifts.

We were facing the strong wind, and every little while he, who later became the "Man of the Place," must stop the team, get out in the snow, and by putting his hands over each horse's nose in turn, thaw the ice from them where the breath had frozen over their nostrils. Then he would get back into the sleigh, and on we'd go until once more the horses could not breathe for the ice.

When we reached the journey's end, it was 40 degrees below zero; the snow was blowing so thickly that we could not see across the street; and I was so chilled that I had to be half carried into the house. But I was home for Christmas, and cold and danger were forgotten.

Such magic there is in Christmas to draw the absent ones home, and if unable to go in the body, the thoughts will hover there! Our hearts grow tender with childhood memories and love of kindred, and we are better throughout the year for having, in spirit, become a child again at Christmastime.

CHAPTER 7

Give me just one
logical reason

Five Dollar Prize for Women
October 1920
by John F. Case

For more than eight years Mrs. A. J. Wilder of Mansfield has been [our] farm home editor. During these years, her column has provided a ray of sunshine for every issue. But Mrs. Wilder hasn't been wholly happy. Folks do not write to her often enough. The editor thinks it's because her address hasn't been printed, and he believes that now it's known farm women will respond. Remember that Mrs. Wilder is one of you farm women folks. You never have attempted a task on your farm that Mrs. Wilder hasn't tried out at Rocky Ridge. She knows your problems and desires.

Mrs. Wilder has been disturbed because of the reports of lessened rural population. She believes that if the women folks were willing to stay, there would be few farm families going to town. And so she wants you to write her before November 10 on "Why I Should Like to Leave the Farm." Put your heart into this letter and write to our farm home editor as you would to your own sister. Your confidence will not be abused. The letter will be published, perhaps, but only the initials will appear. It must be signed, however, and the address given. The best letter sent to Mrs. A. J. Wilder, Mansfield, Mo., before November 10 will win $5, the second $2, the third $1.

If you like Mrs. Wilder's department, write and tell her so. Like every other woman, Mrs. Wilder loves flowers—and a bouquet in October or November is especially welcome.*

---

*Editor's Note: Apparently, Laura's request for feedback, particularly about the difficulties facing farm women, brought a deluge of letters. Three of these appear in "Dear Farm Women." Worn to exasperation, women quite willingly unburdened their hearts to Laura about the hardships of second-generation pioneering in the Ozarks, and elsewhere in Missouri (these women, not being the first settlers necessarily, still had to "prove up" in some way that a real life could be made on the homestead, not merely an existence).

By this time, Laura and Almanzo had been so successful on their own farm that one is tempted to wonder if Laura still remembered her remark to Almanzo, before they were even married, that she "didn't want to be a farmer's wife" (see *The First Four Years*), just the same attitude many of her correspondents fervently expressed to her.

"Pioneering on an Ozark Farm" appears to be Laura's enthusiastic reply to all of the women who wrote on the topic "Why I Should Like to Leave the Farm." Judge for yourself as to whether it is convincing or not.

Dear Farm Women
January 1921

For several years I have been talking and talking, hearing no reply, until I came to feel that no one was listening to me. And to find that you are really there and will answer back is truly delightful.

Thank you all so much for the kind things you have said about my department. To know that I have helped you a little or made a day brighter will make my own work easier and cause the sun to shine on the dark days, for we all have them.

'Tis then a little place of sunshine in the heart helps mightily. And there is nothing that puts so much brightness there as having helped someone else.

Why I Should Like to Leave the Farm

Why Should I Stay?
(First Prize Letter)

Mrs. A. J. Wilder—Give me just one logical reason why I should try to keep my boy and girl on the farm where all the odds are against them; where they are exploited in the marketplace; where they get less for their toil than in any other calling; where they have longer hours of harder work than do the folks in the city and get poorer pay for doing it.

We are told that many great men were born on the farm. But they did not become great on the farm. Every mother's son of them left the farm before he became great!

Why should I keep my boy and girl on the farm where they must attend the poorest schools on earth?

Why should I desire them to remain through life where they are made the butt of every stale joke sprung by every cheap joke-smith in the land when the city offers a ten to one better chance to rise in the world than is afforded in the country?

Why should I want them to remain among a class that by many is looked upon as a harmless group of "ignoramuses," a class who suspect their kind to such a degree that they will not take any measures to protect one another against the abuses that are heaped upon them by their exploiters?

In the country, we must travel over the worst roads in the world and we are exposed to the worst weather conditions. We have poor churches and poorer schools; we cannot hear the best lectures, nor attend the best entertainment as can the folks in town.

We are told that many great men were born on the farm. But they did not become great on the farm. Every mother's son of them left the farm before he became great!

Why should I desire to remain on the farm where the men do not have time to keep posted on at least some of the news of the day and where women do not have time to clean their teeth; where men toil from twelve to fourteen hours a day and grow crops that they must sell for less than the cost of producing them, and the women work from twelve to eighteen hours a day to care for babies and to cook for harvest hands until, when the supper work is over, they are too tired to sleep.

Now can you, with a clear conscience, insist that I remain on the farm under its unfair terms?

Mrs. W.M.

Church and School Privileges

Dear Mrs. Wilder—Why would I like to get off the farm? There are many reasons.

First, I would like to leave the farm because it is possible to attend church and Sunday school every Sunday when living in town.

Second, the children would have the advantages of school and high school without having to leave home when most they need their parents' guiding hands, not to mention the expense of sending children away from home.

I'd like to be where I could see more folks during the days when all the family are away at work and school.

Third, I would leave the farm because I'd like some social life and rest, also would like time to read and do fancy work.

Fourth, I'd like to be where I could see more folks during the days when all the family are away at work and school.

I also would like time to keep up my personal appearance. And I'd like a modern house.

In the country, so much money must go to pay for the farm home. There is nearly always a mortgage on it, and then the interest and taxes and living expenses eat up all the income, and it is drudge along year after year with no labor-saving devices in the house, and finally when enough money has been accumulated to take life easy, folks have lost the power of enjoyment. For instance, one of our neighbors who had accumulated enough to rent his farm, buy a modern bungalow, and move to town had so lost his sense of values that he had the electric lights cut off. The furnace stood fireless, and they used stoves to heat one or two of the smaller rooms. The telephone was taken out of the house, and every possible economy used as in their early married life when they were trying to save for a happy life of ease in town in their old age.

Next door to these most unhappy poor-rich folks lived a family in a similar bungalow. The father had bought the home with all its modern equipment in the first years of their married life, and they have had the use of it all the time. They have a fine family; each child as it shows any decided talent is encouraged and fitted for that which is his or her vocation. The father's income is derived from a clerkship and literary work and is very modest compared to that of the first family.

This city father and mother are the light of their home. They have been able to keep pace with their very interesting family of growing youngsters. They are the heart and life of all church and social affairs and are also ready to boost every civic improvement regardless of the increase in taxes.

The mother, with the aid of her young daughters and the modern conveniences, does all her own work and enjoys all the pleasures with her husband and children. And she looks ten years younger than her neighbor, the country woman, whose children, reared on the farm, are not fitted by education as they should have been to take their places in the world.

These are the reasons why I would leave the farm and live in town. And yet none of these are past redemption if the proper attention were given schools, modern conveniences in the homes, good roads, and too much stress were not given to the thought of owning all the land that joins us.

Mrs. A.E.T.

Here's Hope Deferred

Dear Mrs. Wilder—For several months, I have had in my mind just what you have given me the opportunity to write.

I was reared on a farm, and ten years ago my husband and I bought an old place, forty acres, at the edge of town.

It was in awful condition, but I believed we could make a home of it until we could build a modern house. It is a fine location, good drainage, an ideal place for a home.

My husband worked in a store so most of the work on the farm fell on me, but I was willing to work and almost did the work of two.

I had to carry water a long distance for a large flock of chickens, clean and spray the hen house, milk cows, set out trees, bushes and small fruits; did the gardening, all my sewing, washing, ironing, and cared for three children.

---

*My husband is a good man, but
like most men does not see
how hard the work is.*

Most of the land was in pasture. I hired very little of even the hard work done, for I thought every dollar saved was one earned. And I would think, "Now I have saved enough for a sink in the kitchen," or something else I wanted.

We did not keep a separate pocketbook, for I wanted to save for the home alone. How I have wished for a car, but no, I wanted that modern home more.

I did without furniture, clothes, and all luxuries. All this work and denying was done willingly. For how happy I was dreaming of and planning clothes closets, baths, sink and water in the kitchen, basement, a place to store fruits and vegetables, a power or electric washer and iron, and lights.

Today, I am no nearer those conveniences than when we moved here. And my health is broken so that I am not able to do all the work, yet there is as much work to be done as in the first years.

My husband is a good man, but like most men does not see how hard the work is. Our lives are more than half gone. I do not want money spent on a fine casket and flowers when I am dead. I want a kitchen with a sink, now, and a walk around to the back door and a fence to keep the chickens out of the yard, and the flowers growing while I can see them. I shall teach my boys never to take a wife on a farm and let her drudge just because their mother had no better.

I believe that is why wives want to move to town. We work so hard to make money and are real helpmates. We do not want to escape work; we want conveniences so we can do our work easier and in less time. If men would let their wives know they were never going to have modern homes, many a woman would go where she could have electricity and wash for a living and then have more spare time.

I do not believe in debt, but if a wife dies, the money is found for funeral expenses. Why not put in a light and water system so she can manage her work better and spend more time with the chickens to help pay for it? How we love to work when there is something to look forward to, but if I cannot have even a part of these conveniences, I would leave the farm.

Mrs. J.V.M.

Pioneering on an Ozark Farm
*A Story of Folks Who Searched—and Found Health,
Prosperity and a Wild Frontier in the
Mountains of Our Own State*
June 1921

The days of wilderness adventure are not past! The pioneer spirit is not dead!

We still have frontiers in our old, settled states where the joys of more primitive days may be experienced with some of their hardships and, now and then, a touch of their grim humor.

---

*Mr. Frink fretted at the confinement of
his law office and longed for wider
spaces and the freedom of the old West
he had known as a boy.*

Nestled in a bend of the Gasconade River 1¾ miles south of Hartville, the county seat of Wright County, Missouri, is a little home which is gradually being made into a productive farm while losing none of its natural, woodland beauty. Its wild loveliness is being enhanced by the intelligent care it is receiving and by the determination of its owners to take advantage of, and work with, nature along the lines of her plans, instead of forcing her to change her ways and work according to man's ideals altogether—a happy cooperation with nature instead of a fight against her.

Mr. and Mrs. Frink, owners and partners in the farm, come of pioneer stock and never were quite content with town and village life. They often talked of the joys of pioneering and dreamed of going to the western frontiers somewhere.

And the years slipped by, leaving their imprint: here and there a touch of snow in their dark hair, a few more lines around the eyes. Worst of all, they found their health breaking. Mrs. Frink's nerves were giving way under the constant strain of teaching music, and the combined efforts of each failed to pay the expenses of the many reverses, including doctor's bills with accompanying enforced idleness, and leave any surplus to be laid away for the old age that was bound to arrive with time.

Then Nature Called

All through the sweet days of spring and summer as Mrs. Frink sat hour after hour working with some dull music pupil, she heard the call of the big outdoors and would forget to count the beat as she dreamed of pioneering in some wild, free place, where, instead of hearing the false notes of beginners on the piano, she might listen to the music of the wild birds' song, the murmur of the wind among the treetops and the rippling of some silver stream. And Mr. Frink fretted at the confinement of his law office and longed for wider spaces and the freedom of the old West he had known as a boy. But still they knew deep down in their hearts that there is no more frontier in the old sense.

By chance, Mr. Frink found the little nook, embraced by the bend of the river, tucked securely away in its hidden corner of the world, and Mrs. Frink said, "This is our frontier; we will pioneer here!"

There were only twenty-seven acres on the farm, mostly woodland, some flat, some set up edgeways, and the rest at many different angles as is the way of land in the Ozarks, where, as has been said, we can farm three sides of the land thus getting the use of many more acres than our title deeds call for.

I think at no time did Mr. and Mrs. Frink see the farm as it actually was, but instead they saw it with the eyes of faith as it should be later. What they bought were possibilities and the chance of working out their dreams. Mrs. Frink believed that here they could make their living and a little more. Mr. Frink was doubtful but eager to take a chance.

It required courage to make the venture, for the place was in a bad state. There were some six or seven acres of good bottom land in rather a poor state of cultivation and seven acres of second bottom, or bench land, on which was an old thrown-out, worn-out field. The rest was woodland, a system of brush thickets a rabbit could hardly penetrate. The valleys and glens were overgrown with grapevines and poison ivy, the abiding place of rattlesnakes and tarantulas. There were no fences worth the name.

The farm was bargained for in June, but negotiations were long and tedious, for it was necessary to bring three persons to the same mind at the same time; and it proved to be a case of many men of many minds instead. But at last the transaction was completed, and one sunny morning in August, 1918, Mr. and Mrs. Frink gathered together their household goods and departed for the new home, on the frontier of the Ozarks, leaving Hartville without a mayor and its most prominent music teacher, with one closed law and insurance office.

They went in a delapidated hack, containing household goods and a tent, drawn by a borrowed horse. Hitched at the back of the hack was Mat, the Jersey cow, and Bessie Lee, her nine-month-old calf. Dexter, a four-month-old colt, about twenty chickens, and three shoats had been sent ahead with a lumber wagon.

At four o'clock that afternoon the tent was pitched at Campriverside, and the Frinks were at home on their own farm. As Mr. Frink says, "The great problem was solved; we would not live our whole lives on a half-acre lot."

For supper they feasted on roasting ears and ripe tomatoes from their own fields. These were principal articles of fare for some time. The green corn later gave place to "grits," and finally these were replaced by their own grown corn-meal.

The Frinks began their life on the farm in a small way and handicapped by debt. The price of the land was $600; but after paying off old indebtedness, there was left of their capital only $550 to pay for the land, build a house, and buy a horse. For there was no house on the land, and the tent must be the shelter until one could be built, while a horse was absolutely necessary to even a "one-horse farm."

Four hundred dollars was paid on the place and a note given for the balance of $200. Out of the remaining $150 a cabin was built and a horse bought. The material and labor on the house cost $120 and the horse cost $30.

Mr. and Mrs. Frink made up their minds at the start that the place must furnish fencing and building material as far as possible, and, really, log build-ings seemed more in keeping with the rugged surroundings. The log house was built the first fall. It was 14 by 18 feet and a story and a half high. A shed for the stock, a chicken house, and a good many rods of fence have been added since to the improvements.

From the first, they lived from the proceeds of the little place. The land had been rented when bought, and they were to have the owner's share from the five acres of corn on the bottom field. In the fall, the renter put 125 bushels of good, hard, white corn in the hastily constructed crib. The crop could have been cashed for $300.

The next fall there were 100 bushels of corn as their share from the rented field and a bunch of hogs raised on the place were sold for $125.

In fifteen months after moving on the place, the note for $200 and an old bill of $60 was paid off and a cream separator had been bought and paid for.

For the year of 1920 their share of corn was again 100 bushels, but be-cause of the drop in prices, only $70 worth of hogs were sold. The income from cream and eggs averaged a little over a dollar a day for ten months of the year. And from the little new-seeded meadow, two tons of clover hay were cut and stacked.

The stock has been increased. There are now at home on the place three good Jersey cows, a team of horses, two purebred Poland China brood sows, ten shoats, and fifty laying hens.

There are also on hand 600 pounds of dressed meat and stores of fruits and vegetables—the bulk of a year's provisions ahead. And best of all there are no debts but instead a comfortable bank account.

The expense of running the farm has been very little—about $25 a year for help. It is the intention that the eggs and cream shall provide money for running expenses, which so far they have done, leaving clear what money comes from selling the hogs, calves, and surplus chickens.

* *

The start in raising chickens was made under difficulties. Mrs. Frink was eager to begin stocking the place, and early in the spring, when first the bargain was made for the farm, she wished to raise some chickens to take to it. At that time, the law forbade selling hens, so she borrowed one from a neighbor and set her.* And that hen hatched out eleven roosters and only two pullets! Rather a discouraging start in the poultry business. But Mrs. Frink, while seeing the humor of the situation, refused to admit failure. She took the thirteen chickens out to the farm and put their coop up in a hickory tree beside the road. The roosters were fine large Orpingtons and attracted the attention and admiration of the neighbors.

Mrs. Frink refused to sell but offered to exchange for pullets and soon had a flock of twelve pullets and one rooster in the hickory tree. The pullets began laying in November, laid well all winter, and raised a nice bunch of chicks in the spring.

The plans of these Ozark pioneers are not yet completed. Thirteen acres of the woodland are being cleared and seeded to timothy and clover. In the woods pasture, the timber is being thinned, underbrush cleaned out, and orchard grass, bluegrass, and timothy are being sown.

Mr. Frink says, "There is much yet to be done. When the place is all cleared and in pasture, it will support six cows, which means from $50 to $60 a month for cream, and the fields in the bottom and on the bench will furnish grain for them and the hogs and chickens.

And They've Made Good

"We have demonstrated what can be done on a small piece of land even by renting out the fields. An able-bodied man could have done much better because he could have worked the fields himself, and I would like to have more people know what a man with small means can accomplish."

---

*No doubt owing to World War I commodity controls.

Campriverside is located on the main fork of the Gasconade River, a section of country noted for its beautiful river and mountain scenery, and Mrs. Frink's artistic soul has found delight in the freedom and the beauties surrounding her. She says there is magic at Campriverside. An oak tree growing near the south side of the cabin has the power, when atmospheric conditions are right, of seeming to talk and sing, being in some way a conductor of sounds of conversations and singing of neighbors living as far as a mile away. Among the branches of this tree, brushing the sides and roof of the house, birds of brilliant plumage and sweet song build their nests.

The rugged scenery and placid river had a greater charm for Mrs. Frink than the fertile soil of the bottom land, and she took time each day to explore her little kingdom. Many were the beauty spots she discovered.

There were the basins in the rocks below the spring and Pulpit Rock, which she desecrated by setting her tub upon it when she washed.

When the spring rises and makes a brook in the little glen, there are the Cascades and Wildcat Falls.

And there is Wild Cat Den where, at rare intervals, the bobcat screams, calling the mate who has been the victim of encroaching civilization, while just below is Fern Glen where magnificent sword ferns grow.

As if these were not enough natural beauties for one small farm, there are the Castle Rocks and the Grotto and the dens where the woodchucks and minks live.

And there are wild flowers everywhere—"wild flowers that mark the footsteps of the Master as He walks in His garden, and the brilliant coloring of the autumn foliage speaks again of His presence."

Whom Will You Marry?*
June 1919

Elizabeth came out from town this morning to talk over a problem with me. I was kneading bread, and because twenty-five years of it have not taught me to like this part of the work of a farmer's wife, I had put the bread pan near the kitchen window where I could look up now and then at the clean, cool beauty of the budding oak trees. So I saw Elizabeth as she came up the south slope between the gray tree trunks, and I thought she looked like a redbird in her bright sweater and cap.

I felt a twinge of envy. I thought how glad I would be if I could get out into the spring woods. We always forget our own compensations in looking at others who have joys that we have not. But by the time I had opened the door to Elizabeth and had her in by the stove taking off her muddy rubbers, the envy was gone. It is a poor life that does not teach us to shed envy as a duck sheds raindrops, and, besides, I saw that Elizabeth was troubled.

Such a creature as the woman parasite
has never been known among us.
Perhaps this is one reason why
"feminism" has never greatly
aroused us.

There was a time when I would have been ashamed to receive Elizabeth, a banker's granddaughter, in the farm kitchen. Farm kitchens are not like city kitchenettes, nor even like the white-painted, muslin-curtained kitchens that some of the town people have. All the work of a farm centers in the farmer's wife's kitchen. I skim milk, make butter, and cook bran mashes for the chickens and potato parings for the hogs in mine. A big iron pot of parings was steaming on the stove when Elizabeth came in.

I may as well admit that Elizabeth, in her dainty, gay clothes, was out of place in my kitchen. Twenty-five years ago, when I was her age, I would have hustled her into the front room and entertained her there, feeling embarrassed because my rag carpet was not Wilton and my furniture was not mahogany. The bread would have waited until she was gone, and if the family ate sourish bread for a week, I would have felt it was not my fault.

*By 1919, Laura had become a real farm booster, as can be seen by this article she wrote for *McCall's* magazine (June issue), which extols the virtues of being a partner with your husband, even if it means being a farmer's wife.

But this morning I gave her a kitchen chair and went on kneading, thumping the dough and sprinkling flour over the breadboard while she talked. Good bread is my pride now, rather than Wilton rugs, and I have found that friendliness not genuine in a kitchen is not improved by a parlor.

"Jim's coming home next week," Elizabeth said.

"That's good!" I answered, heartily, for I had watched that romance from the time Elizabeth was in pigtails till the day Jim went away in khaki. But Elizabeth's tone made it clear enough that Jim's coming back brought a little doubt to her mind.

"Would—would you be a farmer's wife if you had the chance to live your life over again?" she asked in that breathless rush in which girls blurt out things they have been thinking about for a long time. "I wanted to talk to you about it. Jim says he wants to buy a farm when he comes back. He says he doesn't want to go into the bank again. I don't know what to do about it. I don't know whether I want to be a farmer's wife or not. Would you, if you were me? I guess I could talk him out of it, but—"

I had no doubt she could talk him out of it. Giving advice to Elizabeth seemed to me a heavy responsibility, though the advice we older women give girls now has not the weight it had when I was a girl. It seems to me that girls nowadays handle their lives and the lives of their husbands with much more assurance than we used to. Elizabeth is really the one who is deciding Jim's future, as well as her own.

In my girlhood we had, one might say, the right of veto in some things in our own lives; we married the man who asked us, or we did not marry him. But now girls make their own laws, and, to an astonishing extent, their own husbands' after they have married them.

While I talked to Elizabeth and kneaded the bread, I thought of many things I did not say. Many persons think that a farmer, and, of course, his wife are isolated from the current of affairs in the nation, but sometimes I think we have a better viewpoint on them because we are farther away. The mail carrier brings out our papers and magazines in the morning, and after the chores are done, I usually have a few minutes to run down to the mailbox and bring them up. During the day, I snatch a glance at them now and then, and after chores are done at night, we sit by the fire and read and talk. We have a great deal of time for thinking at our work and for making our own opinions about the happenings in the world.

So Elizabeth's question seemed to me to mean more than the problem of one girl. I thought of Secretary Lane's plan* for placing returning soldiers on farms, and I thought how badly our country needs good farmers and good

*Secretary of the Interior Franklin K. Lane.

farm conditions. I thought of the million dollars asked by the Senate Committee on Public Lands for making surveys of farms for soldiers, and I thought of all the girls and women whose opinions mean far more in the matter than any decision of any Senate committee.

There must be a great many of them who, like Elizabeth, are undecided because of their ignorance of the real conditions of life on a farm, and nothing I have ever read seems to tell the truth about these conditions.

There has been a great deal of pity spent on the farmer's wife, and a great deal of condescending effort has been spent to educate her, while, on the other hand, some very pleasant and poetic things have been written about country life. But I have never seen it pointed out that the farm woman's life combines the desires of the "modern woman" with all the advantages and traditions of homekeeping.

On the farm, a woman may have both economic independence and a home life as perfect as she cares to make it. Farm women have always been wage earners and partners in their husband's business. Such a creature as the woman parasite has never been known among us. Perhaps this is one reason why "feminism" has never greatly aroused us.

---

*It has been rather amusing to . . . read
flaring headlines announcing the fact
that women are at last coming
into their own.*

It has been rather amusing to farm women to read flaring headlines announcing the fact that women are at last coming into their own, that the younger ones at least can now become self-supporting. About the woman past forty there seems to be a little doubt in the papers. But the woman past forty on the farm is still sure of her position, even the woman past fifty or sixty.

There is always plenty of self-supporting, self-respecting work for women on the farm, even though their youth is gone, and the work is within the shelter and quiet security of their own homes. While the discussion for and against women in business has been raging over the country, farm women have always been businesswomen, and no one has protested against it. No one has even noticed it.

Yet I remember well my husband's mother, undisputed head of her household and fully a partner in all the business of the northern Minnesota farm, where I lived for a few months many years ago. She was not a "feminist"; I never heard the words "economic independence" on her lips, and when her daughter, who went to the city and worked in an office, came back to talk of these things, she listened with an indulgent smile.* She was too busy to bother her head with such notions, she said. But her husband was never so rash as to sell a herd of hogs or turn meadowland into cornfields without consulting her, and the butter money went into her own purse without a question.

Perhaps the reason this economic value of farm women has gone unnoticed is because they have taken the advice the small boy gave the hen. When he heard her wildly cackling to announce that she had laid an egg, he exclaimed, "Aw, shut up! What's the use of making such a fuss? You couldn't help it!"

It is true that a farmer's wife can never stop contributing her share to the success of the farm without ruining her husband's business as well. Many times when the churning had to be done and the hens fed, I have felt like running away into the woods, "just to walk and to walk and to stun my soul and amaze it—a day with the stone and the sparrow and every marvelous thing." And I have felt that the life of a parasite woman has its attractions. But it lacks certain sturdy virtues that are good for a woman to have.

Women in the cities have tried the parasite life, and it appears that they do not like it. Yet, in the city, conditions inevitably pull married women into economic dependence and partial idleness.

It is not good for any living creature to be idle. A horse that does not work becomes unmanageable and fractious in his stall; he begins eating the wood of the manger, which is not a good thing for a horse to do. Hens, if they are to be kept healthy, must be kept busy, and every good poultry raiser gives them straw to scratch, so that they may earn part of their food by good, honest toil. I think it is not unreasonable to suppose that women, too, must use their energies to some purpose, good or bad, and no woman can make a success of her marriage if she uses her energies in eating the wood of the manger.

Yet, if, in order to avoid the restlessness and uneasiness that go with idleness, the city woman works outside her home, her business interests and occupations pull away from the home life and from marriage.

A species of business rivalry enters into the relations of herself and her husband, and, if she is successful, she has a pride in her pay envelope which is only equaled by her husband's jealousy of it. A man is perhaps slower to adapt himself to new things than a woman, or it may be that there is some deep, possessive instinct in him that resents any rival in the attention of the woman he loves. Combating this feeling in her husband gives a woman a sense of power, and nothing tears the delicate fabric of intimacy between two persons so surely as this sense of power in one and of futile protest in the other.

---

*Laura refers to Almanzo's mother, Angeline Day Wilder, and Almanzo's sister, Eliza Jane Wilder. Long after the time of *Farmer Boy*, the large Wilder clan moved to better farming opportunities in Minnesota.

With separated interests, differing ambitions, a different set of business friends, and a jealous rivalry between them, it is no wonder that so many fine men and women in the cities are finding marriage impossible. The divorce court makes legal a separation which already exists, and their marriage is a failure, whatever their business successes may be.

It is in the cities that the divorce statistics pile higher with every year. Divorce is rare in the country.

The farm woman's economic independence pulls in the direction of making her marriage a success. Her interests and those of her husband are the same; their success is a mutual success of which each may be equally proud. In the event of a threatened failure, their interests still hold them together, instead of pulling them apart, and failure may often be averted because of the simple fact that two heads are better than one.

A farmer's wife may and should be—I may almost say must be—her husband's partner in the business, and she may be this without detracting from the home life.

Meals on time; the surplus of garden and orchard preserved; meats properly cured at butchering time; the young creatures on the farm cared for as only a woman has the patience to care for them; work in the dairy and with the poultry contribute very largely to the success of the average farmer.

The farm woman does such work as this at home, without bringing any alien influence to bear upon the home life. A farmer never becomes jealous of his wife's success with the poultry, however large a check it brings in, nor does she feel that it makes her independent of him.

I cannot say there is no rivalry between them, remembering that only last year our farm was the scene of a long and serious contest. Over the supper table one night my husband and I found ourselves suddenly disputing vigorously over the relative value of hens and cows as moneymakers.

I suppose I was bitter about the hens. For a week I had been coaxing them to lay, by every means in my power, and they had responded with beautifully bright combs and shining feathers, but not with eggs. Night after night, I came in past the barnyard with the egg basket rattling lightly on my arm, to find brimming milk pails standing by the separator. I contended that cows paid far better than hens.

My husband takes care of the cows, and during the war, it seemed that the stock might as well be living on minted gold as on mill feed. The summer had been dry, and we faced a winter in which we might have to buy hay. He was strongly prejudiced in favor of hens.

The argument finally became a contest. Each of us was to keep exact accounts, and at the end of six months we were to compare figures. We played fair, each working to prove the other right by taking the best care of our charges; and when, at last, we held an executive session to determine the results, we found that we were both right. The same time was required to care for three cows as for one hundred hens, and the same profit was made.

That is the kind of business rivalry which lends zest to a year's work on a farm. It also gives point to a bit of conversation between our hired man and a neighbor, which my husband overheard and repeated to me with a twinkle in his eye. The hired man was to be married. Our neighbor, stopping beside the fence to talk, was told the news.

"Married!" he exclaimed. "Why, you can't make a living for yourself!"

"Well," the hired man said cheerfully, "I figure she'll help a little."

I am not saying that the life of a farmer's wife is an easy one. We never get anything for nothing, though we may have almost anything in the world if we are willing to pay the price.

Economic independence is not an easy thing for a woman to earn, even on a farm, and part of the price that must be paid for it is responsibility. A farm woman cannot expect to be full partner in pleasures and profits and not share troubles and labor.

I know one farmer's wife who insists in having a voice in all the farm affairs and then, when things go wrong, blames her husband. She fails in her own part of the work. Her hens never lay; she will not help out in harvesting time, when help is scarce, by feeding the horses or turning the cream separator; she cannot raise a calf nor have the meals ready on time. Yet she complains because her husband does not make a better living for her.

This woman does not belong on a farm. There are times when a farmer's wife must neglect her own special part of the work and help her husband, in order that a crop may be saved or the livestock cared for. If the farmer is injured or ill, there may be no one but his wife to take over the entire farm management and a large part of the physical labor besides.

Sometimes a woman must work in this way to pay off the mortgage or meet some unexpected loss caused by bad weather, and in that case, she must help or see the business fail utterly. Every farmer's wife who begins her married life with little money must be prepared to meet such emergencies, but the words of Lord Halifax are as true of women as of men. He said: "A difficulty raiseth the spirit of a great man. He hath a mind to wrestle with it and give it a fall. A man's mind must be very low if the difficulty doth not make part of his pleasure."

There is a joy of spirit and a pride of power that come to a farm woman who is fully alive to her opportunities, meeting and solving problems, confronting and overcoming difficulties, refusing to become petty though attending to numberless details, or to be discouraged before threatened disaster. She wins to a valiant courage of the soul, which holds itself above all harassments, serene and unconquered.

Just as the physical labor of a farm exercises and makes strong every part of a woman's body, so the many interests of the farm life, in threads which reach to it from all parts of the world, exercise her mind.

When the price of eggs goes down, with a corresponding cut in the amount of her weekly check, she will want to know the reason why. When there is an increase in the price of cut bone and meat scraps, which she must feed the hens to produce those eggs, she will ask the reason for that.

Why, she will wonder, does the farmer need helpful laws for his business, more than the grocer, or the banker, or the doctor?

Why is it necessary, in spite of all the natural advantages offered by country life, in spite of the real need of our country for more and better farmers, for our government to use all its efforts of persuasion and inducement in order to turn back that tide of movement from the farms to the cities?

These are problems that can be solved, conditions that can be altered only by the wisdom and efforts of the farmers themselves. There is scope here for all that a woman has of intelligence and fine spirit. There is an opportunity here for the woman who will do her part in remaking a world that has been shaken to its foundations by discoveries the war has forced upon us.

Altogether aside from the feeling of independence and security that comes to a woman through her position as a farmer's wife, she has a deep satisfaction in knowing she is not struggling against someone else for advancement; that her success will not be built upon the downfall of others. Her rise to prosperity is not over the broken fortunes or through the suffering or oppression of those weaker than herself.

Instead, by the labor of her hands, she is producing food for humanity and is, in the old and delightful sense, a lady, a "bread-giver."

Farm life has its ample compensations for all its hardships, and the greatest of these is a sense and enjoyment of the real values of life.

These are not the modern improvements of which we hear so much, the telephone, the rural free delivery, the automobile, and the labor-saving machinery, which are bringing many of the city's advantages to the country. They are not even the beauties of nature, which give so much daily joy and always help over the hard places.

The real values of farm life are simplicity, money honestly earned, difficulties overcome, service lovingly given, respect deserved; in short, the exercise of physical, mental, and spiritual muscles until a rounded, complete, individual character is built.

These are the things I have learned in twenty-five years as a farmer's wife, and so, turning to Elizabeth this morning, I tried to say to her something like this:

"Whether or not you are fitted for the life of a farmer's wife depends on what you want to get from your marriage.

"If you want ease, unearned luxuries, selfish indulgence, a silken-cushioned, strawberries-and-cream life, do not marry a man who will be a farmer.

"If you want to give, as well as to take; if you want to be your husband's full partner in business and in homemaking; if you can stand on your own feet and face life as a whole, the troubles and difficulties and the real joys and growth that come from them; if you want an opportunity to be a fine, strong, free woman, then you are fitted for the life of a farmer's wife, to be his partner, the providence of your own little world of the farm and bread-giver to humanity, the true lady of the world."

CHAPTER 8

A new day
for women

Shorter Hours for the Farm Home Manager
June 1913

When so much is being done to better the conditions of the laboring men all over the world, it is good to know that the work of farm women is receiving its share of attention. Thinking persons realize that the woman on the farm is a most important factor in the success or failure of the whole farm business, and that, aside from any kindly feeling toward her, it pays in dollars and cents to conserve her health and strength. Women on the farm have not, as a rule, the conveniences that city housekeepers have; and their work includes much outside work, such as gardening, caring for chickens, and gathering as well as putting up fruits and vegetables.

It doesn't pay to be like the woman of years ago in old Vermont who opened the stairway door at 5 o'clock on Monday morning and called to the hired girl: "Liza! Liza! Hurry up and come down! Today is wash day and the washing not started; tomorrow is ironing day and the ironing not begun; and the next day is Wednesday and here's the week half gone and nothing done yet."

Farm women have been patient and worked very hard. It has seemed sometimes as though they and their work were overlooked in the march of progress. Yet improvement has found them out, and a great many helps in their work have been put into use in the last few years. Farm homes with modern heating, lighting, and water equipment are increasing in number, and although the majority have not yet advanced so far as that, a great number have passed the stage of the bucket brigade from the spring or the hand-over-hand hauling of water from deep wells. It is getting to be quite the common thing to have the water piped down from the spring with a ram, or forced up from the bottom of deep wells by the compressed air pump. So, many steps have been saved the women folks, for they did most of the water carrying. It is so much easier to turn a faucet when one wants a bucket of water; and the time and strength saved can be used to so much better advantage in other ways.

Cream separators are taking the place of the troublesome setting of milk;

gardens are being planted in rows so that a horse will do in a few minutes what would be a work of hours by hand; home canning outfits are lessening the labor of canning fruits and vegetables; kitchen cabinets are saving steps in the kitchen; and bread and cake mixers save tired hands and arms. Just the change from heavy ironware utensils to graniteware and tin has made more difference than one would think at first.

Vacuum cleaners have almost done away with house-cleaning time for many farm women. In place of the above-ground cellar there is the simple little hanging cellarette. Several shelves of convenient size, either round or square, are fastened together the required distance apart. A close fitting case or cover of two thicknesses of burlap or bran sack is made which completely encloses all the shelves and is closely buttoned down one side for the door. The "cellar" is then hung from the ceiling in some convenient place; a leaky bucket full of water is hung above it so that the water will drip on it, keeping all the burlap wet; a pan is set under it to catch the drips—and there you have a handy cellar for keeping cool the butter and the milk. One will save many a trip up and down cellar stairs or perhaps down to the spring. This hanging cellar is kept cool by the evaporation of the water from its surface.

A friend of mine was unable to stand the heat of the cookstove in summer, so she bought an inexpensive oil stove and a fireless cooker. Anything which required long cooking she started on the oil stove, then placed in the fireless cooker, finishing off, if necessary, when the time came, by a few minutes browning on the oil stove. The combination worked perfectly. There was only a little heat from the oil stove and none at all from the fireless cooker. There was none of the labor of carrying in fuel and keeping up fires and of taking up ashes; and the cleaning up of the dust and dirt was all saved, and there was no increase in the running expenses, for the wood on the farm sold and bought the coal oil for the oil stove.

Another labor-saving idea is the use of a small worktable on casters, which can be easily moved from place to place. If cupboards, stove, and table are some distance apart, this is a great step saver. At one trip it can take from the cupboard to the stove all the things necessary in the getting of a meal. The meal can be dished up on it, and all taken to the dining table at once. The dishes can be taken away to wash upon it.

It was while recovering from a serious illness that I discovered the uses and value of a high stool. It is surprising how much of the housework can be done while sitting—ironing, washing dishes, preparing vegetables and dishes to cook or bake and even such cooking as frying griddle cakes can be accomplished while sitting. There should be a footrest on the stool so the feet will not hang, and it should be light so it can be easily moved. The movable table and the high stool form a combination for saving steps and tiresome standing that is hard to beat.

Ideas for using the things at hand to make our work easier will come to us if we notice a little. For instance, if we keep some old newspapers on hand in the kitchen, the uses we find for them will multiply. Rub the stove over with one when washing the dishes, and the disagreeable task of blackening the stove can be delayed much longer. The paper can be burned and our hands remain clean. Put papers on the worktable to set the pots and pans on while working, and the table will not have to be scoured. When the men come to a meal with their work clothes on from some particularly dirty job, newspapers spread over the tablecloth will save a hard job of washing and ironing.

Time and strength saved by the use of one help make it easier to get the next, and the time saved gives leisure to meet with the neighbors and find still other ways of doing the work more easily. Talking things over is a great help as is also the planning of the work so that the whole family can work together to advantage and without friction. As in any other business each one must do his work well and on time so as not to hinder the others in what they are trying to accomplish.

. . . .

It takes careful thought and planning to have the household machinery run smoothly and to the minute, with meals on time so that the farm work will not be hindered; and the woman who can do this and the outside work connected with the house has proven her executive ability and business talent.

While system is a great help in the work, it is best to get a new light on it once in a while, so we will not get in a rut and do things a certain way because we are in the habit, when we might make some improvement. It helps in finding the little kinks that need straightening out in our work, to notice if there is any of it that we dread to do, and if there is, then study that thing and find some way to do it differently. Perhaps just some little change will be a great help. A woman's work on the farm is very interesting if thought and study are given it, and in no other business can a woman so well keep up with her husband in his work. The more the farm is studied with the help of good farm papers and the Experiment Stations, the more interesting it becomes; and the woman on a farm may, if she wishes, become such an expert as to take the place of a farm advisor. Work in which we are interested can never become drudgery so long as we keep up that interest.

One thing is most important if we expect to keep rested and fit to do our best, and that is not to worry over the work nor to try to do it before the time comes. The feeling of worry and strain caused by trying to carry the whole week's work at once is very tiring. It doesn't pay to be like the woman of years ago in old Vermont who opened the stairway door at 5 o'clock on Monday morning and called to the hired girl: "Liza! Liza! Hurry up and come down!

Today is wash day and the washing not started; tomorrow is ironing day and the ironing not begun; and the next day is Wednesday and here's the week half gone and nothing done yet."

Better for a little while each day to be like the tramp who was not at all afraid of work, yet could lie down right beside it and go to sleep. Slipping away to some quiet place to lie down and relax for fifteen minutes each day, if no longer, rests both mind and body surprisingly. This rest does more good if taken at a regular time, and the work goes along so much better when we are rested and bright that there is no time lost.

Change is rest! How often we have proved this by going away from our work for a day or even part of a day, thinking of other things and forgetting the daily round for a little while. On coming back, the work is taken up with new interest and seems much easier.

If it is not possible to go away, why not let the mind wander a little when the hands can do the task without our strict attention? I have always found that I did not get so tired, and my day seemed shorter when I listened to the birds singing or noticed from the window the beauties of the trees or clouds. This is a part of the farm equipment that cannot be improved upon, though it might be increased with advantage. Perhaps someday we will all have kitchens like the club kitchen lately installed in New York where everything from peeling the potatoes to cooking the dinner and washing the dishes is done by electricity, but the birds' songs will never be any sweeter nor the beauties of field and forest, of cloud and stream, be any more full of delight, and these are already ours.

A Woman's Power and the Vote
April 1916

It is astonishing what an effect a child's early training has upon its whole life. When one reflects upon the subject, one is inclined to agree with the noted clergyman who said, "Give me the child for the first seven years of his life, and you may have him all the rest of the time." What a wonderful power mothers have in their hands! They shape the lives of children today, through them the lives of the men and women of tomorrow, and through them the nations of the world.*

The men who are responsible are largely what their mothers have made them, and their wives usually have finished the job.

I see by the papers that one of the suffrage leaders of the state will tour the Ozarks this spring in the interest of women suffrage, bringing light into the dark places as it were.

A great many seem to regard the securing of the ballot as the supreme attainment and think that with women allowed to vote, everything good will follow as a matter of course. To my mind the ballot is incidental, only a small thing in the work that is before the women of the nation. If politics are not what they should be, if there is graft in places of trust, and if there are unjust laws, the men who are responsible are largely what their mothers have made them, and their wives usually have finished the job. Perhaps that sounds as if I were claiming for the women a great deal of influence, but trace out a few instances for yourself without being deceived by appearances and see if you do not agree with me.

During the controversy between Dr. Cook and Commodore Perry over the discovery of the North Pole,** the subject was being discussed in a home where

---

*Here is a description of what women were supposed to accomplish according to Walter Lord's *The Good Years* (New York: Harper & Brothers, 1960). "After that was won [the right to vote], the women would continue working together for a better, finer, more beautiful world. . . . There would be Democrats, Republicans—and Women. . . . The women would always hold the balance, always throwing their weight on the side of truth and light. United this way, there was no limit to the good they could do (p. 287)."

**The controversy over who really got to the North Pole first has never quite ended. Robert E. Peary and Dr. Frederick A. Cook vied for the claim of first place until Dr. Cook's lack of evidence put an end to his claim. As for Peary, although there have always been strong reservations, the *National Geographic* continues to support his claim.

I happened to be. It was when Cook was being paid such a high price for his lectures, and the mother of two young men present exclaimed, "It makes no difference whether Cook is faking or not! He is getting the money, isn't he, and that's what counts!" She was a woman of whom one expected better things, a refined, educated woman and a devout church member, but her influence on her boys would teach them that money was what counted regardless of truth or honor.

The Woman's Place
March 1922

Reading of an agricultural conference in Washington, D.C., I was very much interested in the address of Mrs. Sewell of Indiana on the place of the farmer's wife in agriculture. She drew a pathetic picture, so much so as to bring tears to the eyes of the audience.

Now I don't want any tears shed over my position, but I've since been doing some thinking on the farm woman's place and wondering if she knows and has taken the place that rightfully belongs to her.

To a woman who has been an "auxiliary" until she is tired of the word, it seems like a start toward the promised land.

Every good farm woman is interested as much in the business part of farm life as she is in the housework, and there comes a time, after we have kept house for years, when the housekeeping is mostly mechanical, while the outside affairs are forever changing, adding variety and interest to life.

As soon as we can manage our household to give us the time, I think we should step out into this wider field, taking our place beside our husbands in the larger business of the farm. Cooperation and mutual help and understanding are the things that will make farm life what it should be.

And so, in these days of women's clubs from which men are excluded, and men's clubs that permit women to be honorary members only, I'm glad to know [there is a club] whereby farm men and women work together on equal terms and with equal privileges. To a woman who has been an "auxiliary" until she is tired of the word, it seems like a start toward the promised land.

. . . .

Two Heads Are Better Than One
August 1919

"We are going to be late getting the hay in from the west meadow. Can't you come and rake it for us?" said the Man of the Place.

I could and did; also I drove the team on the hay fork to fill the big barn, for such is the life of a farmer's wife during the busy season.

"The colt has sprained his ankle. Come pet him while I rub on some liniment, and while you are there, I wish you'd look at the red heifer's bag and see what you think best to do for that swelling on it."

The farmer's wife must know her own business, which includes the greatest variety of trades and occupations ever combined in one all-around person. Think of them! Cook, baker, seamstress, laundrywoman, nurse, chambermaid, and nurse girl. She is a poultry keeper, an expert in dairy work, a specialist in canning, preserving, and pickling, and besides all else, she must be the mother of the family and a smiling hostess.

And so I halter broke the colt while the Man of the Place bathed the lame ankle, and then we decided that the red heifer had been bee stung and bathed her udder with salt and water.

I have finally got the weakly calf into good growing condition and turned it out in the pasture with the others, for I am by way of being an understudy for the veterinarian.

"What would you raise next year on that land we cleared of brush down by the creek? The hay on it is too thin, and it must be broken up." This was the question for my consideration at the breakfast table, and my answer was, "Raise the same crop on that as you do on the remainder of the land on that side of the creek. One large field is better than two small ones, and time is saved in working. Put it into the regular rotation with the rest."

Not that the Man of the Place would do as I said unless he agreed with me, but getting my ideas helps him to form his own opinions, and he knows that two heads are better at planning than one.

One of my neighbors is managing the farm this summer during the absence of her husband. She planted and cultivated and has attended to the harvesting and threshing and haying. She, with the children, cares for the horses and cows, the pigs and poultry. She buys and sells and hires and fires. In short, she does all the work and business that her husband would do if he were here and keeps up her own work besides.

. . . .

A farmer, to be successful, must understand his machinery and be a sort of blacksmith. He must be a carpenter, a road builder, enough of a civil engineer to know how to handle the creeks and washouts on his farm. He must, of course, understand all about the care of the animals on the farm in sickness and in health; he must know all about the raising of crops and handling of soils, the fighting of pests and overcoming of weather conditions and, in addition, must be a good businessman so that he shall not lose all the fruits of his toil in the buying and selling end of the game.

Besides being a helper in all these things with brains—and muscle if necessary—the farmer's wife must know her own business, which includes the greatest variety of trades and occupations ever combined in one all-around person. Think of them! Cook, baker, seamstress, laundrywoman, nurse, chambermaid, and nurse girl. She is a poultry keeper, an expert in dairy work, a specialist in canning, preserving, and pickling, and besides all else, she must be the mother of the family and a smiling hostess.

Women's Work?
April 1919

Flaring headlines in the papers have announced that "women will fight to hold jobs," meaning the men's jobs which they took when the men went to war. What to do about the situation seems to be a very important question. One would think that there must have been a great number of women who were idle before the war. If not, one wonders what has become of the jobs they had. To paraphrase a more or less popular song—I Wonder Who's Holding Them Now?

With men by the thousands out of work and the unemployment situation growing so acute as to cause grave fears of attempted revolution, women by the hundreds are further complicating affairs by adding their numbers to the ranks of labor, employed, unemployed, or striking as the case may be.

We heard nothing of numbers of women who could not find work before the war. They were all busy apparently and fairy well satisfied. Who is doing the work they left to fill the places of men who went into the army, or is that work undone?

It would be interesting to know, and it seems strange that while statistics are being prepared and investigations made of every subject under the sun, no one has compiled the records of "The Jobs Women Left or Women's Work Undone."

Will these women take up their old work and give the men a chance to go back . . . ? The women say not.

But however curious we may be about the past, we are more vitally interested in the future. Will these women take up their old work and give the men a chance to go back to the places they will thus leave vacant? The women say not.

Other women, also, besides those who took men's jobs, have gone out of the places they filled in pre-war days, out into community and social work and government positions which were created by and because of the war. Will these women go back? And again we hear them answer, "Never! We never will go back!" All this is very well, but where are they going and with them all of us?

I think this query could most truthfully be answered by a slang expression, which, though perhaps not polished, is very apt: "We don't know where we're going, but we're on our way."

It makes our hearts thrill and our heads rise proudly to think that women were found capable and eager to do such important work in the crisis of war-time days. I think that never again will anyone have the courage to say that women could not run world affairs if necessary. Also, it is true that when men or women have advanced, they do not go back. History does not retrace its steps.

But this too is certain. We must advance logically, in order, and all together if the ground gained is to be held. If what has hitherto been women's work in the world is simply left undone by them, there is no one else to take it up. If in their haste to do other, perhaps more showy things, their old and special work is neglected and only half done, there will be something seriously wrong with the world, for the commonplace home work of women is the very foundation upon which everything else rests.

So if we wish to go more into world affairs, to have the time to work at public work, we must arrange our old duties in some way so that it will be possible. We cannot leave things at loose ends, no good housemother can do that; and we have been good housekeepers so long that we have the habit of finishing our work up neatly.

Women in towns and villages have an advantage over farm women in being able to cooperate more easily. There is talk now of community kitchens for them from which hot meals may be sent out to the homes. They have, of course, the laundries and the bake shops already.

We farm women, at least farm mothers, have stayed on the job, our own job, during all the excitement. We could not be spared from it, as we realized, so there is no question of our going back or not going back. We are still doing business at the old place, in kitchen and garden and poultry yard; and no one seems to be trying to take our job from us.

But we do not wish to be left too far behind our sisters in towns and cities. We are interested in social and world betterment, in religion and politics; we might even be glad to do some work as a side line that would give us a change from the old routine. We would like to keep up, if any one can keep up with these whirling times, and we must have more leisure from the treadmill if we are to do any of these things.

We must arrange our work differently in some way. Why not a laundry for a farm neighborhood and a bakery also, so situated that they will be easily accessible to a group of farms?

Perhaps if we study conditions of labor and the forward movement of the world as related to the farm, we may find some way of applying the best of them to our own use.

Women's Duty at the Polls
April 1919

Now that women in Missouri have been given the right to vote for president of the United States, and the prospect is good that they will be granted full franchise in the state, it will be interesting to observe how they will respond to the new duty laid upon them.

That it is a duty for every self-respecting woman to discharge faithfully there can be no question; and as these women are not in the habit of failing in their duties, there is no danger that they will do so now if they understand the situation.

We must get rid of the habit of classing all women together politically and thinking of the "woman's vote" as one and indivisible.

We must get rid of the habit of classing all women together politically and thinking of the "woman's vote" as one and indivisible. When the question of woman suffrage was last before the voters of the state, one ardent advocate of the measure, who was also a strong prohibitionist, made the remark, "When women have the ballot, we'll do away with this whisky business."

But when women secured the ballot in California, the state rejected the prohibition amendment and just lately, with the women voting, Chicago went wet, "wringing wet" as one editor says.

This simply shows what we have all really known: that there are all kinds of women as well as of men and that woman's vote will no more bring purity into politics and can no more be counted on as a unit than can man's vote.

It is easy to forecast the effect of woman's suffrage on politics if the home-loving, home-keeping women should refuse to use their voting privilege, for the rougher class of women will have no hesitancy in going to the polling places and casting their ballots. There must be votes enough from other women to offset these in order to keep the balance as it has been.

Then, too, there is legislation which is needed to protect farming interests. Shall farm women fail to use the power given them by the ballot to help secure this legislation?

And so, as I said before, instead of being a privilege to be taken advantage of or neglected according to individual fancy, voting has now become, for the better class of women, a duty to be bravely and conscientiously done, even though it may be rather distasteful. It is "up to them" to see to it that the power of their ballot is behind their influence for good clean government; for an honest administration of public affairs; for justice for all and special privilege for none.

In short, as they have stood behind their soldiers at home and abroad who were fighting for freedom and democracy, they now need to stand shoulder to shoulder with them and keep up the fight.

I fear that we are not quite ready to use the ballot intelligently. Though there has been warning enough that the responsibility was coming to rest upon us, we have been careless about informing ourselves of the conditions which the people of the United States must handle and the questions they must answer.

In this reconstruction period, the most serious time which our nation and the world has ever been called upon to face, we come into the responsibility of helping to decide the fate of the world for perhaps hundreds of years without being prepared.

We women know in our hearts, though
we would not admit it, that our men
are not infallible.

Women can no longer hide behind their husbands and fathers and brothers by saying, "I don't pay any attention to politics. That is the men's business," nor can they safely vote as their men folks do without any other reason for so doing. We women know in our hearts, though we would not admit it, that our men are not infallible. They do sometimes make mistakes and have wrong ideas. Frankly now, is it not true? This being the case, now that the responsibility is ours, we shall be obliged to think things out for ourselves if we are honest and fair to them and ourselves.

If we expect to be fit companions of the men who did their duty so bravely, fighting and working to save our country, we must do our part in upholding our ideals in time of peace. In plain words, as the other women will vote, we must do so in order to keep things properly balanced, and though we may be unprepared at present, there is no reason why we should not be able to vote intelligently by the time we are called upon to exercise the privilege.

Daily Tasks Are Not Small Things
May 1923

"The days are just filled with little things, and I am so tired doing them," wailed a friend recently. Since then I have been thinking about little things or these things we are in the habit of thinking small, although I am sure our judgment is often at fault when we do so.

"Feeding the World"

Working in the garden; taking care of the poultry, calves, and lambs; milking the cows; and all the other chores that fall to the lot of farm women may each appear small in itself; but the results go a long way in helping to "feed the world." Sometimes I try to imagine the people who will eat the eggs I gather or the butter from my cream and who will wear the clothes made from the wool of the lambs I help to raise.

---

*It belittles us to think of our daily tasks
as small things, and if we continue to
do so, it will in time make us small.*

Doing up cut fingers, kissing hurt places, and singing bedtime songs are small things by themselves; but they will inculcate a love for home and family that will last through life and help to keep America a land of homes.

Putting up the school lunch for the children or cooking a good meal for the family may seem very insignificant tasks as compared with giving a lecture, writing a book, or doing other things that have a larger audience; but I doubt very much if, in the ultimate reckoning, they will count for as much.

If when cooking you will think of yourselves as the chemist that you are, combining different ingredients into a food that will properly nourish human bodies, then the work takes on a dignity and an interest. And surely a family well nourished with healthful food so that the boys and girls grow up strong and beautiful, while their elders reach a hale old age, is no small thing.

It belittles us to think of our daily tasks as small things, and if we continue to do so, it will in time make us small. It will narrow our horizon and make of our work just drudgery.

There are so many little things that are really very great, and when we learn to look beyond the insignificant appearing acts themselves to their far-reaching consequences, we will, "despise not the day of small things." We will feel an added dignity and poise from the fact that our everyday round of duties is as important as any other part of the work of the world.

And just as a little thread of gold, running through a fabric, brightens the whole garment, so women's work at home, while only the doing of little things, is like the golden gleam of sunlight that runs through and brightens all the fabric of civilization.

Thoughts on the Role of Women and Divorce
May 1916

"The Athenians" is a woman's club just lately organized in Hartville,* for purposes of study and self-improvement. Hartville was already well supplied with social organizations. There was an embroidery club, also a whist club, and the usual church aid societies and secret orders which count for so much in country towns. Still, there were a few busy women who felt something lacking. They could not be satisfied altogether with social affairs. They wanted to cultivate their minds and increase their knowledge, so they organized the little study club and have laid out a year's course of study.

The membership of the club is limited to twenty. If one of the twenty drops out then some one may be elected to take the vacant place. Two negative ballots exclude anyone from membership. There are no dues. "The Athenians" is, I think, a little unique for a town club, as the membership is open to town and country women alike and there are several country members. Well, why not? "The Colonel's lady and Judy O'Grady are sisters under the skin." (Mind I have not said whether Judy O'Grady is a town or country woman. She is just as likely, if not a little more likely, to be found in one place as the other.)

Surely the most vital subjects in which women are interested are the same in town and country, while the treasures of literature and the accumulated knowledge of the world are for all alike. Then why not study them together and learn to know each other better? Getting acquainted with folks makes things pleasanter all around. How can we like people if we do not know them? It does us good to be with people whose occupation and surroundings are different from ours; it will broaden our minds to get their point of view and we will likely find that they are right in part at least, while it may be that a mutual understanding will lead to a modification of both opinions.

While busily at work one afternoon I heard the purr of a motor and, going to the door to investigate, I was met by the smiling faces of Mr. and Mrs. Frink and Mr. and Mrs. Curtis of Hartville. Mrs. Curtis and Mrs. Frink have taken an active part in organizing "The Athenians," and they had come over to tell me of my election to membership in that club. What should be done when there is unexpected company and one is totally unprepared and besides must be at once hostess, cook, and maid? The situation is always so easily handled in a story. The lovely hostess can perform all kinds of conjuring tricks with a cold bone and a bit of leftover vegetable, producing a delicious repast with no trouble whatever and never a smut on her beautiful gown. In real life it sometimes

---

*The county seat of Wright County, Missouri.

is different, and during the first of that pleasant afternoon my thoughts would stray to the cook's duties. When the time came, however, it was very simple. While I made some biscuits, Mrs. Frink fried some home-cured ham and fresh eggs, and Mrs. Curtis set the table. The Man of the Place opened a jar of preserves, and we all had a jolly, country supper together before the Hartville people started on the drive home.

> *"Woman has found out that, with education and freedom, pursuits of all kinds are open to her, and by following these pursuits, she can preserve her personal liberty and avoid the grave responsibilities, the almost inevitable sorrows and anxieties which belong to family life."*

It is such a pleasure to have many friends and to have them dropping in at unexpected times that I have decided when it lies between friendship and feasting (and something must be crowded out) the feasting may go every time.

At a recent meeting of The Athenians, some very interesting papers, prepared by the members, were read. Quoting from the paper written by Mrs. George Hunter: "The first societies of women were religious and charitable. These were followed by patriotic societies and organizations of other kinds. At present there exists in the United States a great number of clubs for women which may be considered as falling under the general heads—educational, social, and practical. The clubs which may be classified as practical include charitable organizations, societies for civic improvement or for the furthering of schools, libraries, and such organizations as have for their object the securing, by legislation, of improved conditions for working women and children. In 1890 the General Federation of Women's Clubs was formed. There were in the United States at the last enumeration more than 200,000 women belonging to clubs." Get the number? Two hundred thousand! Quite a little army this.

A very interesting paper and one that caused serious thought was that prepared by Mrs. Howe Steel on "The Vocation of Woman." "Woman," says Mrs. Steel, "has found out that, with education and freedom, pursuits of all kinds are open to her, and by following these pursuits, she can preserve her personal liberty and avoid the grave responsibilities, the almost inevitable sorrows and anxieties which belong to family life. She can choose her friends and change them. She can travel and gratify her tastes and satisfy her personal ambitions. The result is that she frequently is failing to discharge satisfactorily some of the most imperative demands the nation makes upon her. I think it was Longfellow who said: 'Homekeeping hearts are happiest.' Dr. Gilbert said, 'Through women alone can our faintest dreams become a reality. Woman is the creator of the future souls unborn. Though she may be cramped, enslaved, and hindered, though she may never be able to speak her ideal, or touch the work she longs to accomplish, yet in the prayer of her soul is the prophecy of her destiny.'

> *Here's to woman, the source of all our bliss.*
> *There's a foretaste of Heaven in her kiss.*
> *From the queen upon her throne to the maiden in the dairy,*
> *They are all alike in this."*

✳✳

In "Soldiers of the Soil," a story of country life in California by Rose Wilder Lane, a real country woman says: "It is my opinion there are lots more happy homes in the country than there are in the city. If everybody lived in the country, you wouldn't hear all this talk about divorce." I wonder how true that is and if true, or if not true, what are the reasons for it? I suppose there are statistics on the subject. There are on most things; but you know "there are three kinds of lies—lies, d———d lies, and statistics," so why bother about them? The reasons given by the woman quoted were that while the woman in the country worked to help out the family income, her work was at home; while if the woman in the city worked she must leave home to do so; that, working together, man and wife were drawn together, while working apart they drifted apart.

There may be fewer divorces in the country without its necessarily following that there are more happy homes. It seems to me that the deadly monotony of working with, and playing with, the same person in the same place for days and weeks and months and years would be more apt to drive a person to divorce or suicide than if they were separated during the working day and could meet when it was over, with different experiences to talk about and to add variety to their companionship. To be sure, in the city a woman can live in one apartment as well as another so long as her pay envelope comes to hand regularly. While in the country, when a woman leaves her home, she leaves her job too. Perhaps this has more effect in lessening divorce in the country than the happy home idea.

We carry our own environment with us to a certain extent and are quite likely to stand or fall by the same principles wherever we may live.

The Home Beauty Parlor
April 1914

"Beauty is but skin deep" says the old adage, and most of us would be glad to know it was as deep as that. Why ugliness should have been made a virtue in the teaching of our youth is passing strange. We all admire beauty of character, but the possession of it is no excuse for neglecting our personal appearance. Indeed it seems to me there must be a fault in the character when one is satisfied with anything less than the best she can make of herself. It is not vanity to wish to appear pleasing to the eyes of our home folks and friends, nor is it a matter of small importance. To be well groomed and good to look at will give us an added self-respect and a greater influence over others.

It is more difficult for country women than for those in the city to make a well-groomed appearance, for they usually do rougher work, and they cannot go to a beauty parlor and have themselves put in trim as the city woman can. However many barber shops there may be in a country town, there is almost never a beauty parlor for the women.

---

*Oh yes, the barber shop is a man's
beauty parlor!*

(Oh yes, the barber shop is a man's beauty parlor! They have things put on their hair to prevent its falling out and to make it grow; they have soothing lotions and astringents and powder put on their faces. Don't let any of them tell you a beauty parlor is foolish or unnecessary or any of those things.)

Until we can make a change in things, and have our beauty parlor in town where we can have the same attention that men do at theirs, we must do these things for ourselves.

We can make a very good job of it, too, with some good, pure soap, a bottle of dioxogen* and some orange wood sticks, a bottle of glycerine and rosewater, and a good toothbrush. With these aids, we can take care of our complexion, our hair, our hands, and our teeth, and with these in good condition, we shall have all the skin-deep beauty necessary for practical purposes; and this will help rather than hinder us in making a beautiful character.

There are a few simple things to remember in caring for the complexion. When washing the face it should first be thoroughly cleansed with warm water, using a good soap, then the soap should be well rinsed off with clear warm

*Perhaps hydrogen peroxide?

water. The warm water opens the pores of the skin and, with the soap, thoroughly cleanses them; the clear warm water rinses out the soap so it will not clog the pores. The face should then be well rinsed with cold water, the colder the better, to close the pores and tighten the skin to prevent flabbiness. Cold water is one of the best aids in keeping a good complexion if it is used in this way. It keeps the pores of the skin from becoming enlarged and brings the blood to the face, thus keeping up a good circulation in the minute blood vessels; and this makes the skin look fresh and youthful.

Cheap perfumed soaps are apt to be injurious to the skin and their use is risky. A good castile soap is always good and not expensive when bought a large bar at a time.

The skin should always be rubbed upward and outward, because it is the gradual sagging down of the muscles of the face that causes wrinkles.

When washing the face, the skin should always be rubbed up and outward, because it is the gradual sagging down of the muscles of the face that causes wrinkles. You can satisfy yourself of this by a few experiments before a glass. A good cold cream rubbed into the skin just before the cold water is used, and then wiped lightly off with a soft cloth, will help to keep the wrinkles away and make the skin softer.

Face and hands should always be well dried after washing. If they are not, the skin will become rough. Keep the bottle of glycerine and rosewater close by the washpan, and after the hands are washed and dried, while they are still damp, rub a few drops of this over them. Do this as many times a day as the hands are washed, and they will keep soft and white.

Wrap a little cotton around the point of one of the little orange wood sticks, dip it into the bottle of dioxygen, and wipe out the dirt from under the fingernails. Then take a little dry cotton on the stick and dry under them. This will do away with the annoying black line, for it cleanses and bleaches and does not make the nail rough, to catch more dirt, as a knife or scissors will when used to clean the nails.

There are many simple things in daily use on a farm that are splendid beautifiers. Washing in buttermilk will whiten the hands and face. Fresh strawberries rubbed on the skin will bleach it, and rhubarb or tomatoes will remove stains from the fingers. None of these things will do the least harm. Common table salt is one of the best tooth powders, and, with a good brush and water, will keep the teeth clean and white.

The hair should not be washed too often, for this will cause it to fall. Still, the scalp should be kept clean. Wearing a little dust cap over the hair while doing the work will help greatly in this, and such frequent washings will not be necessary.

When washing the hair, it is best to dissolve the soap in a little water, making a soft soap. Rub this into the hair with water until it lathers well, then wash it off. Repeat if necessary. When the hair is clean, rinse it well with clear warm water until the soap is all out, then pour some cold water over the scalp to close the pores of the skin. This will prevent taking cold and also act as a tonic to the scalp. The addition of a little baking soda to the water will lighten the hair and help to make it fluffy.

A tea made from common garden sage will darken the hair and help it grow.

What Women Can Add to Politics
December 1919

Is one any more of a lawbreaker, I wonder, for trying to take that to which he is not entitled from those above him in the social scale, than for taking more than he is entitled to from those below him in the social scale?

Some public speakers and some editorials are saying that the farmers hold the balance of power [in the "unsettled times" following WWI] and will have to take control and handle the situation. But farmers are only partly organized, and it will be difficult for them to handle anything so few understand; besides, they are all divided among political parties and stand by their particular party regardless, even though by so doing they lower the price of [their own] hogs.

I think the idea of a woman's party, a political division on sex lines, is distasteful to women.

I heard some farmers talking politics not long ago, and they violently disagreed, passing insults on one another's popular leaders. In this they were following the lead of their daily papers.

. . . .

Some writers are expressing the hope that the women will "clean house" in politics, sweeping out from both parties those who only clutter up the place and hinder the day's work.

I think the idea of a woman's party, a political division on sex lines, is distasteful to women, especially farm women. It seems as if the time has come to reason together instead of dividing into another antagonistic group.

. . . .

If women, with their entrance into a free discussion of politics, can do away with the "hot air" and insults, with "making the Eagle scream," and "twisting the Lion's tail," and "shaking the bloody shirt," and all the rest of the smoke screen, bringing politics into the open air of sane, sensible discussion—a discussion of facts and conditions, not personal discussions of leaders—they will have rendered the country a great service.

This and That—A Neighborly Visit With Laura
February 1916

I wonder if Missouri farm women realize the value in dollars and cents of the work they do from day to day in raising farm products for the market? How many persons when reading the astonishing amount received in a year for Missouri poultry and eggs think of the fact that it is practically all produced by the women, and as a sideline at that! For, of course, a woman's real business is the keeping of the house and caring for the family. Not only the care of the poultry but also the raising of garden products and small fruits is largely women's

We are told that the life of a woman on a farm is narrow and that the monotony of it drives many farm women insane.

work; and in many instances the greater part of the labor of producing cream and butter also falls to women. The fact is that while there has been a good deal of discussion for and against women in business, farm women have always been businesswomen, and I have never heard a protest.

. . . .

I find that it adds greatly to the interest of life to keep careful accounts of the business of housekeeping with its sidelines of poultry and small fruits.

Especially do the account books add a spice when the Man of the Place gets angry because the hens get into the barn and scratch things around, or when the grain is getting low in the bins in the spring and he comes to you and says: "Those durn hens are eating their heads off!"

Then, if you can bring your little account book and show him that the feed for the hens cost so much, and the eggs and poultry sold brought so much, leaving a good little profit besides the eggs and poultry used in the house, he will feel better about things in general and especially the hens.

A woman I know kept for one year the accounts of the household and her own especial little extra work and surprised herself by finding that by her own efforts she had made a clear profit of $395 during the year, and this without neglecting in any way her household or home duties.

The total for household expenses and her own personal expenses for the same time was $122.29. There is after all, you see, some excuse for the man who told a friend he was going to be married. "Be married!" the friend exclaimed, in surprise. "Why, you can't make a living for yourself!" To which the first man replied, sulkily: "Well, it's a pity if she can't help a little."

My friend proved that she could "help a little." Her books made such a good showing that her husband asked her to keep books for the farm, and so she was promoted to the position of farm accountant (without salary).

Considering the amount of time, labor, and capital invested, the farm books did not balance out so well as her own, and she became interested in hunting the reason why. So now she has become a sort of farm advisor with whom her husband consults on all matters of farm business.

We are told that the life of a woman on a farm is narrow and that the monotony of it drives many farm women insane. That life on a farm as elsewhere is just what we make it, that much and no more, is being proved every day by women who, like this one, pick up a thread connecting farm life with the whole, great outside world.

In the study of soils, of crops, their origin and proper cultivation and rotation; in the study of the livestock on the place, their proper selection and care; with the care of her house and poultry, always looking for a shortcut in the work to gain time for some other interesting thing, there does not seem to be much chance for monotony to drive her insane.

＊＊

That "all work and no play makes Jack a dull boy" is very true, I think. It is just as dull for Jill as it is for Jack, and so they formed a "neighborhood crochet club" down in "Happy Hollow." The women met and learned the new crochet patterns and visited (?)—well, gossiped, then—as the men do when they go to town on Saturday and have so much business (?) to attend to that they cannot go home until late chore time.

By the way, did you ever think that as much good can be done by the right kind of gossip as harm by the unkind sort? The crochet club made a little playtime mixed with the work all summer until bad weather and the grippe interfered in the fall. Jill was not so dull, and plans are made for the club to meet again soon.

＊＊

We do enjoy siting around the fireplace in the evening and on stormy days in the winter.

When we planned our new house, we determined that we would build the fireplace first, and the rest of the house if we could afford it—not a grate, but a good old-fashioned fireplace that will burn a stick of wood as large as a man can carry. We have seen to it besides that there is a wood lot left on the farm to provide those sticks. So far we have escaped having the grippe while all the neighborhood has been suffering with it. We attribute our good fortune to this same big fireplace and the two open stairs in the house. The fresh air they furnish has been much cheaper as well as pleasanter to take than the doctor's medicine.

Some old-fashioned things like fresh air and sunshine are hard to beat. In our mad rush for progress and modern improvements let's be sure we take along with us all the old-fashioned things worthwhile.

The magazines say that the spring fashions will return to the styles of our grandmothers, ruffles, pantalettes, ribbon armlets and all. It will surely be delightful to have women's clothes soft and fluffy again, and we need not follow the freak styles, you know. There is a distinct advantage in choosing the rather moderate, quiet styles, for the up-to-the-minute freaks soon go out, and then they call attention to their out-of-dateness by their striking appearance, while others in equally as good style, but not so pronounced, will be a pleasure for more than one season.

New Day for Women
June 1918

How long has it been since you have seen an old maid? Oh, of course, one sees unmarried women every day, but it has been a good many years since I have seen a real, "old maid" or "maiden lady." Even the terms sound strange and lead one back and back into memories.

There were old maids when I was a girl. Later, some of the older girls protested against being called "old maids" and insisted on being called "bachelor girls." There was some controversy over the question of whether women should be given such a title, I remember; but not having any special interest in the subject, I lost sight of it and awakened later to the fact that both old maids and bachelor girls had disappeared, how or when I do not know. In their place are simply women, young women, older women (never old women), married and unmarried women, divorced women and widows, with the descriptive adjective in the background; but nowhere in the world, I think, are there any old maids.

Although still a vital part of a woman's life, marriage is not now the end and aim of her existence.

As one considers the subject, it becomes plain that this one fact contains the whole story and explanation of the change in the world of women, the broadening and enriching of their lives. In the days when old maids flourished, the one important fact in a woman's life was whether or not she was married, and as soon as a girl child reached maturity, she was placed in one of two classes and labeled accordingly. She was either Mrs. —— or else an old maid.

The World Is Open to Us

As women became more interested in other things; as the world opened up to them its storehouse of activities and absorbing interests; when the fact that a woman was a doctor, a lawyer, a farmer or what not; when her work in and for the world became of more importance to the world than her private life, the fact of whether or not she was married did not receive the emphasis that it formerly did.

To be sure, everyone knows that a woman's most important work is still her children, but other interests enter so largely into her life today that she is not classified solely on the one count. Although still a vital part of a woman's life, marriage is not now the end and aim of her existence. There are in the world many, many other ambitions and occupations to take up her attention.

Women are successful lumber dealers, livestock breeders, caterers, curators, bacteriologists, pageant managers, cable code experts, and besides have entered nearly every ordinary profession. They have learned and are learning the most advanced methods of farming and scientific dairy management while it has become no uncommon thing for a woman to manage an ordinary farm. The exigencies of the war have thrust women into many new occupations that otherwise they might not have undertaken for many years, if ever.

Thousands of them have become expert munitions makers and, while we all hope there will be no need for that trade when the present war is ended, still there will be use for the trained technical skill which these women workers have acquired.

Women are running trains; they are doing the work in factories; they are clerks, jurors, representatives in congress, and farm help. By the time the war is over, most of the economic and industrial systems of the world will be in the hands of the women. Quite likely, too, they will have through the ballot the control of the political governments of the world.

If by an inconceivable turn of fate, Germany should conquer in the struggle now going on,* women will be held in control by the military power and without doubt will be again restricted to the home and children according to the rule laid down by Emperor William defining their sphere of activity; but this we will not permit to be possible.

When the democratic nations are victorious and the world is ruled by the ballot instead of the cannon, there is scarcely a doubt but what women will be included in the universal suffrage. Already the franchise has been given to six million women in England. A suffrage amendment to the Constitution of the United States missed being brought before Congress by only a few votes, and there is no doubt but that the women of the United States will soon have the ballot.

In Russia, when the revolution occurred, the women took the franchise with the men as a matter of course and without question. In France, the old idea that women should rule through their influence over men is still alive but growing feeble. More and more women and men are coming to stand together on terms of frankness and equality.

Women Shall Rule

Italy is far behind the other nations in the emancipation of its women; still the women of Italy have a great influence. It was the use of German propa-

---

*World War I.

ganda among the Italian peasant women that weakened Italy and caused the late reverse there.

We all realize with aching hearts that there is a great slaughter of men on the battle fronts and with the sexes about equal over the world before the war, what will be the result when millions of men are killed? When at last the "Beast of Berlin" is safely caged and the soldiers of freedom return home to settle quietly down into civil life once more, the women are going to be largely in the majority over the world. With the ballot in their hands, they are going to be the rulers of a democratic world.

There is a great deal of speculation about the conditions that will prevail after the war. Nearly all writers and thinkers are looking for a new order, a sort of social and industrial revolution; and they all expect it to come through the returned soldiers. No one, so far as I have found, is giving a thought to the fact that in a free democratic world the power will be in the hands of the women who have stayed quietly at home, working, sorrowing, and thinking.

Will we be wise and true and strong enough to use this power for the best or will we be deceived through our ignorance or driven on the wrong way by storms of emotion or enthusiasm? We have been privileged to look on and criticize the way the world has been run. "A man-made world" we have called it now and then, implying that women would have done so much better in managing its affairs. The signs indicate that we are going to have a chance to remake it nearer to the heart's desire. I wish I might be sure that we would be equal to our opportunity.

I suggested this idea of the coming power of women to a liberal-minded man, a man who is strongly in favor of woman suffrage and he replied: "The women are no more ready for such a responsibility than the people of Russia were; they are ignorant along the lines of government and too uncontrolled in their emotions."

I wonder if he is right? The majority vote in a democratic league of nations will be a great power to hold in inexperienced hands, a great responsibility to rest upon the women of the world.

CHAPTER 9

If we would but
open our eyes

The Creative Chemistry of Life
July 1921

It is hot in the kitchen these days cooking for the men in the hay harvest fields. But perhaps we are making ourselves more warm and tired than necessary by fretting and thinking how tired and warm we are. We would be much cooler and less tired if, instead of thinking of the weather and our weariness, we would try to remember the bird's songs we heard in the early morning or notice the view of the woods and hills or of the valley and stream. It would help us to think of the cooling breeze on the porch where we rest in the evening's lengthening shadows when the long, hot day is over.

---

*There are pleasant things to think
about and beauty to be found
everywhere, and they grow
by dwelling on them.*

There are pleasant things to think about and beauty to be found everywhere, and they grow by dwelling on them. If we would but open our eyes to the beauty of our surroundings, we would be much happier and more comfortable. The kingdom of home, as well as the Kingdom of Heaven, is within us. It is pleasant and happy or the opposite according as our minds and hearts atune themselves to the beauty and joy around us or vibrate to thoughts of ugliness and discomfort.

Which leads me to conclude that our lives are like coal tar. This sounds rather unpleasant, but I'm sure I'll be pardoned for using the simile when it is clearly understood that I have no intention of blackening anyone's character. Coal tar is not altogether what it appears to be. A great many things can be taken from it. That's like life, isn't it—everybody's life?

Until recently I always thought of coal tar as a black, sticky, unpleasant substance, fit only for use as a roofing paint. But it is a wonderful combination of elements out of which may be made what one wills. The most beautiful colors, delightful perfumes, and delicious flavors are contained within its blackness and may be taken from it. It also contains valuable food elements and the most dreadful poisons. From it also are made munitions of war, and the precious medicines that cure the wounds made by those same munitions.

And so our lives are similar in that we may make of them or get out of them what we choose—beauty and fragrance and usefulness or those things that are ugly and harmful. It is necessary to understand chemistry to extract from coal tar its valuable properties, and we must practice the "creative chemistry" of life to get true values from life.

Just as the chemist in his laboratory today is carrying on the work of the old-time alchemist, so we may practice magic arts. We may change unloveliness into beauty and, from the darkness of life, evolve all the beautiful colors of the rainbow of promise by developing the bright rays of purity and love, the golden glow of constancy, the true-blue of steadfastness, and the ever-green home of immortality.

The Light We Throw
February 1922

A wonderful way has been invented to transform a scene on the stage, completely changing the apparent surroundings of the actors and their costumes without moving an article. The change is made in an instant. By an arrangement of light and colors, the scenes are so painted that with a red light thrown upon them, certain parts come into view while other parts remain invisible. By changing a switch and throwing a blue light upon the scene, what has been visible disappears and things unseen before appear, completely changing the appearance of the stage.

Things and persons appear to us
according to the light we throw
upon them.

This late achievement of science is a good illustration of a fact we all know but so easily forget or overlook—that things and persons appear to us according to the light we throw upon them from our own minds.

When we are down-hearted and discouraged, we speak of looking at the world through blue glasses; nothing looks the same to us; our family and friends do not appear the same; our home and work show in the darkest colors. But when we are happy, we see things in a brighter light and everything is transformed.

How unconsciously we judge others by the light that is within ourselves, condemning or approving them by our own conception of right and wrong, honor and dishonor! We show by our judgment just what the light within us is.

What we see is always affected by the light in which we look at it so that no two persons see people and things alike. What we see and how we see depends upon the nature of our light.

A quotation, the origin of which I have forgotten, lingers in my mind: "You cannot believe in honor until you have achieved it. Better keep yourself clean and bright; you are the window through which you must see the world."

A Few Minutes with a Poet
January 1919

Among my books of verse, there is an old poem that I could scarcely do without. It is "The Fool's Prayer" by Edward Rowland Sill, and every now and then I have been impelled in deep humiliation of spirit to pray the prayer made by that old-time jester of the king.

Even though one is not in the habit of making New Year's resolutions, to be broken whenever the opportunity arises, still, as the old year departs, like Lot's wife, we cannot resist a backward glance. As we see in retrospect the things we have done that we ought not and the things we have left undone that we should have done, we have a hope that the coming year will show a better record.

---

*To laugh and forget is one
of the saving graces.*

In my glance backward and hope for the future, one thing became plain to me—that I valued the love and appreciation of my friends more than ever before, and that I would try to show my love for them; that I would be more careful of their feelings, more tactful, and so endear myself to them.

A few days later a friend and I went together to an afternoon gathering where refreshments were served, and we came back to my friend's home just as the evening meal was ready. The Man of the Place failed to meet me, and so I stayed unexpectedly. My friend made apologies for the simple meal, and I said that I preferred plain food to such as we had in the afternoon, which was the same as saying that her meal was plain and that the afternoon refreshments had been finer. I felt that I had said the wrong thing, and in a desperate effort to make amends, I praised the soup which had been served. Not being satisfied to let well-enough alone, because of my embarrassment I continued, "It is so easy to have delicious soups, one can make them of just any little things that are left."

And all the way home as I rode quietly beside the Man of the Place I kept praying "The Fool's Prayer": "Oh Lord, be merciful to me, a fool."

We can afford to laugh at a little mistake such as that, however embarrassing it may be. To laugh and forget is one of the saving graces, but only a little later I was guilty of another mistake over which I could not laugh.

Mrs. G and I were in a group of women at a social affair; but having a little business to talk over, we stepped into another room where we were almost immediately followed by an acquaintance. We greeted her and then went on with our conversation, from which she was excluded. I forgot her presence, and then I looked her way again; she was gone. We had not been kind, and to make it worse, she was comparatively a stranger among us.

> *Our hearts are mostly in the right place, but we seem to be weak in the head.*

In a few minutes everyone was leaving without my having had a chance to make amends in any way. I could not apologize without giving a point to the rudeness, but I thought that I would be especially gracious to her when we met again so she would not feel that we made her an outsider. Now I learn that it will be months before I see her again. I know that she is very sensitive and that I must have hurt her. Again and from the bottom of my heart, I prayed "The Fool's Prayer":

> *These clumsy feet, still in the mire,*
> *Go crushing blossoms without end;*
> *These hard, well-meaning hands we thrust*
> *Among the heart-strings of a friend—*
> *Oh Lord, be merciful to me, a fool.*

As we grow old enough to have a proper perspective, we see such things work out to their conclusion or rather to a partial conclusion, for the effects go on and on endlessly. Very few of our misdeeds are with deliberate intent to do wrong. Our hearts are mostly in the right place, but we seem to be weak in the head.

> *'Tis not by guilt the onward sweep*
> *Of truth and right, Oh Lord, we stray;*
> *'Tis by our follies that so long*
> *We hold the earth from heaven away.*
> *Our faults no tenderness should ask;*
> *The chastening stripes must cleanse them all;*
> *But for our blunder—oh, in shame*
> *Before the eyes of heaven we fall.*

Without doubt each one of us is fully entitled to pray the whole of "The Fool's Prayer" and more especially the refrain: "Oh Lord, be merciful to me, a fool."

Success
October 1922

I was told to go into a certain community and get the story of the most successful person in it.

"There are no successes there," I said, "just ordinary people; not one of whom has contributed to the progress of the world. I can get no story there worth anything as an inspiration to others."

"I can get no story there worth anything as an inspiration to others."

Then came the reply: "Surely someone has lived a clean life, has good friends, and the love of family. Such a one must have contributed something of good to others."

Rearranging my standard of "success" to include something besides accumulated wealth—achieved ambition of a spectacular sort—I thought of Grandpa and Grandma Culver, poor as church mice, but a fine old couple, loved by everybody and loving everybody. Home meant something to their children who return there year after year. I went to see them.

"No," Grandma told me over the jelly she was making for the sick, "Pa and I never have been well-off in money, but, oh, so very rich in love of each other, of family, and friends.

"We've tried to see every little submerged virtue in each other, in the children, and in everybody. I had the gift of cheerfulness; Pa had patience; we cultivated these traits.

"Every day we have tried to be of a little use to somebody, never turning down a single opportunity to help someone to a glimpse of things worthwhile. What we have lacked in money and brilliance, we have tried to make up in service."

But ever the world has let the flash of more dazzling successes blind it to the value of such lives as these.

Good Neighbors
May 1917

There are two vacant places in our neighborhood. Two neighbors have gone ahead on "the great adventure."

We become so accustomed to our neighbors and friends that we take their presence as a matter of course, forgetting that the time in which we may enjoy their companionship is limited; and when they are no longer in their places, there is always a little shock of surprise mingled with our grief.

When we came to the Ozarks more than twenty years ago, neighbor Deaver was one of the first to welcome us to our new home, and how he has moved on ahead to that far country from which no traveler returns. Speaking of Mrs. Case's illness and death, a young woman said, "I could not do much to help them, but I did what I could, for Mrs. Case was mighty good to me when I was sick." That tells the story. The neighborhood will miss them both for they were good neighbors. What remains to be said? What greater praise could be given?

*I half expected him to come back once
more and borrow the hog.*

I wonder if you all know the story of the man who was moving from one place to another because he had such bad neighbors. Just before making the change, he met a man from the neighborhood to which he was going and told him in detail how mean his old neighbors were, so bad in fact that he would not live among them any longer. Then he asked the other man what the neighbors were like in the place to which he was moving. The other man replied, "You will find just the same kind of neighbors where you are going as those you leave behind you."

It is true that we find ourselves reflected in our friends and neighbors to a surprising extent, and if we are in the habit of having bad neighbors, we are not likely to find better by changing our location. We might as well make good neighbors in our own neighborhood, beginning, as they tell us charity should, at home.

If we make good neighbors of ourselves, we likely shall not need to seek new friends in strange places. This would be a tiresome world if everyone were shaped to a pattern of our own cutting, and I think we enjoy our neighbors more if we accept them just as they are.

Sometimes it is rather hard to do, for certainly it takes all kinds of neighbors to make a community. We once had a neighbor who borrowed nearly everything on the place. Mr. Skelton was a good borrower but a very poor hand to return anything. As he lived just across a narrow road from us, it was very convenient—for him. He borrowed the hand tools and the farm machinery, the grindstone and the whetstone, and the harness and saddles, also groceries and kitchen tools.

One day he came over and borrowed my wash boiler in which to heat water for butchering. In a few minutes he returned, and making a separate trip for each article, he borrowed both my dishpans, my two butcher knives, the knife sharpener, a couple of buckets, the boards on which to lay the hog, some matches to light his fire, and as an afterthought while the water was heating, he came for some salt. There was a fat hog in our pen, and I half expected him to come back once more and borrow the hog, but luckily he had a hog of his own. A few days later when I asked to borrow a paper, I was told that they never lent their papers. And yet this family were kind neighbors later when we really needed their help.

The Smiths moved in from another state. Their first caller was informed that they did not want the neighbors "to come about them at all," didn't want to be bothered with them. No one knew the reason, but all respected their wishes and left them alone. As he was new to the country, Mr. Smith did not make a success of his farming, but he was not bothered with friendly advice either.

A Constant Friend
January 1917

A group of friends was gathered around a glowing fire the other evening. The cold outside and the warmth and cheer and soft lights within had opened their hearts, and they were talking freely together as good friends should.

"I propose that we eliminate the word 'can't' from our vocabularies for the coming year," said Mrs. Betty. "There ain't no such animal anyhow."

"But sometimes we just c——t" began sister Sue, then stopped abruptly at the sound of an amused chuckle.

"Oh, well—if you feel that way about it!" rejoined Mrs. Betty, "but I still insist that if you see such an animal, it is only a creature of the imagination. When I went to school they tried to teach me that it was noble to say, 'I'll try' when confronted with a difficult thing to be done, but it always sounded weak to me. Why, the very expression presupposes failure!" she went on with growing earnestness. "Why not say I will and then make good? One can, you know, for if there is not one way to do a thing there are usually two."

"That word 'can't' with its suggestion of failure!" exclaimed George. "Do you know a man came up to me on the street the other day and said, 'You can't lend me a dollar, can you?' He expected to fail in his request—and he most certainly did," he added grimly.

Remember well and bear in mind
A constant friend is hard to find.

"After all," said brother James slowly, "people do a good deal as they are expected to do, even to saying the things they are expected to say. The power of suggestion is very strong. Did you ever notice how everyone will agree with you on the weather? I have tried it out many a time just for fun. Before the days of motor cars, when we could speak as we passed driving along the road, I have said to the first man I met, 'This is a fine day'; and regardless of what the weather might be, he never would fail to answer, 'Sure, it's a fine day,' or something to that effect and pass on smiling. To the next man I met I would say, 'Cold weather we're having,' and his reply would always be, 'Coldest I ever knew at this season,' or 'Mighty cold this morning,' and he would go on his way shivering.

"No matter if it's raining, a man usually will agree with you that it's awfully dry weather if you suggest it to him right."

"Speaking of friends," said Philip, which no one had been doing, though all could trace the connecting thought, "Speaking of friends—I heard a man say not long ago that he could count all the friends he had on the fingers of one hand. I wonder"—and his voice trailed off into silence as his thought carried him away. A chorus of protest arose.

"Oh, how awful!" exclaimed Pansy, with tender eyes. "Anyone has more friends than that. Why, if anybody is sick or in trouble everybody is his friend."

"It all depends on one's definition of friend," said Mrs. Betty in a considering tone. "What do we mean when we say 'friend'? What is the test for a friend?" A silence fell upon the little group around the glowing fire.

"But I want to know," insisted Mrs. Betty. "What is the test for a friend? Just what do you mean, Philip, when you say, 'He is my friend'?"

"Well," Philip replied, "when a man is my friend I expect he will stand by me in trouble, that he will do whatever he can to help me if I am needing help, and do it at once even at cost of inconvenience to himself."

"Now, Pansy! How do you know your friends?" still insisted Mrs. Betty.

"My friends," said Pansy, with the tender eyes, "will like me anyway, no matter what my faults are. They will let me do as I please and not try to change me but will be my friends whatever I do."

"Next," began Mrs. Betty, but there were exclamations from every side. "No! No! It's your turn now! We want to know what your test of friendship is!"

"Why! I was just asking for information," answered Mrs. Betty with a brilliant smile, the warmth of which included the whole circle. "I wanted to know—"

"Tell us! Tell us!" they all insisted.

"Well, then," earnestly, "my friends will stand by me in trouble. They will love me even though I make mistakes and in spite of my faults, but if they see me in danger of taking the wrong course, they will warn me. If necessary, they will even tell me of a fault which perhaps is growing on me unaware. One should dare anything for a friend, you know."

"Yes, but to tell friends of a fault is dangerous," said gentle Rosemary. "It is so likely to make them angry."

"To be sure," Mrs. Betty answered. "But if we are a friend, we will take it thankfully for the sake of the spirit in which it is given as we do a Christmas present which otherwise we would not care for."

> *Remember well and bear in mind*
> *A constant friend is hard to find*
> *And when you find one good and true*
> *Change not the old one for the new,*

quoted Philip as the group began to break up.

"No, don't change, 'em," said George, in the bustle of putting on of wraps. "Don't change 'em! Just take 'em all in!"

What Would You Do?
April 1918

What would you do if you had a million dollars?

I asked the question once of a young man of my acquaintance. He was the only son of rich parents and had been reared like the lilies of the field to "toil not." Then suddenly his father decided that he must learn to work. Working for a salary was supposed to teach him the value of money, and learning the business would teach him how to care for his father's property when he should inherit it. But he did not take kindly to the lessons. He had been a butterfly so long he could not settle down to being a busy bee. Office hours came too early in the morning, and why should he keep office hours, anyway, when the fishing and hunting were good?

"If I had a million dollars,
I would buy a bulldog."

"Bert," I said to him one day, "what would you do if you had a million dollars?"

Bert looked at me gravely a moment and then, with a twinkle in his eye, said earnestly: "If I had a million dollars, I would buy a bulldog, a big brindled one. I would keep him under my office desk and if anyone came in and said 'business' to me, I would say, 'Take him, Tige.'"

I read in a California paper last week of an altogether different type of man who had arrived at somewhat the same conclusion as Bert, but by exactly the opposite route. This man was an old desert prospector, "desert rat" as they are called in the West, who had spent years hunting for gold in the desert. He came out to the nearest town with his burro and packs after supplies and found that he was heir to a fortune, and that there had been quite a search through the country to find him. He did not want the money, and at first refused to take it. But it was his and he must make some disposition of it, so he insisted that a trustee be appointed to take care of it for him.

The old "desert rat," with all his worldly possessions in a pack on the back of a burro, and Bert, who had grown to manhood with no wish unsatisfied that money could gratify, had both come to the same decision—the burden of riches was more than they could bear.

The real character of men and women comes to the surface under stress, and sudden riches is as strong a test as any.

* *

Just now there is a chance of fortune coming to unexpected places in the Ozark hills through the boom in mining operations. Several farm women were talking over the prospects.

"What will you do when they strike it rich on your place?" someone asked.

"Oh! I'll get some new spring clothes and some more Holsteins," answered Mrs. Slade.

"Clothes, of course, but who would stop there?" exclaimed Mrs. Rice. "I shall buy motor cars and diamonds."

"I'll sell out the place and leave these hills," said Mrs. Wade. "How about you, Mrs. Woods?"

"I wouldn't go away," said Mrs. Woods slowly. "I should just like to help, and I can help better where I am accustomed to people and things."

Her serious face lighted and her eyes shone as she continued: "I do so desire to help a little, and there is so much one could do with a little money, not just ordinary charity—there are so many persons looking after that—but some playthings for children here and there who do not have any; the pleasure of paying a mortgage now and then for some hard-working family who could not pay it themselves; just helping those who need it before they become discouraged. It would be so much better than taking care of them after they have given up trying to help themselves. I'm going to do some of these things if they find ore on our place."

And so they showed their different characters and dispositions and the objects of their lives—business and show and snobbishness on the one hand, and love for others, with a sincere desire to share good fortune with those less fortunate on the other.

What would you do if you should suddenly become rich? Think out the answer and then look at yourself impartially by the light that answer will throw upon you! It is surprising what an opinion one sometimes forms of one's self by mentally standing off and looking on as at a stranger.

Opportunity
November 1918

"Grasp opportunity by the forelock, for it is bald behind," says the old proverb. In other words, we must be ready to meet and take advantage of opportunities as they come, or we will lose the chance. We cannot have any hold on

---

Even though we never become one of the great persons of the world, the chance is sure to come to us to use whatever knowledge we acquire.

---

them once they have passed by. Nor is time and endeavor spent in preparing ourselves ever wasted, for if we are ready, opportunity is sure to come.

. . . .

No one can become great who is not ready to take the opportunity when it comes, nor indeed succeed in smaller matters; and whatever we prepare ourselves to do or become, the opportunity will come to us to do or become that thing.

Even though we never become one of the great persons of the world, the chance is sure to come to us to use whatever knowledge we acquire.

I knew a woman who denied herself in other things in order that she might pay for French lessons. There seemed no chance that it would ever be an advantage to her except as a means of culture, but she now has a good position at a large salary which she would have been unable to fill but for her knowledge of French.

There is unfortunately a reverse side to this picture I have drawn of efforts crowned by success. Just as achievements are made possible by a careful preparation, a lack of effort to reach forward and beyond our present position works inversely and again examples are too numerous to mention.

A hired man on a farm who always needs a boss, who is unable mentally and by disposition to work unless his employer is present and leading, who never fits himself by being responsible and trustworthy for the responsibility of owning and running his own farm, will always be a hired man either on a farm or elsewhere.

The tenant farmer who is not preparing himself for being an owner by putting himself mentally in an owner's place, getting his point of view and realizing his difficulties, is the tenant farmer who is always having trouble with his landlord and almost never comes to own his own farm. Realizing the difficulties and solving the problems of the next step up seem to lead inevitably to taking that step.

If we do a little less than is required by the position we now fill, whether in our own business or working for someone else; if we do not learn something of the work of the person higher up, we are never ready to advance, and then we say, "I had a good chance if I had only known how," and so forth.

If we spend on our living every cent of our present income, we are not ready to take that opportunity which requires a little capital, and then we say, "That was a good chance if I could only have raised the money."

There is also a touch of humor to be found in the fact that what we prepare for comes to us, although it is rather pitiful. Humor and pathos are very close "kin."

When the influenza came to our town, Mrs. C called a friend and tried to engage her to come and nurse her through the illness.

"Have you the influenza?" asked the friend.

"Oh, no!" replied Mrs. C. "None of us has it yet, but I'm all ready for it. I have my bed all clean and ready to crawl into as soon as I feel ill. Everything is ready but a nurse, and I want you to come and take care of me."

In very few days, Mrs. C was in bed with an attack of influenza. She had prepared for the visit, and she could say with the psalmist: "The thing that I feared has come upon me."*

---

*Actually, the quote is from Job 3:25.

To Stand by Ourselves
April 1920

Out in the woods the other day, I saw a tree that had branches on only one side. Evidently, other trees had grown so near it that there had been room for it to grow in only the one way, and now that it was left to stand alone its lack of good development and balance showed plainly.

It was not a beautiful thing. It looked lopsided and freakish and unable to stand by itself, being pulled a little over by the weight of its branches. It reminded me of a person who has grown all in one direction; in his work perhaps, knowing how to do only one thing as those workmen in factories who do a certain thing to one part of a machine day after day and never learn how to complete the whole, depending on others to finish the job.

Lives never were meant to grow that way, lopsided and crippled!

Or a woman who is interested in nothing but her housework and gossip, leaving her life bare of all the beautiful branches of learning and culture which might have been hers.

Or that person who follows always the same habits of thought, thinking always along the same lines in the same safe, worn grooves, distrusting the new ideas that begin to branch out in other directions leading into new fields of thought where free winds blow.

And so many are dwarfed and crooked because of their ignorance on all subjects except a very few with the branches of their tree of knowledge all on one side!

Lives never were meant to grow that way, lopsided and crippled! They should be well-developed and balanced, strong and symmetrical, like a tree that grows by itself against the storms from whatever direction they may come—a thing of beauty and satisfaction.

The choice lies with us as to which we shall resemble. We may be like the young woman devoted to dress and fancywork who, when asked to join a club for the study of current events, replied, "What! Spend all the afternoon studying and talking about such things as that! Well, I should say not!"

Or, if we prefer, we may be like Mr. and Mrs. A. Mr. A is a good farmer; his crops and livestock are of the best, and besides he is a leader in farm organizations. Mrs. A is a good housekeeper; her garden is the best in the neighborhood, and her poultry is the pride of her heart.

As you see, they are very busy people, but they keep informed on current affairs and, now that the son and daughter are taking charge of part of the farm work, are having more time for reading and study. Their lives are branching out more and more in every direction for good to themselves and other people, for it is a fact that the more we make of our lives the better it is for others as well as ourselves.

You must not understand me to mean that we should selfishly live to ourselves. We are all better for contact and companionship with other people. We need such contact to polish off the rough corners of our minds and our manners, but it is a pitiful thing when anyone cannot, if necessary, stand by himself sufficient to himself and in good company even though alone.

Challenges
August 1918

"A difficulty raiseth the spirit of a great man. He hath a mind to wrestle with it and give it a fall. A man's mind must be very low if the difficulty doth not make part of his pleasure." By the test of these words of Lord Halifax, there are a number of great persons in the world today.

After all, what is a difficulty but a direct challenge? "Here I am in your way," it says, "you cannot get around me nor overcome me! I have blocked your path!" Anyone of spirit will accept the challenge and find some way to get around or over or through that obstacle. Yes! And find pleasure in the difficulty for the sheer joy of surmounting it, as well as because there has been an opportunity once more to prove one's strength and cunning and, by the very use of these qualities, cause an increase of them.

Yes! And find pleasure in the difficulty
for the sheer joy of surmounting it.

The overcoming of one difficulty makes easier the conquering of the next until finally we are almost invincible. Success actually becomes a habit through the determined overcoming of obstacles as we meet them one by one.

If we are not being successful, if we are more or less on the road toward failure, a change in our fortunes can be brought by making a start, however small, in the right direction and then following it up. We can form the habit of success by beginning with some project and putting it through to a successful conclusion, however long and hard we must fight to do so, by "wrestling with" one difficulty and "giving it a fall." The next time it will be easier.

For some reason, of course, according to some universal law, we gather momentum as we proceed in whatever way we go; and just as by overcoming a small difficulty, we are more able to conquer the next, though greater; so if we allow ourselves to fail, it is easier to fail the next time, and failure becomes a habit until we are unable to look a difficulty fairly in the face, but turn and run from it.

There is no elation equal to the rise of the spirit to meet and overcome a difficulty, not with a foolish overconfidence but by keeping things in their proper relations by praying, now and then, the prayer of a good fighter whom I used to know: "Lord, make me sufficient to mine own occasion."

An Autumn Day
October 1916

King Winter has sent warning of his coming! There was a delightful freshness in the air the other morning, and all over the low places lay the first frost of the season.

What a beautiful world this is! Have you noticed the wonderful coloring of the sky at sunrise? For me there is no time like the early morning when the spirit of light broods over the earth at its awakening. What glorious colors in the woods these days! Did you ever think that great painters have spent their lives trying to reproduce on canvas what we may see every day? Thousands of dollars are paid for their pictures which are not so beautiful as those nature gives us freely. The colors in the sky at sunset, the delicate tints of the early spring foliage, the brilliant autumn leaves, the softly colored grasses and lovely flowers—what painter ever equalled their beauties with paint and brush?

*Why is the world so beautiful
if not for us?*

I have in my living room three large windows uncovered by curtains which I call my pictures. Ever changing with the seasons, with wild birds and gay squirrels passing on and off the scene, I never have seen a landscape painting to compare with them.

As we go about our daily tasks the work will seem lighter if we enjoy these beautiful things that are just outside our doors and windows. It pays to go to the top of the hill now and then to see the view and to stroll through the wood-lot or pasture forgetting that we are in a hurry or that there is such a thing as a clock in the world. You are "so busy"! Oh, yes, I know it! We are all busy, but what are we living for anyway, and why is the world so beautiful if not for us? The habits we form last us through this life, and I firmly believe into the next. Let's not make such a habit of hurry and work that when we leave this world, we will feel impelled to hurry through the spaces of the universe using our wings for feather dusters to clean away the star dust.

The true way to live is to enjoy every moment as it passes, and surely it is in the everyday things around us that the beauty of life lies.

*I strolled today down a woodland path—
A crow cawed loudly and flew away.
The sky was blue and the clouds were gold*

And drifted before me fold on fold;
The leaves were yellow and red and brown
And patter, patter the nuts fell down,
On this beautiful, golden autumn day.

A squirrel was storing his winter hoard,
The world was pleasant: I lingered long,
The brown quails rose with a sudden whirr
And a little bundle, of eyes and fur,
Took shape of a rabbit and leaped away.
A little chipmunk came out to play
And the autumn breeze sang a wonder song.

CHAPTER 10

The war, the terrible . . .

Each in His Place
May 1917

I know a farm woman who is wearing overalls this spring at her outdoor work. "They wear overalls in the munition factories," she says. "Isn't the raising of food to preserve life as important as the making of shells to take it? Why should I be hampered in my work and tormented by skirts flapping around my ankles when I am out in the field?"

---

*"I can't feel right about doing this! It
does not seem to me that this is a time
to be feasting and frolicking."*

Why, indeed! When every bit of one's time and strength can be put to such good use in work that is so very necessary to the world, it seems foolish to spend any of it uselessly. The simpler and more suitably we can dress the better. This year of our Lord 1917 is no time for giving much attention to frills; and when we remember the tight skirts of recent date, we surely cannot accuse overalls of being immodest. As the Man of the Place said to me, "Just hunt up a couple of your old tight skirts and sew them together, then you'll have a pair of overalls."

We all feel that we would like to do something to help our country in these perilous times, however much we may regret the necessity. We may do this; may do our share of the work and bear our share of the burden of the world without leaving our homes or exposing ourselves to new and fearful dangers. Not that country women would hesitate to take these risks if it were necessary, but it is natural to be glad that we may help as much or more in our own accustomed ways. Women in the towns and cities can be spared to work in the factories, to make munitions, to join the navy, or to go as nurses with the Red Cross; but what would happen to the world if the farm women should desert their present posts?

Our work is not spectacular, and in doing it faithfully we shall win no war medals or decorations, but it is absolutely indispensable. We may feed the field hands, care for the poultry, and work in the garden with the full assurance that we are doing as much for our country as any other person.

Here in the hills, we have helped plant the potatoes and corn; we help with the milking and feed the calves and hogs; and we will be found on the line just behind the trenches, "fighting for Uncle Sam," as I heard one woman say; and every extra dozen eggs, pound of meat, or bushel of vegetables we raise will help beat back the enemy, hunger.

. . . .

Some women were talking over an entertainment that had been planned for the crowd. They seemed to be taking only a half-hearted interest in the subject, and finally one of them exclaimed: "I can't feel right about doing this! It does not seem to me that this is a time to be feasting and frolicking. I do not think we ought to eat an unnecessary mouthful, and sometimes I feel like choking on the food I do eat when I think of the people in the world who are hungry and starving."

I fully agreed with her. When there seems not to be enough food to go around, we ought to be as careful and economical with it as possible. If it is true, as we are told, that most of us have the bad habit of overeating, now is a good time to break that habit.

I am sure that we farm women will not be found second to those of any other occupation in willingness to bear our part in effort or in self-denial, and if, as experts say, "armies travel on their stomachs," we are doing our best to enable the soldiers of the United States to go as far as those of any other nation.

Left Out and Pushed About
July 1917

In answer to the call sent out by the State College of Agriculture, the park in Mansfield was filled with a crowd of farm folks and town folks to listen to the address of the man from the college who was organizing farmers' clubs throughout the county.

As I looked around at the people, I thought of what a representative gathering it was. Judging from the appearance of the crowd, the women were as much interested in the subject of food production as a means of national defense as the men were, for fully as many women as men were present, and they were seemingly as eager to learn from the speaker of anything that farmers could do to increase the food supply.

Her working day is already somewhere
from fourteen to sixteen hours long.

A farmers' club was formed after the address, but the women took no part in the organization nor were they included in any way. As arrangements were being made for a meeting of the club, someone near the speaker said, "The women must come, too," but it was only after a broad and audible hint from a woman that this remark was made; and it was so plainly because of the hint, instead of from a desire for the women's presence and cooperation, that it made no impression.

At the first meeting of the club the following week, there were only two women present. Quite likely, it was the women's own fault, and if they had taken part as a matter of course, it would have been accepted as such; but it seems rather hard to do this unless we are shown the courtesy of being mentioned. We will get over this feeling in time, no doubt, and take the place we should; for a farmer may be either a man or a woman, and farmers' clubs are intended for both.

. . . .

What would happen to the "increase of production" if the women did not cook for the harvest hands, to say nothing of taking care of the hired help the remainder of the year?

. . . .

As one farm paper says, "The women and children can do it! Eliminate all waste from the kitchen! It is conceded that it will take more time and work to do all this, but it is a patriotic duty and will increase the farm profits."

Why shouldn't farm women's work be recognized by state authorities and others in ways other than urging her to more work, when her working day is already somewhere from fourteen to sixteen hours long?

✳✳

There is a woman's commission of the Council of National Defense and under this commission committees are being organized in every state for the purpose of cooperating with the National Woman's Trade Union League of America. The league is fighting to protect the women and children who are working in factories and in the cities. It asks that the American people demand the eight-hour day, the living wage, and one day of rest in seven.

But mark this! These things are for women and children working in the cities. They are not intended to extend to the women and children on farms. There is not yet, so far as I know, any committee to cooperate with the farm women in obtaining for them either an eight-hour day or a living profit, and if they are denied an active part in the farmers' clubs, they are the only class of workers who are absolutely without representation.

The War, the Terrible . . .
August 1917

Once upon a time, a crowd of men were working in the woods where they had to do their own cooking. They took turns at being cook, and they made a rule that when any one of them found fault with the food provided, that man must take the cook's place, until he in turn was released from the distasteful job by someone's finding fault with his cooking.

As he nearly strangled, he exclaimed,
"These beans are sure salty!"

This worked very well, with frequent changes in the occupancy of the cook shanty, until the men had learned better than to criticize the food. No one wanted to take the cook's place, so they became very careful about what they said; and the poor unfortunate who was cooking for the hungry crew saw no chance of escape. He was careless as to how his work was done but no one found fault; he burned the biscuits, then he made the coffee too weak, but still no one objected.

At last he cooked a mess of beans and made them as salt as brine. One of the men at supper that night took a huge mouthful of the beans, and as he nearly strangled, he exclaimed, "These beans are sure salty!" Then, as the eye of the cook, alight with hope, glanced in his direction, he added, "But my, how good they are!"

It is so much easier to find fault with what others do than to do the thing right one's self. Besides, how much pleasanter to let someone else do it. Of course, a mere woman is not expected to understand politics in Missouri, but there is no objection to her understanding human nature; and it is certainly amusing to watch the effects of the working of human nature on men's political opinions.

I know some men who were all for war during President Wilson's first term. "The United States soldiers ought to go down there and take Mexico! A couple of months would do it! The United States should fight if our shipping is interfered with. It would be easily settled." There was much more to the same effect.

But now that the fight is on, and there is a chance for them to show what they can do, their fighting spirit seems to have evaporated. It was easy to find fault, but rather than do the work themselves, almost anything is good enough. It is the quiet ones who hoped we might be able to keep out of war that are volunteering.

One after another our young men are enlisting. Eight in a body volunteered a few days ago. The war, the terrible, has been something far off, but now it is coming closer home and soon we shall have a more understanding sympathy with those who have been experiencing its horrors for so long. There is nothing quite like experience to give one understanding, and nothing more sure than that if we could be in the other fellow's place for a while, we would be less free with our criticisms.

* *

In the days of long ago when armored knights went journeying on prancing steeds, two knights, coming from opposite directions, saw between them a shield standing upright on the ground. As the story goes, these fighting men disagreed about the color of the shield, and each was so positive, the one that it was black, and the other that it was white, that from disputing about it, they came to blows and charged each other right valiantly.

The fury with which they rode their steeds carried each one past the shield to where the other had stood before, and as they turned to face each other again, each saw the side of the shield which the other had first seen; and the man who had said the shield was white found the side he was now looking at to be black, while the one who had declared the shield was black found himself facing the white side, so each got the other's point of view and felt very foolish that they had fought over so simple a thing.

It makes a difference when you're in the other fellow's place.

Getting Down to First Causes
June 1919

Germany is finding that as a nation that has for four years deliberately broken its pledged word, that word is of no value; that it is bankrupt in moral guarantees.

The entente* is in the position with Germany of the hill man who fought another man for telling an untruth about him.

"Don't you hear him hollering 'enough'?" "Oh, yes!" replied the hill man, "but he is such a liar I don't know whether he is telling the truth or not."

He had knocked his enemy down and was still beating him though he was crying "enough" when a stranger came along and interfered.

"Stop! Stop!" he exclaimed. "Don't you hear him hollering 'enough'?"

"Oh, yes!" replied the hill man, "but he is such a liar I don't know whether he is telling the truth or not."

* *

When I was a girl at home, my father came in from the harvest field one day at noon and with great glee told what had befallen my cousin Charley. Father and Uncle Henry were harvesting a field of wheat in the old-fashioned way, cutting it by hand with cradles, and Charley, who was about ten years old, followed them around the field for play. He lagged behind until the men were ahead of him and then began to scream, jumping up and down and throwing his arms around. Father and Uncle Henry dropped their cradles and ran to him thinking a snake had bitten him or that something in the woods close by was frightening him; but when they came to Charley, he stopped screaming and laughed at them.

Charley fooled them this way three times, but they grew tired and warm and had been deceived so many times that when, for the fourth time, he began to scream, they looked back at him as he jumped up and down, then turned away and went on with their work.

---

*A name used for Britain and France as allied against Germany after World War I.

But Charley kept on screaming, and there seemed to be a new note in his voice, so finally they walked back to where he was and found that he was in a yellow jackets' nest; and the more he jumped and threw and screamed the more came to sting him.

"I'd like to have the training of that young man for a little while," said father, "but I don't believe I could have thought of a better way to punish him for his meanness."*

Boys or men or nations, it seems to be the same, if they prove themselves liars times enough, nobody will believe them when they do tell the truth.

"Getting down to first causes, what makes one nation choose the high way and another nation choose the low way? What produces character and conscience in a nation anyhow? What produces the other thing?" asks a writer in an article in the *Saturday Evening Post*. And the question is left unanswered.

In a country ruled as Germany has been, there is no doubt the character of the nation received the impress of the rulers, coming from them down to the people. In a country such as ours, the national character is also like that of the rulers; but in this case the rulers are the people, and it is they who impress themselves upon it. The character of each individual one of us affects our national character for good or bad.

Getting down to first causes, what forms the character of individuals?

Training! School training; home training; mother's training! And there you are back to the first causes in the making of an honorable, truthful, upright individual, the kind of citizen who collectively makes an honorable, treaty-keeping nation, a nation that chooses the high way instead of the low.

---

*This story is retold in chapter eleven of *Little House in the Big Woods*.

Are We Too Busy?
October 1917

The sunlight and shadows in the woods were beautiful that morning, the sunlight a little pale and the air with that quality of hushed expectancy that the coming of autumn brings. Birds were calling to one another and telling of the wonderful Southland and the journey they must take before long. The whole, wide outdoors called me, and tired muscles and nerves rasped from the summer's rush pleaded for rest; but there was pickle to make, drying apples to attend to, vegetables and fruits that must be gathered and stored, the Saturday baking and the thousand things of the everyday routine to be done.

"You need not lose your power of enjoyment nor your sense of the beautiful if you desire to keep them."

"Oh, for a little time to enjoy the beauties around me," I thought. "Just a little while to be free of the tyranny of things that must be done!" A feeling of bitterness crept into my soul. "You'll have plenty of leisure someday when you are past enjoying it," I thought. "You know, in time, you always get what you have longed for, and when you are old and feeble and past active use, then you'll have all the leisure you ever have wanted. But my word! You'll not enjoy it!"

I was horrified at these thoughts, which almost seemed spoken to me. We do seem at times to have more than one personality, for as I gave a dismayed gasp at the prospect, I seemed to hear a reply in a calm, quiet voice.

"You need not lose your power of enjoyment nor your sense of the beautiful if you desire to keep them," it said. "Keep the doors of your mind and heart open to them, and your appreciation of such things will grow and you will be able to enjoy your well-earned leisure when it comes even though you should be older and not so strong. It is all in your own hands and may be as you wish."

We are all beginning to show the strain of the busy summer. Mrs. Menton has put up a full two-year's supply of canned and dried fruits and vegetables. She says that, even though no part of it should be needed to save anyone from starving, she will feel well repaid in the smallness of their grocery bills the coming year. She also confessed she was glad the lull in work was in sight for there wasn't "a whole pair of socks on the place."

Several women were comparing notes the other day. Said one, "My man says he doesn't mind a decent patch, but he does hate to go around with a hole in his khakis." Everyone smiled understandingly and another took up the tale.

"Joe said this morning that he wished I'd make a 'working' and call the neighbors in to fix up his clothes," she said, "but I told him you were all too busy to come."

There has been no time this summer to do the regular work properly. Mrs. Clearly says that if the rush of work does not stop soon she will have to stop anyway. She is a recent comer to the Ozarks, and through the dry seasons she has hoped for a good crop year. Now she does not know whether she will pray for rain next year or not.

A good crop year does bring work with it, and though the worst may be over, there are still busy days ahead. There are the late fruits and garden truck to be put up, potato harvest and corn harvest, the second crop of timothy and clover, and more cutting of alfalfa. There is the sorghum to make and the silos to fill and everything to be made snug for winter.

Some of us will help in the actual work, and others will be cooking for extra help. Whatever may be expected of us later, women have certainly done their utmost during this summer so nearly gone.

* *

The Man of the Place and I have realized with something of the shock of a surprise that we do not need to buy anything during the coming year. There are some things we need and much that we would like to get, but if it were necessary, we could go very comfortably through the year without a thing more than we now have on the place.

There is wheat for our bread and potatoes, both Irish and sweet; there are beans and corn and peas. Our meat, milk, cream, butter, and eggs are provided. A year's supply of fruit and sweetening are at hand and a plentiful supply of fuel in the wood lot. All this, to say nothing of the surplus.

During the summer when I have read of the high wages paid in factories and shops, there has been a little feeling of envy in the back of my mind; but I suppose if those working people had a year's supply of fuel and provisions and no rent to pay, they would think it wonderful good fortune. After all, as the Irishman said, "Everything is evened up in this world. The rich buy their ice in the summer, but the poor get theirs in the winter."

The Man of the Place and I had known before that farmers are independent, but we never had realized it; and there is a difference between knowing and realizing. Have you realized it personally or do you just know in a general way? Thanksgiving will soon be here, and it is time to be getting our blessings in order.

But why wait for Thanksgiving? Why not just be thankful now?

Make Every Minute Count
March 1918

Spring has come! The wild birds have been singing the glad tidings for several days, but they are such optimistic little souls that I always take their songs of spring with a grain of pessimism. The squirrels and chipmunks have been chattering to me, telling the same news, but they are such cheerful busybodies that I never believe quite all they say.

I knew then that spring was here, for the sign of picnickers is more sure than that of singing birds.

But now I know that spring is here, for as I passed the little creek on my way to the mailbox this morning, I saw scattered papers caught on the bushes, empty cracker and sandwich cartons strewn around on the green grass, and discolored pasteboard boxes soaking in the clear water of the spring.

I knew then that spring was here, for the sign of the picnickers is more sure than that of singing birds and tender green grass, and there is nothing more unlovely than one of nature's beauty spots defiled in this way. It is such an unprovoked offense to nature, something like insulting one's host after enjoying his hospitality. It takes just a moment to put back into the basket the empty boxes and paper, and one can depart gracefully leaving the place all clean and beautiful for the next time or the next party.

Did you ever arrive all clean and fresh, on a beautiful summer morning, at a pretty picnic place and find that someone had been there before you, and that the place was all littered with dirty papers and buzzing flies? If you have and have ever left a place in the same condition, it served you right. Let's keep the open spaces clean, not fill them up with rubbish!

* *

It is so easy to get things cluttered—one's days, for instance, as well as picnic places—to fill them with empty, useless things and so make them unlovely and tiresome. Even though the things with which we fill our days were once important, if they are serving no good purpose now, they have become trash like the empty boxes and papers of the picnickers. It will pay to clean this trash away and keep our days as uncluttered as possible.

There are just now so many things that must be done that we are tempted to spend ourselves recklessly, especially as it is rather difficult to decide what to eliminate; and we cannot possibly accomplish everything. We must continually be weighing and judging and discarding things that are presented to us if we would save ourselves and spend our time and strength only on those things that are important. We may be called upon to spend our health and strength to the last bit, but we should see to it that we do not waste them.*

"Oh, I am so tired that I just want to sit down and cry," a friend confided to me, "and here is the club meeting on hand and the lodge practice and the Red Cross workday and the aid society meeting and the church bazaar to get ready for, to say nothing of the pie supper at the schoolhouse and the spring sewing and garden and—Oh! I don't see how I'm ever going to get through it all!"

Of course, she was a little hysterical. It didn't all have to be done at once, but it showed how over-tired she was, and it was plain that something must give way—if nothing else, herself. My friend needed a little open space in her life.

We must none of us shirk our responsibilities. We must do our part in every way, but let's be sure we clear away the rubbish, that we do nothing for empty form's sake nor because someone else does, unless it is the thing that should be done.

---

*World War I priorities were making themselves felt in the Ozarks.

A Wish for the Present
April 1918

We read so much in the papers of graft and price profiteering, of federal investigation of first one business and then another, of treachery and double-dealing and strikes and riots that one is tempted to be discouraged with people in general, until one remembers that crimes and criminals are news and, as such, are given prominence with glaring headlines on first pages of newspapers. It is seldom that good deeds and their doers have such startling news value, but there are still plenty of them in the world. People are still kind and neighborly and are quietly and unobtrusively helping each other over hard places as they always have done.

A common cause, and the work we are doing together is making us appreciate one another more.

Mrs. Sells was left a widow last winter, and this spring she wishes to make a start with poultry in order to be self-supporting and able to keep her home. The neighbors have contributed the eggs, and one will hatch them in her incubator to give Mrs. Sells her start.

Mr. Ashton was unable, because of illness, to put in his crop of oats. His neighbors have done the work for him.

I know a busy, up-to-date farmer who, in his own way, is helping his neighbors and his country. He is selling for seed a particular high-priced kind of bean and some especially good cowpeas at just half the price charged in the seed catalogs.

His price makes him a good profit, he says, and that is enough. Poultry is a specialty on his farm, but he is selling eggs for hatching at a great reduction from his usual price. He wishes his neighbors to be successful in their farming and to increase the supply of food.

Isn't it refreshing to think of such a man as a change from excess profits? There is more of this kind of thing being done than appears on the surface, for it is not given publicity. The spirit of helpfulness and comradeship is moving us all more or less.

Haven't you noticed a kinder feeling in your heart for your friends lately—a little more thoughtfulness for their comfort and well-being; just a touch more tenderness for your dear ones, even those who are in no danger of being called by the draft? It seems to me there is a drawing closer together, a feeling of

---

standing shoulder to shoulder with my friends and neighbors that I have never experienced before. I am sure it is not all imagination.

* *

There had been a little misunderstanding and consequently bad feelings in an organization to which I belong. It has been causing quite a little tempest in a teapot, as such things always do, even though they should not break out where they have more room for mischief. I was surprised to hear one of the parties in the controversy say: "I wish we might all go on and forget it. That's the only thing to do—just go on and forget it!"

Another person who has been a strong partisan on the other side said to me the same day: "What's the use of chewing the rag forever? It is much better to let it all drop and work together. There is no time to keep hashing things over and stirring up trouble." How long can any quarrel last when the parties to it begin to talk in that way?

Our common danger, a common cause, and the work we are doing together is making us appreciate one another more and making us understand the littleness of petty jealousies and disagreements. The big things of life are crowding out the little unpleasant differences.

How can I hold a grudge against my neighbor when I know that his son, "somewhere in France," is interposing his body as a shield between my home and the danger that threatens it? How is it possible for me to do an unkind thing to my acquaintance when her son is braving the dangers of submarines and enemy warships while convoying my son safely to France to do his part in the fighting or perhaps helping to protect the ship that is bringing him home from foreign shores?

Then, too, if I can help my neighbor to raise a better crop or have better success with his stock, it will be just so much more to feed all our "kinfolks" at home and abroad. Under these circumstances, how can we be selfish and self-centered? The old saying that "Everybody's business is nobody's business" is certainly all wrong now, and anybody's business is everybody's business instead.

We will feel differently toward one another than ever before when we have had time to realize these things, and if there has been any friction or misunderstanding, we will surely "just go on and forget it."

Glory! What Days in Which to Live!
September 1918

The world is growing smaller each day. It has been shrinking for centuries; but during these later years it is diminishing in size with an ever-increasing-swiftness, yet so gradual is the change that we do not realize what is taking place unless we compare the present with the past.

It is only a few years ago that our neighbors were only those who lived within a few miles of us. Now we make an afternoon call on our neighbors twenty miles away with no greater effort.

---

*It seems to me such a wonderful thing
that the people of all the different
nations of the earth are becoming
so well acquainted.*

The King and Queen of Belgium called on the English sovereigns not long ago. Their conveyance was an airplane, and it took them only a short time to make the trip from Belgium to their destination in England.

Students of the future tell us that flying machines will come into general use after the war and perhaps we shall then drop in on our friends in England and France for afternoon tea just as casually as we used to "happen in" at our next door neighbors. We shall have friends in France and England by that time, and those countries will never again seem far away. Even now, it is just "over there," and with so many persons passing back and forth, with millions of our common, everyday folks becoming intimately familiar with all the countries at war, the world will be much, much smaller when peace comes again.

It seems to me such a wonderful thing that the people of all the different nations of the earth are becoming so well acquainted. When people have fought and struggled and worked and gone hungry and eaten together, they can never again be indifferent and distant toward one another. These people whom we have always carelessly bunched together in our minds as foreigners will be our friends and neighbors from this time on. Already we have shared our food with them; we have gone to their aid in danger and sickness, in misfortune and misery, as is and always has been the privilege of good neighbors the world over; and in doing this, we are only returning the neighborly kindness of France shown to the United States in the War of Independence and that of England in protecting us from Germany during the war with Spain.*

---

*Spanish American War; the Germans sought to intervene against American interests.

As nations, we have been neighbors for many years, and now we are beginning to realize it as individuals. The people of the allied nations have learned that our sympathy is quick and our purse open to the needy, and now they are finding out that our boys are good to fight beside.

As we who stay at home follow the operations on the various battle fronts, we have come to feel a personal interest in the heroic Belgian soldiers, holding the small corner of their country in spite of the worst the enemy could do; in the gallant French soldiers who set the bounds and said, "They shall not pass!"; in the Italian soldiers who accomplished almost unbelievable feats fighting above the clouds, on snowclad mountain peaks, thousands of them having left security in the United States to take part in the terrific combat; and in the Russian soldiers, surely as brave as any, who went out against armed Germans and artillery with their bare hands when there were no arms and ammunition, and yet who were so simple-minded and gentle-minded as to be overcome with fair words and false promises.*

Our admiration and sympathy has drawn us near to the soldiers of these different armies and to the people of their countries. We have been proud of their bravery and fortitude; we have rejoiced with them in their successes and sorrowed with them in their sufferings. This is what makes of people friends and neighbors. Never again can we be strangers.

If we can but broaden our vision to see world happenings as a whole, we cannot fail to be in accord with that young and eager person who exclaimed, "Glory! What days in which to live!"

---

*The Russians were probably not "deceived" by false promises; internal conditions in Russia, namely revolution, made it necessary for them to sue for peace with Germany.

Our Code of Honor
October 1918

What is your personal code of honor? Just what do you consider dishonorable or disgraceful in personal conduct? It seems to me that we had all grown rather careless in holding ourselves to any code of honor and just a little ashamed of admitting that we had such a standard. At best, our rules of life were becoming a little flexible, and we had rather a contemptuous memory of the knights of King Arthur's roundtable, who fought so often for their honor and still at times forgot it so completely, while we pitied the Pilgrim Fathers for their stern inflexibility in what they considered the right way of life.

*Another woman's code of honor is to be
fair, to always give the "square deal" to
the other person.*

Just now, while such mighty forces of right and wrong are contending in the world, we are overhauling our mental processes a little and finding out some curious things about ourselves. We can all think of examples of different ideas of what is dishonorable. There are persons who strictly fulfill their given word. To them, it would be a disgrace not to do as they agree, not to keep a promise, while others give a promise easily and break their word with even greater ease.

Some persons have a high regard for truth and would feel themselves disgraced if they told a lie, while others prefer a lie even though the truth were easier.

There are persons who have no scruples to prevent them from eavesdropping, reading letters not intended for them, or any manner of prying into other persons' private affairs, and to others the doing of such things is in a manner horrifying.

There are scandalmongers who are so eager to find and scatter to the four winds a bit of unsavory gossip that they are actually guilty in their own souls of the slips in virtue that they imagine in others and, contrasting with these, are people so pure minded that they would think themselves disgraced if they entertained in their thoughts such idle gossip.

I know a woman whose standard of honor demands only "The greatest good to the greatest number, including myself." The difficulty with this is that a finite mind can scarcely know what is good for other persons or even one's self.

Another woman's code of honor is to be fair, to always give the "square deal" to the other person, and this is very difficult to do because the judgment is so likely to be partial.

There is a peculiar thing about the people who hold all these differing ideas of what they will allow themselves to do. We seldom wish to live up to the high standard to which we hold the other fellow. The person who will not keep his word becomes very angry if a promise to him is broken. Those who have no regard for truth in what they say expect that others will be truthful when talking to them. People who pry into affairs which are none of their business consider the same actions disgraceful in others, and gossips think that they should be exempt from the treatment they give to other people. I never knew it to fail, and it is very amusing at times to listen to the condemnation of others' actions by one who is even more guilty of the same thing.

It does one good to adhere strictly to a rule of conduct if that rule is what it should be. Just the exercise of the will in refusing to follow the desires which do not conform to the standard set is strengthening to the character, while the determination to do the thing demanded by that standard, and the doing of it, however difficult, is an exercise for the strengthening of the willpower, which is far better than anything recommended for that purpose by books.

If you doubt that it pays in cash and other material advantages to have a high code of honor and live up to it, just notice the plight of the German government. At the beginning of the war, they threw away their honor, broke their pledged word, and proclaimed to the world that their written agreements were mere scraps of paper. Now when they ask for a conference to discuss a "peace by agreement," the allies reply, in effect, "but an agreement with you would in no sense be binding upon you. We cannot trust again to your word of honor since your signed pledge is a mere 'scrap of paper' and your verbal promises even less."

It is plain, then, that nations are judged by their standards of honor and treated accordingly; and it is the same with individuals. We judge them by their code of honor, and the way they live up to it. It is impossible to hold two standards, one for others—for what is dishonorable in them would be the same for us, and that seems, in the end, to be the only sure test, embracing and covering all the rest, the highest code of honor yet voiced: "Whatsoever ye would that men should do to you, do ye even so to them!"

When the War Ended
December 1918

I am sure that a great many persons felt a sort of flatness and staleness in life when the war ended [Armistice Day: November 11, 1918]. Although they were glad and deeply thankful, there was an unpleasantness in going back to ordinary things, a letting down from the heights to which they had attained, a silence in place of the bugle call to duty to which their spirits had become attuned.

The American spirit as it has been displayed is really the spirit . . . of Christianity, a practical example of loving and serving and giving.

But here is a chance to exercise still further those qualities which, in spite of all the horrors, have made of the war a glorious thing by showing how the good still rises triumphant over the bad in the heart of humanity.

The appeal of Dr. Wilbur* comes most appropriately at this time, for the American spirit as it has been displayed is really the spirit of Christmas or, in other words, the spirit of Christianity, a practical example of loving and serving and giving.

It is a wonderful thing for us to have accepted as our own such national ideals, but we cannot hold them as a nation unless we accept them for our own as individuals. So the responsibility rests upon each of us to keep our country true to the course it has taken and up to the high standard it has reached.

---

*Ray Lyman Wilbur was president of Stanford University. He had called upon Americans to be generous with food relief for war-ravaged Europe.

Peace on Earth
December 1919

Peace upon earth the angel sang,
Good will unto men the chorus rang.

But that was many, many years ago at the first Christmas time. We could scarcely hear the angels if they were singing now for the clamor of disputing and wrangling which is going on where peace is supposed to be.

In our own country there is a gathering into groups with mutterings and threats of violence, with some bloodshed and danger of more, and there is still war and threat of war over most of the world. This would be bad enough at any time, but just now when we are thinking of all the blessed meanings of Christmastide, it becomes much more terrible.

It is rather the lack of Christianity that has brought us where we are. Not a lack of churches or religious forms but of the real thing in our heart.

A great deal is said and written about natural, national boundaries and learned discussions of racial antagonisms as causes of the restlessness and ill-temper of the nations; and there are investigations and commissions and inquiries to discover what is the matter with the world and to find a remedy.

But the cause of all the unrest and strife is easily found. It is selfishness, nothing else, selfishness deep in the hearts of the people.

It seems rather impossible that such a small thing as individual selfishness could cause so much trouble, but my selfishness added to your selfishness and that added to the selfishness of our neighbors all over the big, round world is not a small thing.

We may have thought that our own greed and striving to take unfair advantage were not noticed and never would be known, but you and I and our neighbors make the neighborhood and neighborhoods make the states and states make the nations and the nations are the peoples of the world.

No one would deny that the thoughts and actions and spirit of every person affect his neighborhood, and it is just as plain that the spirit and temper of the communities are reflected in the state and nation and influence the whole world.

The nations of Europe are selfishly trying to take advantage of one another in the settlement of boundaries and territory, and so the World War is like a fire that has been stopped in its wild advance only to smoulder and break out here and there a little farther back along the sides.*

At home, in the troubles between labor and capital, each is willing to stop disputes and eager to cure the unrest of the people if it can be done at the expense of the other party and leave them undisturbed in their own selfish gains.

Following all the unrest and unreason on down to its real source where it lurks in the hearts of the people, its roots will be found there in individual selfishness, in the desire to better one's own condition at the expense of another by whatever means possible; and this desire of each person infects groups of people and moves nations.

Here and there one sees a criticism of Christianity because of the things that have happened and are still going on. "Christian civilization is a failure," some say. "Christianity has not prevented these things; therefore, it is a failure," say others.

But this is a calling of things by the wrong names. It is rather the lack of Christianity that has brought us where we are. Not a lack of churches or religious forms but of the real thing in our hearts.

There is no oppression of a group of people but that which has its root and inception in the hearts of the oppressors. There is no wild lawlessness and riot and bloodlust of a mob but that which has its place in the hearts of the persons who are that mob. Just so, if justice and fairness and kindness fill the minds of a crowd of persons, those things will be shown in their actions.

So, if we are eager to help in putting the world to rights, our first duty is to put ourselves right, to overcome our selfishness and be as eager that others shall be treated fairly as we are that no advantage shall be taken of ourselves; and to deal justly and have a loving charity and mercy for others as we wish them to have for us. Then we may hear the Christmas angels singing in our own hearts, "Peace upon earth! Good will unto men."

---

*Many historians judge that the Treaty of Versailles, ending World War I, so exacerbated poor economic conditions in Europe that it made World War II almost inevitable.

CHAPTER 11

Surely worth
the effort

Administer Advice in Small Doses
January 1917

I have just learned something new! Isn't it a wonderful thing that we are "never too old to learn," and also sometimes isn't it strange that no matter how many years we have numbered, we still learn best from that old, old teacher: experience? For instance, there was the time when I read, (not in a farm paper) that the addition of a little vinegar to the lard in which doughnuts were fried would keep them from soaking fat. I was preparing a company dinner not long afterward and, wishing to have my doughnuts especially good, was about to pour the vinegar into the lard when the Man of the Place came into the kitchen.

"Oh, it will be all right," I answered easily, "or it would not have been in that paper."

From long association with the cook, he knew that she was doing something different and demanded to know why. When I had explained, he advised me not to try any experiments at that particular time. "Oh, it will be all right," I answered easily, "or it would not have been in that paper."

I added the vinegar and learned it was perfectly true that the doughnuts would not soak the grease. They would hardly soak anything, they were so tough. Experience had taught me one more lesson!

It is so easy to give advice. It is one thing with which the most of us are well-supplied and with which we are perfectly willing to part. Sometimes I think we are too quick to do this, too free in handing out, unasked, an inferior article. There is no way of estimating the mischief done by the well-meant but ill-considered advice of friends and acquaintances.

Knowing only one side of a question, seeing imperfectly a part of a situation, we say: "Well, I wouldn't stand for that a minute," or "You'll be foolish if you do," or "I would do this or that," and go lightheartedly on our way never thinking that by a careless word or two we may have altered the whole course of human lives, for some persons will take advice and use it.

There were once two men who had different ways of treating their horses when they went around them in the barn. One always spoke to his horses as he passed so that they might know he was there and not kick. The other never spoke to them. He said it was their business to look before they kicked. This last man often spoke of his way as being much the best.

One day he advised the other to change his way of doing because someday he would forget to speak and get kicked. Not long after, this actually happened and the man was seriously injured. His wife said to me, "If he had spoken to the horse when he went into the barn as he used to do, he would not have been hurt, but lately he had stopped doing that and the horse kicked before it saw him."

I have seen so often where what was best for me might not be just the thing for the other fellow.

I always have thought that the accident happened because of his friend's advice, and I have seen so often where what was best for me might not be just the thing for the other fellow that I have decided to keep my advice until asked for and then administer it in small doses.

There are ways of profiting by the experience of others, besides taking advice carelessly given. We might watch, you know, while someone else tried the vinegar on the doughnuts.

And that brings me back to where I started to tell of the new thing I had learned. It is a great help with the work of sewing to cover the tread of the sewing machine with a piece of soft, thick carpet. The carpet will act as a cushion, and one's feet will not become so tired as they otherwise would when using the machine a great deal.* There is another advantage in the use of the carpet in cold weather, as it is much warmer for the feet to rest on than the cold iron of the machine.

---

*Of course, before electricity, all sewing machines were pedal-powered.

Keeping Friends
March 1919

Sometimes we are a great trial to our friends and put an entirely uncalled-for strain upon our friendships by asking foolish questions.

The Man of the Place and I discovered the other day that we had for some-time been saying to our friends, "Why don't you come over?" Can you think of a more awkward question than that? Just imagine the result if that question should always be answered truthfully. Some would reply, "Because I do not care to visit you." Others might say, "Because it is too much trouble," while still others who might care to come would be swamped in trying to enumerate the many little reasons why they had not done so. We decided that we would break ourselves of such a bad habit.

I once had a neighbor who, whenever we met, invariably asked me why I had not been to visit her. Even when I did go she met me with the query, "Why haven't you been over before?" It was not a very pleasant greeting, and natu-rally one shuns unpleasantness when one may.

Even when I did go she met me with the query, "Why haven't you been over before?"

I have another neighbor who will call me on the phone and say: "It has been a long time since we have seen you, and we do want a good visit. Can't you come over tomorrow?" And immediately I wish to go. It does make such a difference how things are said.

Friendship is like love. It cannot be demanded or driven or insisted upon. It must be wooed to be won. The habit of saying disagreeable things or of being careless about how what we say affects others grows on us so easily and so surely if we indulge it.

"Mrs. Brown gave me an unhappy half hour a few days ago," said Mrs. Gray to me. "She said a great many unpleasant things and was generally disagree-able, but it is all right. The poor thing is getting childish, and we must over-look her oddities."

Mrs. Gray is a comparative newcomer in the neighborhood, but I have known Mrs. Brown for years; and ever since I have known her, she has prided herself on her plain speaking, showing very little regard for others' feelings. Her unkindness appears to me not a reversion to the mentality of childhood but simply an advance in the way she was going years ago. Her tongue has only become sharper with use, and her dexterity in hurting the feelings of others has grown with practice.

I know another woman of the same age whom no one speaks of as being childish. It is not necessary to make such an excuse for her because she is still, as she has been for twenty years, helpful and sweet and kind. And this helpfulness and sweetness and kindness of hers has grown with the passing years. I think no one will ever say of her, "poor old thing, she is childish," as an excuse for her being disagreeable. I know she would hope to die before that time should come.

People do grow childish in extreme old age, of course, and should be treated with tenderness because of it; but I believe that even then the character which they have built during the years before will manifest itself. There is a great difference in children, you know, and I have come to the conclusion that if we live to reach a second childhood, we shall not be bad-tempered, disagreeable children unless we have indulged those traits.

Then there are the people who are "peculiar." Ever meet any of them?

The word seems to be less used than formerly, but there was a time when it was very common, and I longed to shriek everytime I heard it.

"Oh! You must not do that, George will be angry. He is so peculiar!"

"Of course, she doesn't belong with the rest of the crowd, but I had to invite her. She is so peculiar, you know, and so easily offended."

"I wouldn't pay any attention to that. Of course, she did treat you abominably, but it is just her way. She is so peculiar."

And so on and on. I thought seriously of cultivating a reputation for being peculiar, for like charity such a reputation seemed to cover multitudes of sins; but I decided that it would be even more unpleasant for me than for the other fellow; that it would not pay to make myself an unlovely character for the sake of any little, mean advantage to be gained by it.

We Always Pay for That "Need"
September 1917

I have been very much impressed by a sentence I read in an advertisement of farm machinery, and here it is for you to think about. "The minute we need a thing, we begin paying for it whether we buy it or not."

That is true of farm machinery on the face of it. If a farm tool is actually needed, it will, without question, have to be bought in time; and the farmer begins paying for it at once in loss of time or waste or damage resulting from not having it. He might even, if buying was put off long enough, pay the whole price of the machine and still not have it.

We begin to pay the dentist when our teeth first need attention whether they have that attention or not.

A dentist once said to me, "I don't care whether people come to me when they should or put off coming as long as they possibly can. I know they'll come in time, and the longer they put it off the bigger my bill will be when they do come." We begin to pay the dentist when our teeth first need attention whether they have that attention or not.

"I can't afford to build a machine shed this year," said farmer Jones, and so his machinery stood out in the weather to rot and rust. The next year he had to spend so much for repairs and new machines that he was less able than before to build the shed. He is paying for that protection for his machinery, but he may never have it.

We think we cannot afford to give children the proper schooling. "Besides, their help is needed on the farm," we say. We shall pay for that education which we do not give them. Oh! We shall pay for it! When we see our children inefficient and handicapped, perhaps through life, for the lack of the knowledge they should have gained in their youth, we shall, if in no other way, pay in our hurt pride and our regret that we did not give them a fair chance, though quite likely we shall pay in money too. The children, more's the pity, must pay also.

Mr. Colton's work kept him outdoors in all kinds of weather, and one autumn he did not buy the warm clothing he needed. He said he could not afford to do so and would make the old overcoat last through. The old coat outlasted him, for he took a chill from exposure and died of pneumonia. So he paid with his life for the coat he never had, and his widow paid the bills which amounted to a great deal more than the cost of an overcoat.

Instances multiply as one looks for them. We certainly do begin paying for a thing when we actually need it, whether we buy it or not; but this is no plea for careless buying as it is just as great a mistake to buy what we do not need as it is not to buy what we should.

In the one case we pay before, and in the other, we usually keep paying after the real purchase. One thing always leads to another or even to two or three, and it requires good business judgment to buy the right thing at the right time.

Learning Something New
April 1924

The topic that had been given me for my club lesson was music. Now the only instrument I can play is the phonograph, and I venture to sing only in a crowd where I can drown my voice in the volume of sound. To be sure, I have a little music in my feet, but that would not answer for a club paper, so it seemed rather hopeless; but never yet have I been "stumped." I began to dig up just plain facts about music and seldom have I found anything so interesting.

I began to dig up just plain facts about music and seldom have I found anything so interesting.

The simple fact of how music came to have written form takes us away into the days of chivalry in the sixteenth century. To guide the choir boys in following the melody when singing masses, the monks wrote the Latin words, not in a straight line but up and down, to indicate their place in the musical scale. Later, to shorten the time and labor of writing, the words were replaced by circles, and the horizontal lines of the staff were added to more clearly indicate their position. Slowly, from time to time, the different forms of notes were made and music was standardized into the base and treble cleffs so that our music of today takes its printed form directly from the manuscripts so laboriously written by hand in the monasteries of the sixteenth century.

This is only one of the many things I learned about music, but I learned also that it isn't what one already knows that adds interest to the preparation of a club paper so much as the learning something new in order to be able to go on with it.

Learning things is most fascinating, and I think it adds joy to life to be continually learning things so that we may be able to go on with it creditably.

The Hidden Cost of Getting What We Want
April 1917

We were speaking of a woman in the community who was ignoring the conventions, thereby bringing joy to the gossips' hearts and a shock to those persons who always think first of what people will say.

"Well, of course," said my friend, "it is all perfectly harmless, and she has the satisfaction of doing as she pleases; but I'm wondering whether it's worth the price."

There are very few things in this world that we may not have if we are willing to pay their price. You know, it has been said that "Every man has his price," which may or may not be true; but without doubt nearly every other thing has its market value, and we may make our choice and buy. We must pay, in one way or another, a greater or lesser amount for everything we have, and sometimes we show very poor judgment in our purchases.

Many a woman and girl has paid her good eyesight for a few pieces of hand embroidery or her peace of mind for a new gown, while many a man's good health or good standing in the community goes to pay for his indulgence in a bad habit.

Is there something in life that you want very much? Then pay the price and take it, but never expect to . . . avoid paying the bills.

Is there something in life that you want very much? Then pay the price and take it, but never expect to have a charge account and avoid paying the bills. Life is a good collector and sooner or later the account must be paid in full. I know a woman who is paying a debt of this kind on the installment plan. She wanted to be a musician and so she turned her children into the streets and neglected her husband that she might have more time for practice. She already has paid too high a price for her musical education, and the worst of it is that she will keep on paying the installments for the rest of her life.

There are persons who act as if the things life has to offer were on sale at an auction, and if someone else is likely to secure an article, they will raise their bid without regard to the value of the goods on sale. Indeed, most of us are like people at an auction in this respect, that during the excitement and rivalry, we buy many things we do not need, nor want, nor know just what to do with, and we pay for them much more than they are worth.

Is it your ambition to outshine your neighbors and friends? Then you are the foolish bidder at the auction, raising your bid just because someone else is bidding. I knew a man like this. He owned a motor car of the same size and make as those of his friends but decided he would buy a larger, more powerful, and much more expensive one. His old car was good enough for all his needs, he said, but he was going to have a car that would be "better than the other fellows'."

I suppose he figured the cost of the car in dollars and cents, but the real price he paid was in his integrity and business honor, and, for a bonus, an old and valued friendship. He had very poor judgment as a buyer, in my opinion.

Do you desire an education? No matter who pays the money for this, you cannot have it unless you also pay with long hours of study and application.

Do you wish to be popular? Then there is a chance to buy the real, lasting thing, which means to be well thought of and beloved by people worthwhile, or [to have] the shoddy imitation, a cheap popularity of the "hail fellow well met" sort depending mostly on one's ability to tell a good story and the amount one is able to spend on so-called pleasure. As always, the best is the cheapest, for poor goods are dear at any price: the square dealing, the kindness and consideration for others, the helpfulness and love, which we must spend if we wish lasting esteem to enrich us in the paying besides, bringing us what we so much desired.

On the other hand, in buying a cheap popularity, people sometimes bankrupt themselves in things the value of which cannot be estimated. If popular favor must be paid for by the surrender of principles or loss of character, then indeed the price is too high.

Early Training Counts
October 1918

"Don't open that door again, Tom! It lets in too much cold," said Tom's mother with what I thought was an unnecessarily sharp note in her voice.

It was the first chilly day of early autumn, and there was no fire in the house except in the kitchen stove. As I was making an afternoon visit, we, of course, sat in the front room—and shivered. In a moment, the outside door opened again and Tom and a gust of raw wind entered together.

His mother screamed after him, "Tom!
If you open that door again,
I'll skin you alive!"

"I told you not to open that door! If you do it again, I'll spank you good!" said Tom's mother, and Tom immediately turned around, opened the door and went out.

We talked on busily for another moment when, feeling more chilly than usual, I looked around and saw Tom standing in the open door, swinging it to and fro.

"Tom!" exclaimed his mother, "I told you not to open that door! Come here to me!" As the door swung shut, Tom turned and faced his mother, took a few steps toward her, raised himself on his tiptoes, with his hands behind him—and turned around, opened the door, and walked out.

His mother screamed after him, "Tom! If you open that door again, I'll skin you alive!"

"You know you wouldn't do that, and Tom knows it too," I said. "Oh, of course," she replied, "but I have to tell him something."

I know Tom's mother is trying to teach her boy to be truthful; but a few days ago, he got into mischief, and when asked who had done the damage he replied, "Sister did it."

Tom was punished for telling a lie, but I imagine it would be rather difficult to explain to him why it was all right to tell a falsehood about what *would* happen and all wrong to tell one about what *had* happened; why he should be punished and his mother not.

* *

While I was busy with my work the other morning, a great commotion arose in the dooryard. There was shouting, the dog was barking furiously, and there was the noise of running and trampling. I hurried to the door and found several boys in the yard darting here and there, shouting to each other, "Catch it! There it goes!"

As I opened the door, a couple of the boys put their feet into the meshes of the woven wire fence and climbed over it as though it had been a stairs, although the gate was only a few steps from them. Evidently, that was the way they had entered the dooryard.

"Boys, what are you doing?" I asked. "Oh! Just chasing butterflies," answered one, while another added as though that excused everything, "Our teacher is just down there," indicating a place well within the fenced field.

When we had taken stock of the damage done by the butterfly chasers, we found that the barbed wire fence had been broken down where they had entered the fields, and the woven wire fence was badly stretched and sagged. Wire fencing is high these days and help impossible to get so that such raids are particularly annoying just now though they are not by any means anything new.

We are engaged just now in a mighty struggle to teach a certain part of the people of the world a respect for truth and for the rights and property of other people.* Are we failing to teach these things at home as we should?

. . . .

If in one generation a gentle, kindhearted people can be changed into fiends by a system of teaching, what might be accomplished if children were as carefully trained in the opposite direction? Truly, "As the twig is bent, the tree inclines."

---

*Laura is talking about World War I and the moral attitude some people took toward Germany.

Don't Call on the Government All of the Time
November 1919

"Isn't it awful, the prices we have to pay for things!" exclaimed my neighbor to me. "Just look at these shoes! I paid $10 for them! Something ought to be done to these profiteers; poor people can't afford to live anymore."

My neighbor's shoes were new, of course, and the heels were extremely high, too high to be really good style; but she seemed very proud of them and proud also in a rather shamefaced way that she had paid $10 for them.

---

*"Pins has saved many lives
by not swallering of 'em."*

"You need not have paid so much," I replied, "through all these high prices for shoes I never have paid quite $4 for a pair, and my shoes always have been correct in style and have worn well."

"Oh!" said my neighbor. "It's too much trouble to hunt bargains, and my foot is not easily fitted. Besides, you order your shoes, do you not?"

"Sometimes," I answered, "but never when I think the home retailer is asking only a fair profit. When I think he is profiteering, I protect myself without calling on the government at Washington. I do for myself at least as much as I can."

. . . .

There are problems that should be handled for us all collectively; but as in so many other things of our national life, it is also a matter for each of us to attend to. If each one of a crowd acting independently does the same thing, it produces a mass action that is powerful; and we can handle this problem of high costs for ourselves much better than we have been doing, if we try.

We all did seemingly impossible things in conserving and producing during the war. We can still do them until the effects of the war have passed away so far as prices are concerned, and it is as much a patriotic duty. Experts in economics say that the rate of production has not kept up with the inflation of currency due to war conditions, and that the remedy for the evils of high prices is increased production.

According to them, prices and production work like a seesaw—when one goes up the other goes down. When money is scarce and products plentiful, a little money buys a large amount of products; but when money is plentiful and products scarce, then it takes a great deal of money to buy a small amount of products, which is where we are today.

Just now to help arrive at that balance we must practice economy and produce as much as possible. This is where everyone of us can help. For instance, if by caring for a garment, we can make that garment last twice as long, we have not only saved money but also helped to increase the volume of products by leaving them on the market. It acts in the same way as the schoolboy described in his essay on pins—"Pins has saved many lives by not swallering of 'em."

Another way to help ourselves through the pinch of these unsettled times and to make it harder for the actual profiteers is to buy as carefully and economically as possible even though it is some trouble, for it is surely worth the effort.

Pies and Poetry
March 1924

"I would rather have made that pie than to have written a poem," said Rose Wilder Lane, pausing midway through the triangular piece upon her plate. It was just a plain, farm apple pie, the kind we all make in Missouri. But listen! "Oh, these Missouri pies," exclaimed the other New York writer.* "Never before have I seen such wonderful pies."

I'll tell you the tale as 'twas told to me, and you shall decide.

So it seems that the center of pie fame as well as the center of population has traveled westward, for pie, you know, was a New England dish not known anywhere else in the world. To this day it is made only in America. And speaking of pies and poems, the first pie as we know pie, invented by a New England woman, was a poem of love and service, full of imagination, spicy with invention.

Oh, of course, what it was really filled with was something very common and homely; but I'll tell you the tale as 'twas told to me, and you shall decide if my description of that first pie as a poem does not hold good.

In one of the New England states away back in Colonial times, a pioneer woman one Saturday was cooking the Sunday dinner. She wanted a sweet meat for the ending but had nothing of which to make anything of the kind she ever had seen. But she did want to please and satisfy the good man and the children, so using her imagination and Yankee invention, she made a dough with bear's grease for shortening, spread it in a pan, and filled it with a mixture of vinegar and water thickened with flour, sweetened with maple sugar and flavored with a bit of spice bush.

She baked it and, behold, the first American pie! In fact, it was the first pie, spicy and sweet, of custard-like consistency and crispy crust, a poem in cookery. Its originator was truly an artist, as though she had written a poem or painted a picture, for she had used her creative instinct and imagination with a fine technique.

Thinking of pies and poems, I am more content with pie making, for surely it is better to make a good pie than a poor poem.

---

*Such famous writers as Sinclair Lewis and Dorothy Thompson visited Laura's home in the Ozarks on the invitation of her daughter, Rose Wilder Lane.

Simplify, Simplify
July 1919

Rummaging through a closet in the attic a few days ago, I unearthed some fashion magazines of the summer of 1908 and was astonished to discover that since that short time ago, women have apparently changed the form of their bodies and the shape of their faces, as well as the style of their gowns and hair dressing.

Perhaps the pensive lines and die-away expression of the faces in the old-fashioned plates were due to the tightly drawn-in waists and the overdrawn-check effect of the choker collars, or it may be that faces with such an expression just naturally called for that style of dressing.

There used to be 207 kinds of lawn mowers. Now there are only six.

However that may be, a comparison of those fashions with the easy, comfortable styles of this summer, which give beauty and grace of line with freedom of movement and plenty of breathing room, is enough cause for celebrating a special Thanksgiving Day months ahead of the regular time.

There is still room for improvement in children's clothes. They are much too fussy to be either beautiful or becoming. Why trouble with fancy, changeable children's styles? There will be plenty of time for them to learn all the vanities of dress later, and it is better to keep them simple and sweet as long as possible. It would do away with a lot of needless bother and vexation if we copied the English in their way of dressing little girls as their mothers were dressed, in the same kind of a simple little smock frock.

Fashions in other things than clothes have been and are still being simplified for the sake of a more economic production, thus lessening the cost of manufacturing by saving time, labor, and material.

Furniture makers cut down the number of their patterns several hundred percent during the war, cutting out just that many varieties of furniture. This was done on the advice of the War Industries Board to reduce the cost of production and save materials and labor for other work. It was found to be such a benefit that it has been decided to keep on in the same way, and so we shall have fewer styles in furniture.

In the hardware trade the same plan is being used. There are something like 4,450 fewer styles of pocket knives for Johnnie to buy and lose than there were before the war, but it does seem that he should be able to please himself by a choice from the 250 kinds left him.

There used to be 207 kinds of lawnmowers. Now there are only six. This number does not include the regular mowing machine which the Man of the Place uses so effectively in the front yard nor the pet colt who mows the lawn and puts the clippings to such good use.

The idea of doing away with useless, unnecessary things is at work in architecture also in the planning and building of houses, so that we are hearing a great deal these days of the dining-roomless house.

The dining room, if kept strictly as a dining room, is used for only a few minutes three times a day, which is not enough return for the work and thought and expense of keeping up an extra room. The fact is that most dining rooms are used by the family as a living room as well, and so in the new plans, the rooms are frankly combined into one.

Sometimes where the kitchen is large, it is the kitchen *and* dining room and many steps are saved. Either of these combination rooms may be made very attractive and have been in small houses where people did not wait for it to become the fashion.

Everyone is complaining of being tired, of not having time for what they wish to do. It is no wonder when they are obliged to pick and choose from such multitudes of thoughts and things.

The world is full of so many things, so many of them useless, so many, many varieties of the same thing creating confusion and a feeling of being overwhelmed by their number. It would be a wonderful relief if, by eliminating both wisely and well, life might be simplified.

Think for Yourself
February 1920

Cooperation is the keynote of affairs today, and our lives seem to be governed mostly by the advice of experts. These both are greatly needed, and I heartily say, more power to them. But every good becomes evil when carried to excess by poor, faulty mortals. Thrift and economy overdone become miserliness; even religion may be carried so far as to become fanaticism and intolerance, the faith that should cause love and gentleness instead causing hatred and persecution.

And if, just so, the power of cooperation and the privilege of having expert advice are not to become harmful, then individual thinking and initiative must keep pace with them. We must still do our own thinking and act upon it, for even though we make mistakes, experience is still the best teacher, and thinking and experimenting develop character.

---

*But every good becomes evil when
carried to excess.*

The more we think for ourselves, the less we shall need advice; and high-priced experts would not need to waste their time and government money, which is really our money, in telling us things we should think out for ourselves.

I read an item a short time ago in a farm paper stating that government experts advised the use of oil on shoes to prolong their life and usefulness and in so doing beat the high cost of living. Full instructions were given for this treatment of shoes.

Now the weekly cleaning and greasing of the family shoes was a regular thing with the grandparents and the parents of most of us, and they charged nothing for advising and instructing us in the process. In fact, there was at times a compelling quality about their advice that is lacking in that of government experts. But at least our grandparents, and their "old-fashioned notions" are at last vindicated.

"Scrape off all that dirt and clean those shoes up good, then rub that grease into them," said they, perhaps a bit sharply.

"The shoes should be thoroughly cleaned and warm oil then rubbed well into the leather," say the experts smoothly.

So you see that expert advice was given in our homes years ago. And after all, that is the best place for teaching many things, first and most important of which is how to think for one's self.

The Blessings of the Year
November 1922

Among all the blessings of the year, have you chosen one for which to be especially thankful at this Thanksgiving time or are you unable to decide which is the greatest?

Sometimes we recognize as a special blessing what heretofore we have taken without a thought as a matter of course, as when we recover from a serious illness; just a breath drawn free from pain is a matter for rejoicing. If we have been crippled and then are whole again, the blessed privilege of walking forth free and unhindered seems a gift from the gods. We must needs have been hungry to properly appreciate food, and we never love our friends as we should until they have been taken from us.

---

*We must needs have been hungry to
properly appreciate food.*

As the years pass, I am coming more and more to understand that it is the common, everyday blessings of our common everyday lives for which we should be particularly grateful. They are the things that fill our lives with comfort and our hearts with gladness—just the pure air to breathe and the strength to breathe it; just warmth and shelter and home folks; just plain food that gives us strength; the bright sunshine on a cold day; and a cool breeze when the day is warm.

Oh, we have so much to be thankful for that we seldom think of it in that way! I wish we might think more about these things that we are so much inclined to overlook and live more in the spirit of the old Scotch table blessing.

*Some hae meat wha canna' eat
And some can eat that lack it.
But I hae meat and I can eat
And sae the Laird be thankit.**

---

*From "The Selkirk Grace" by Robert Burns.

CHAPTER 12

The greatness
and goodness
of God

Everyday Implications of the Golden Rule
May 1922

Some small boys went into my neighbor's yard this spring and with sling-shots killed the wild birds that were nesting there. Only the other day, I read in my daily paper of several murders committed by a nineteen-year-old boy.

At once there was formed a connection in my mind between the two crimes, for both were crimes of the same kind, though perhaps in differing degree—the breaking of laws and the taking of life cruelly.

I am sure we will all agree that these laws of ours should be as wise and as few as possible.

For the cruel child to become a hard-hearted boy and then a brutal man is only stepping along the road on which he has started. A child allowed to disobey without punishment is not likely to have much respect for law as he grows older. Not that every child who kills birds becomes a murderer nor that everyone who is not taught to obey goes to prison.

The Bible says, if we "train up a child in the way he should go, when he is old, he will not depart from it."* The opposite is also true, and if a child is started in the way he should not go, he will go at least some way along that road as he grows older. It will always be more difficult for him to travel the right way even though he finds it.

The first laws with which children come in contact are the commands of their parents. Few fathers and mothers are wise in giving these, for we are all so busy and thoughtless. But I am sure we will all agree that these laws of ours should be as wise and as few as possible, and, once given, children should be made to obey or shown that to disobey brings punishment. Thus they will learn the lesson every good citizen and every good man and woman learns sooner or later—that breaking a law brings suffering.

If we break a law of nature, we are punished physically; when we disobey God's law we suffer spiritually, mentally, and usually in our bodies also. Man's laws, being founded on the ten commandments, are really mankind's poor attempt at interpreting the laws of God, and for disobeying them there is a penalty. The commands we give our children should be our translation of these

---

*Proverbs 22:6.

laws of God and man, founded on justice and the law of love, which is the Golden Rule.

And these things enter into such small deeds. Even insisting that children pick up and put away their playthings is teaching them order, the law of the universe, and helpfulness, the expression of love.

The responsibility for starting the child in the right way is the parents'—it cannot be delegated to the schools or to the state, for the little feet start on life's journey from the home.

Thanks for Benefits Bestowed
November 1923

We are inclined to think of Thanksgiving Day as a strictly American institution, and so, of course, it is in date and manner of celebration. But a harvest feast with the giving of praise and thanks to whatever gods were worshiped is a custom much older than our Thanksgiving that has been, and still is, observed by most races and peoples.

Mankind is not following a blind trail.

It seems to be instinctive for the human race to give thanks for benefits bestowed by a Higher Power. Some have worshiped the sun as the originator of blessings through its light and heat, while others have bowed the knee to lesser objects. Still, the feeling of gratitude in their hearts has been the same as we feel toward a beneficent Providence who has given us the harvest as well as countless other blessings through the year. This is just another touch of nature that makes the whole world kin and links the present with the far distant past.

Mankind is not following a blind trail; feet were set upon the true path in the beginning. Following it at first by instinct, men stumbled from it often in the darkness of ignorance even as we do today, for we have much to learn. But even more than for material blessings, let us, with humble hearts, give thanks for the revelation [given] us and our better understanding of the greatness and goodness of God.

Thanks for the Harvest
November 1921

The season is over, the rush and struggle of growing and saving the crops is past for another year, and the time has come when we pause and reverently give thanks for the harvest. For it is not to our efforts alone that our measure of success is due, but to the life principle in the earth and the seed, to the sunshine and to the rain—to the goodness of God.

*His goodness and mercy does follow us
all the days of our lives.*

We may not be altogether satisfied with the year's results, and we can do a terrific amount of grumbling when we take the notion. But I am sure we all know in our hearts that we have a great deal for which to be thankful. In spite of disappointment and weariness and perhaps sorrow, His goodness and mercy does follow us all the days of our lives.

As the time approaches when we shall be called upon by proclamation to give thanks, we must decide whether we shall show our thankfulness only by overeating at the Thanksgiving feast. That would seem a rather curious way to show gratitude—simply to grasp greedily what is given!

When a neighbor does us a favor, we show our appreciation of it by doing him a favor in return. Then when the Lord showers favors upon us, how much more should we try to show our gratitude in such ways acceptable to Him, remembering always the words of Christ, "Inasmuch as ye have done it unto one of the least of these, ye have done it unto me."*

*Matthew 26:40.

Harvest of the Soul
October 1920

There is a purple haze over the hilltops and a hint of sadness in the sunshine because of summer's departure; on the low ground down by the spring the walnuts are dropping from the trees and squirrels are busy hiding away their winter supply. Here and there the leaves are beginning to change color and a little vagrant autumn breeze goes wandering over the hills and down the valleys whispering to "follow, follow," until it is almost impossible to resist. So I should not be too harshly criticized if I ramble a little even in my conversation.

The time of gathering together the visible results of our year's labor is a very appropriate time to reckon up the invisible, more important harvest.

We have been gathering the fruits of the season's work into barns and bins and cellars. The harvest has been abundant, and a good supply is stored away for future needs.

Now I am wondering what sort of fruits and how plentiful is the supply we have stored away in our hearts and souls and minds from our year's activities. The time of gathering together the visible results of our year's labor is a very appropriate time to reckon up the invisible, more important harvest.

When we lived in South Dakota where the cold came early and strong, we once had a hired man (farmers had them in those days), who was a good worker, but whose money was too easily spent. In the fall when the first cold wind struck him, he would shiver and chatter and, always he would say, "Gee Mighty! This makes a feller wonder what's become of his summer's wages!"

Ever since then, Harvest Home time has seemed to me the time to gather together and take stock of our mental and spiritual harvest, and to wonder what we have done with the wealth of opportunity that has come to us, and the treasures we have had in our keeping. Much too often I have felt like quoting the hired man of other days.

Have we found a new friendship worthwhile? Have we even kept safely the old friendships, treasures worth much more than silver and gold? People in these history-making days hold their opinions so strongly and defend them so fiercely that a strain will be put upon many friendships; and the pity of it is that these misunderstandings will come between people who are earnestly striving for the right thing. Right seems to be obscured and truth is difficult to find.

But if the difficulty of finding the truth has increased our appreciation of its value, if the beauty of truth is plainer to us and more desired, then we have gathered treasure for the future.

We lay away the gleanings of our years in the edifice of our character where nothing is ever lost. What have we stored away in this safe place during the season that is past? Is it something that will keep sound and pure and sweet or something that is faulty and not worth storing?

As a child I learned my Bible lessons by heart in the good old-fashioned way, and once won the prize for repeating correctly more verses from the Bible than any other person in the Sunday school. But always my mind had a trick of picking a text here and a text there and connecting them together in meaning. In this way there came to me a thought that makes the stores from my invisible harvest important to me. These texts are familiar to everyone. It is their sequence that gives the thought.

"Lay not up for yourselves treasures upon earth, where moth and rust doth corrupt, and where thieves break through and steal. But lay up for yourselves treasures in Heaven, where neither moth nor rust doth corrupt, and where thieves do not break through nor steal."*

And then: "Neither shall they say, Lo here! for behold, the Kingdom of God is within you."**

---

*Matthew 6:19–20.
**Luke 17:21.

A Dog's a Dog for A' That
August 1916

A redbird swinging in the grape arbor saw himself in the glass of my kitchen window not long ago. He tried to fly through the glass to reach the strange bird he saw there, and when his little mate came flitting by, he tried to fight his reflection. Apparently, he was jealous. During all one day he fretted and struggled to drive the stranger away. He must have told his little wife about it that night, I think, for in the morning they came to the arbor together, and she alighted before the window while he stayed in the background. She gave Mr. Redbird one look after glancing in the glass, then turned and flew fiercely at her reflection, twittering angrily. One could imagine her saying: "So, that's it! This strange lady Redbird is the reason for your hanging around here instead of getting busy building the nest. I'll soon drive her away!" She tried to fight the strange lady bird until her husband objected to her paying so much attention to her rival; and then they took turns, he declaring there was a gentleman there, she vowing there was a lady and doing her best to drive her away. At last between them, they seemed to understand; and now they both come occasionally to swing on the grapevine before the window and admire themselves in the glass.

There are many interesting things in the out-of-doors life that come so close to us in the country, and if we show a little kindness to the wild creatures, they quickly make friends with us.

There are many interesting things in the out-of-doors life that come so close to us in the country, and if we show a little kindness to the wild creatures, they quickly make friends with us and permit us a delightful intimacy with them and their homes. A bird in a cage is not a pretty sight to me, but it is a pleasure to have the wild birds and the squirrels nesting around the house and so tame that they do not mind our watching them. Persons who shoot or allow shooting on their farms drive away a great deal of amusement and pleasure with the game, as well as do themselves pecuniary damage, while a small boy with a stone handy can do even more mischief than a man with a gun.

It is surprising how like human beings animals seem when they are treated with consideration. Did you ever notice the sense of humor animals have? Ever see a dog apologize—not a cringing fawning for favor, but a frank apology as one gentleman to another?

Shep was trying to learn to sit up and shake hands, but try as he would, he could not seem to get the knack of keeping his balance in the upright position. He was an old dog, and you know it has been said that, "It is hard to teach an old dog new tricks." No sympathy has ever been wasted on the dog, but I can assure you that it also is hard for the old dog. After a particularly disheartening session one day, we saw him out on the back porch alone and not knowing that he was observed. He was practicing his lesson without a teacher. We watched while he tried and failed several times, then finally got the trick of it and sat up with his paw extended. The next time we said, "How do you do, Shep?" he had his lesson perfectly. After that it was easy to teach him to fold his paws and be a "Teddy Bear" and to tell us what he said to tramps. We never asked him to lie down and roll over. He was not that kind of character. Shep never would do his tricks for anyone but us, though he would shake hands with others when we told him to do so.

His eyesight became poor as he grew older, and he did not always recognize his friends. Once he made a mistake and barked savagely at an old friend whom he really regarded as one of the family, though he had not seen him for some time. Later, as we all sat in the yard, Shep seemed uneasy. Evidently, there was something on his mind. At last he walked deliberately to the visitor, sat up, and held out his paw. It was so plainly an apology that our friend said: "That's all right, Shep, old fellow! Shake and forget it!" Shep shook hands and walked away perfectly satisfied.

My little French Poodle, Incubus, is blind. He used to be very active and run about the farm, but his chief duty, as he saw it, was to protect me. Although he cannot see, he still performs that duty, guarding me at night and flying at any stranger who comes too near me during the day. Of what he is thinking when he sits for long periods in the yard with his face to the sun, I am too stupid to understand perfectly, but I feel that in his little doggy heart, he is asking the eternal "Why?" as we all do at times. After a while he seemingly decides to make the best of it and takes a walk around the familiar places or comes in the house and does his little tricks for candy with a cheery good will.

If patience and cheerfulness and courage, if being faithful to our trust and doing our duty under difficulties count for so much in man that he expects to be rewarded for them, both here and hereafter, how are they any less in the life of my little blind dog? Surely, such virtues in animals are worth counting in the sum total of good in the universe.

Let Us Be Just
September 1917

Two little girls had disagreed, as was to be expected, because they were so temperamentally different. They wanted to play in different ways, and as they had to play together, all operations were stopped while they argued the question. The elder of the two had a sharp tongue and great facility in using it. The other was slow to speak but quick to act, and they both did their best according to their abilities.

I hate to write the end of the story. No,
not the end! No story is ever ended!

Said the first little girl: "You've got a snub nose and your hair is just a common brown color. I heard Aunt Lottie say so!* Ah, Don't you wish your hair was a b-e-a-u-tiful golden like mine, and your nose a fine shape? Cousin Louisa said that about me. I heard her!"

The second little girl could not deny these things. Her dark skin, brown hair, and snub nose, as compared with her sister's lighter coloring and regular features, were a tragedy in her little life. She could think of nothing cutting to reply, for she was not given to saying unkind things nor was her tongue nimble enough to say them, so she stood digging her bare toes into the ground, hurt, helpless, and tongue-tied.

The first girl, seeing the effect of her words, talked on. "Besides, you're two years younger than I am, and I know more than you, so you have to mind me and do as I say!"

This was too much! Sister was prettier, no answer could be made to that. She was older, it could not be denied; but that gave her no right to command. At last here was a chance to act!

"And you have to mind me," repeated the first little girl. "I will not!" said the second little girl and then, to show her utter contempt for such authority, this little brown girl slapped her elder, golden-haired sister.

I hate to write the end of the story. No, not the end! No story is ever ended! It goes on, and on, and the effects of this one followed this little girl all her life, showing her hatred of injustice. I should say that I dislike to tell what came next, for the golden-haired sister ran crying and told what had happened, ex-

---

*This story is retold in *Little House in the Big Woods* in chapter ten. Pa was the parent who did the unjust thing.

cept her own part in the quarrel, and the little brown girl was severely punished. To be plain, she was soundly spanked and set in a corner.

She did not cry but sat glowering at the parent who punished her and thinking in her rebellious little mind that when she was large enough, she would return the spanking with interest.

It was not the pain of the punishment that hurt so much as the sense of injustice, the knowledge that she had not been treated fairly by one from whom she had the right to expect fair treatment, and that there had been a failure to understand where she had thought a mistake impossible. She had been beaten and bruised by sister's unkind words and had been unable to reply. She had defended herself in the only way possible for her and felt that she had a perfect right to do so, or if not, then both should have been punished.

Children have a fine sense of justice that sometimes is far truer than that of older persons, and in almost every case, if appealed to, will prove the best help in governing them. When children are ruled through their sense of justice, there are no angry thoughts left to rankle in their minds. Then a punishment is not an injury inflicted upon them by someone who is larger and stronger but the inevitable consequence of their own acts, and a child's mind will understand this much sooner than one would think. What a help all their lives in self-control and self-government this kind of a training would be!

We are prone to put so much emphasis on the desirability of mercy that we overlook the beauties of the principle of justice. The quality of mercy is a gracious, beautiful thing; but with more justice in the world, there would be less need for mercy, and exact justice is most merciful in the end.

The difficulty is that we are so likely to make mistakes, we cannot trust our judgment and so must be merciful to offset our own shortcomings; but I feel sure when we are able to comprehend the workings of the principle of justice, we shall find that instead of being opposed to each other, infallible justice and mercy are one and the same thing.

Do the Right Thing Always
June 1918

"It is always best to treat people right," remarked my lawyer friend.

"Yes, I suppose so in the end," I replied inanely.

"Oh, of course!" he returned, "but that was not what I meant. It pays every time to do the right thing! It pays now and in dollars and cents."

"For instance?" I asked.

"Well, for the latest instance: a man came to me the other day to bring suit against a neighbor. He had good grounds for damages and could win the suit, but it would cost him more than he could recover. It would increase his neighbor's expenses and increase the bad feeling between them. I needed that attorney's fee; but it would not have been doing the right thing to encourage him to bring suit, so I advised him to settle out of court. He insisted, but I refused to take the case. He hired another lawyer, won his case, and paid the difference between the damages he recovered and his expenses.

Is it possible that "honesty is the best policy" after all, actually and literally?

"A client came to me a short time afterward with a worthwhile suit and a good retainer's fee, which I could take without robbing him. He was sent to me by the man whose case I had refused to take and because of that very refusal."

Is it possible that "honesty is the best policy" after all, actually and literally? I would take the advice of my lawyer friend on any other business, and I have his word for it that it pays to do the right thing here and now.

To do the right thing is simply to be honest, for being honest is more than refraining from shortchanging a customer or robbing a neighbor's hen roost. To be sure, those items are included, but there is more to honesty than that. There is such a thing as being dishonest when no question of financial gain or loss is involved. When one person robs another of his good name, he is dishonest. When by an unnecessary, unkind act or cross word, one causes another to lose a day or an hour of happiness, is that one not a thief? Many a person robs another of the joy of life while taking pride in his own integrity.

We steal from today to give to tomorrow; we "rob Peter to pay Paul." We are not honest even with ourselves; we rob ourselves of health; we cheat ourselves with sophistries; we even "put an enemy in our mouths to steal away our brains."

If there were a cry of "stop, thief!"
we would all stand still.

If there were a cry of "stop thief!" we would all stand still. Yet nevertheless, in spite of our carelessness, we all know deep in our hearts that it pays to do the right thing, though it is easy to deceive ourselves for a time. If we do the wrong thing, we are quite likely never to know what we have lost by it. If the lawyer had taken the first case, he might have thought he gained by so doing, for he never would have known of the larger fee which came to him by taking the other course.

The Armor of a Smile
November 1921

Mrs. A was angry. Her eyes snapped, her voice was shrill, and a red flag of rage was flying upon each cheek. She expected opposition and anger at the things she said, but her remarks were answered in a soft voice; her angry eyes were met by smiling ones; and her attack was smothered in the softness of courtesy, consideration, and compromise.

She might as well have tried to break a
feather pillow by beating it.

I feel sure Mrs. A had intended to create a disturbance, but she might as well have tried to break a feather pillow by beating it as to have any effect with her angry voice and manner on the perfect kindness and good manners which met her. She only made herself ridiculous, and in self-defense was obliged to change her attitude.

Since then I have been wondering if it always is so, if shafts of malice aimed in anger forever fall harmless against the armor of a smile, kind words, and gentle manners. I believe they do. And I have gained a fuller understanding of the words, "A soft answer turneth away wrath."*

Until this incident, I had found no more in the words than the idea that a soft answer might cool the wrath of an aggressor, but I saw wrath turned away as an arrow deflected from its mark and came to understand that a soft answer and a courteous manner are an actual protection.

Nothing is ever gained by allowing anger to have sway. While under its influence, we lose the ability to think clearly and lose the forceful power that is in calmness.

Anger is a destructive force; its purpose is to hurt and destroy, and being a blind passion, it does its evil work, not only upon whatever arouses it, but also upon the person who harbors it. Even physically it injures him, impeding the action of the heart and circulation, affecting the respiration, and creating an actual poison in the blood. Persons with weak hearts have been known to drop dead from it, and always there is a feeling of illness after indulging in a fit of temper.

Anger is a destroying force. What all the world needs is its opposite—an uplifting power.

---

*Proverbs 15:1.

Laura and Mary Quarrel at Thanksgiving
November 1916

As Thanksgiving day draws near again, I am reminded of an occurrence of my childhood. To tell the truth, it is a yearly habit of mine to think of it about this time and to smile at it once more.

We were living on the frontier in South Dakota then. There's no more frontier within the boundaries of the United States, more's the pity, but then we were ahead of the railroad in a new unsettled country. Our nearest and only neighbor was twelve miles away, and the store was forty miles distant.

I remember saying in a meek voice to sister Mary, "I wish I had let you have the sage."

Father had laid in a supply of provisions for the winter, and among them were salt meats; but for fresh meat we depended on Father's gun and the antelope which fed in herds across the prairie. So we were quite excited, one day near Thanksgiving, when Father hurried into the house for his gun and then away again to try for a shot at a belated flock of wild geese hurrying south.

We would have roast goose for Thanksgiving dinner! "Roast goose and dressing seasoned with sage," said sister Mary. "No, not sage! I don't like sage, and we won't have it in the dressing," I exclaimed. Then we quarreled, sister Mary and I, she insisting that there should be sage in the dressing, and I declaring there should not be sage in the dressing, until Father returned—without the goose!

I remember saying in a meek voice to sister Mary, "I wish I had let you have the sage," and to this day when I think of it, I feel again just as I felt then and realize how thankful I would have been for roast goose and dressing with sage seasoning—with or without any seasoning—I could even have gotten along without the dressing. Just plain goose roasted would have been plenty good enough.*

This little happening has helped me to be properly thankful even though at times the seasoning of my blessings has not been just such as I would have chosen.

"I suppose I should be thankful for what we have, but I can't feel very thankful when I have to pay $2.60 for a little flour and the price still going up,"

---

*This story appears in chapter twenty-six of *By the Shores of Silver Lake*.

writes a friend, and in the same letter she says, "we are in our usual health." The family are so used to good health that it is not even taken into consideration as a cause of thanksgiving. We are so inclined to take for granted the blessings we possess and to look for something peculiar, some special good luck for which to be thankful.

I read a Thanksgiving story the other day in which a woman sent her little boy out to walk around the block and look for something for which to be thankful.

One would think that the fact of his being able to walk around the block, and that he had a mother to send him, would have been sufficient cause for thankfulness. We are nearly all afflicted with mental farsightedness and so easily overlook the thing which is obvious and near. There are our hands and feet—who ever thinks of giving thanks for them, until indeed they, or the use of them, are lost?

We usually accept them as a matter of course, without a thought, but a year of being crippled has taught me the value of my feet and two perfectly good feet are now among my dearest possessions.* Why, there is greater occasion for thankfulness just in the unimpaired possession of one of the five senses than there would be if someone left us a fortune. Indeed, how could the value of one be reckoned? When we have all five in good working condition, we surely need not make a search for anything else in order to feel that we should give thanks to Whom thanks are due.

I once remarked upon how happy and cheerful a new acquaintance seemed always to be, and the young man to whom I spoke replied, "Oh, he's just glad that he is alive." Upon inquiry, I learned that several years before, this man had been seriously ill; that there had been no hope of his living, but to everyone's surprise he had made a complete recovery, and since then he had always been remarkably happy and cheerful.

*Unfortunately, her husband, Almanzo, was somewhat crippled in both feet following a stroke early on in their marriage. He had become sick, had tried to get back to work too soon, and had suffered the stroke.

Not So Bad Off
December 1922

My community is representative of those rural districts which come in for much solicitude because of their backward state. Our children are among those pitied because of their lack of a chance equal to the negro in the cities for a proper start in life. I used to be mortally sick because I believed this. Today I doubt it.

"Lord, that I may be a little kinder, a little braver to meet temptation, a little more thoughtful of my neighbor." The object of all education is to make folks fit to live.

A chance is not everything. Besides:

In our schoolhouse, where stoves are still unjacketed, the children meet one day out of seven to receive religious training.

In the city, where children are supposed to have everything, thousands are growing up without the most important part of an education—proper home training.

We country mothers, realizing the dearth of so-called advantages, strive that at least home and neighborhood influences shall be of the best.

Because it takes us all to make a go of any cooperative work or pastime, we learn to work harmoniously together. This is good for the children to see.

We read good books. We have our community sings. Also, we have prayer meetings where young mothers pray and where boys and girls get up and say: "Lord, that I may be a little kinder, a little braver to meet temptation, a little more thoughtful of my neighbor."

The object of all education is to make folks fit to live. I guess we are not so bad off.

Swearing
August 1918

I heard a boy swear the other day, and it gave me a distinctly different kind of shock than usual. I had just been reading an article in which our soldiers were called crusaders who were offering themselves in their youth as a sacrifice in order that right might prevail against wrong and that those ideals, which are in effect the teachings of Christ, shall be accepted as the law of nations.

> *I wonder how things came to be so reversed . . . that it should be thought daring and smart to swear instead of being regarded as . . . a sign of weakness.*

When I heard the boy use the name of Christ in an oath, I felt that he had belittled the mighty effort we are making, and that he had put an affront upon our brave soldiers by using lightly the name of the great Leader who first taught the principles for which they are dying. The boy had not thought of it in this way at all. He imagined that he was being very bold and witty, quite a grown man in fact.

I wonder how things came to be so reversed from the right order that it should be thought daring and smart to swear instead of being regarded as utterly foolish and a sign of weakness, betraying a lack of self-control. If people could only realize how ridiculous they appear when they call down the wrath of the Creator and Ruler of the Universe just because they have jammed their thumbs, I feel sure they would never be guilty of swearing again. It is so out of proportion, something as foolish and wasteful as it would be to use the long-range gun which bombarded Paris to shoot a fly. If we call upon the Mightiest for trivial things, upon whom or what shall we call in the great moments of life?

There are some things in the world which should be damned to the nethermost regions, but surely it is not some frightened animal, whom our own lack of self-control has made rebellious, or an inanimated object that our own carelessness has caused to smite us. Language loses its value when it is so misapplied, and in moments of real and great stress or danger we have nothing left to say.

It is almost hopeless to try to reform older persons who have the habit of swearing fastened upon them. Like any other habit, it is difficult to break, and it is useless to explain to them that it is a waste of force and nervous energy. But I think we should show the children the absurdity of wasting the big shells of language on small insignificant objects.

Perhaps a little ridicule might prick that bubble of conceit, and the boy with his mouth full of his first oaths might not feel himself such a dashing, daredevil of a fellow if he feared that he had made himself ridiculous.

Honor and Duty
October 1919

"Now can we depend on you in this?" asked Mr. Jones. "Certainly you can," replied Mr. Brown. "I'll do it!"

"But you failed us before, you know," continued Mr. Jones, "and it made us a lot of trouble. How would it be for you to put up a forfeit? Will you put up some money as security that you will not fail; will you bet on it?"

> *"It is so much easier to say 'yes,' and*
> *then do as I please afterward."*

"No-o-o," answered Mr. Brown. "I won't bet on it, but I'll give you my word of honor."

How much was Mr. Brown's word worth? I would not want to risk much on it. Would you? He evidently considered it of less value than a little cash. Now and then we hear of people whose word is as good as their bond, but far too often we find that "word of honor" is used carelessly and then forgotten or ignored.

Speaking to a friend of the difficulties of putting through a plan we had in mind, I remarked that it was very difficult to do anything with a crowd anymore, for so many would promise and then fail to keep the promise.

"I know," she replied, "I do that way myself; it is so much easier to say 'yes,' and then do as I please afterward."

If my friend had realized how weak and unkind her reason was for disregarding her word, she would be more careful, for she prides herself on her strength of character and is a very kind, lovable woman on the whole.

Mr. Brown and my friend had mistaken ideas of value. One's word is of infinitely more worth than money. If money is lost, more money, and just as good, is to be had; but if you pledge your word and do not redeem it, you have lost something that cannot be replaced. It is intangible perhaps but nevertheless valuable to you.

A person who cannot be depended upon by others, in time, becomes unable to depend upon himself. It seems in some subtle way to undermine and weaken the character when we do not hold ourselves strictly responsible for what we say.

And what a tangle it makes of all our undertakings when people do not keep their promises. How much pleasanter it would be, and how much more would be accomplished, if we did not give our word unless we intended to keep it, so that we would all know what we could depend upon!

When we think of honor we always think of duty in connection with it. They seem to be inseparably linked together. The following incident illustrates this.

Albert Bebe, a French resident of San Francisco, came home from the battlefront in France. He had been in the trenches for two years and four months in an advanced position, a "listening post" only sixty yards from the German trenches. Marie Bebe, the soldier's little daughter, was very much excited over her father's coming and objected to going to school the next morning. She thought she should be allowed to stay at home on the first day of her father's visit.

But her mother said: "No! Your father went to fight for France because it was his duty to go. You must go to school because that is your duty. Your father did his duty and you must do yours!" And Marie went to school.

If everybody did his duty as well in the smaller things, there would be no failures when the greater duties presented themselves.

If We Only Understood
December 1917

Mrs. Brown* was queer. The neighbors all thought so and, what was worse, they said so.

Mrs. Fuller happened in several times, quite early in the morning, and although the work was not done up, Mrs. Brown was sitting leisurely in her room or else she would be writing at her desk. Then Mrs. Powers went through the house one afternoon, and the dishes were stacked back unwashed, the bed still airing, and everything "at sixes and sevens," except the room where Mrs. Brown seemed to be idling away her time. Mrs. Powers said Mrs. Brown was "just plain lazy," and she didn't care who heard her say it.

The safest course is to be as understanding as possible, and, where our understanding fails, to call charity to its aid.

Ida Brown added interesting information when she told her schoolmates, after school, that she must hurry home and do up the work. It was a shame, the neighbors said, that Mrs. Brown should idle away her time all day and leave the work for Ida to do after school.

Later, it was learned that Mrs. Brown had been writing for the papers to earn money to buy Ida's new winter outfit. Ida had been glad to help by doing the work after school so that her mother might have the day for study and writing, but they had not thought it necessary to explain to the neighbors.

I read a little verse a few years ago entitled, "If We Only Understood," and the refrain was

*We would love each other better,
If we only understood.*

I have forgotten the author and last verse, but the refrain has remained in my memory and comes to my mind every now and then when I hear unkind remarks made about people.

The things that people do would look so different to us if we only under-

---

*Mrs. Edward Brown. Ida and Mrs. Brown appear in *Little Town on the Prairie;* see chapters thirteen and twenty-three.

stood the reasons for their actions, nor would we blame them so much for their faults if we knew all the circumstances of their lives. Even their sins might not look so hideous if we could feel what pressure and perhaps suffering had caused them.

The safest course is to be as understanding as possible, and, where our understanding fails, to call charity to its aid. Learn to distinguish between persons and the things they do, and while we may not always approve of their actions, have a sympathy and feeling of kindness for the persons themselves.

It may even be that what we consider faults and weaknesses in others are only prejudices on our own part. Some of us would like to see everybody fitted to our own pattern, and what a tiresome world this would be if that were done. We should be willing to allow others the freedom we demand for ourselves. Everyone has the right to self-expression.

If we keep this genial attitude toward the world and the people in it, we will keep our own minds and feelings healthy and clean. Even the vigilance necessary to guard our thoughts in this way will bring us rewards in better disciplined minds and happier dispositions.

The Things That Matter
January 1924

Standing on the shore with the waves of the Pacific rolling to my feet, I looked over the waters as far as my eyes could reach until the gray of the ocean merged with the gray of the horizon's rim. One could not be distinguished from the other. Where, within my vision, the waters stopped and the skies began I could not tell, so softly they blended one into the other. The waves rolled in regularly, beating a rhythm of time, but the skies above them were unmeasured—so vast and far-reaching that the mind of man could not comprehend it.

We are so overwhelmed with things these days that our lives are all, more or less, cluttered.

A symbol of time and of eternity—time spaced by our counting into years, breaking at our feet as the waves break on the shore; and eternity, unmeasurable as the skies above us—blending one into the other at the farthest reach of our earthly vision.

As the New Year comes, seemingly with ever-increasing swiftness, there is a feeling that life is too short to accomplish the things we must do. But there is all eternity blending with the end of time for the things that really are worthwhile.

We are so overwhelmed with things these days that our lives are all, more or less, cluttered. I believe it is this, rather than a shortness of time, that gives us that feeling of hurry and almost of helplessness. Everyone is hurrying and usually just a little late. Notice the faces of the people who rush past on the streets or on our country roads! They nearly all have a strained, harassed look, and anyone you meet will tell you there is no time for anything anymore.

Life is so complicated! The day of the woman whose only needed tool was a hairpin is long since passed. But we might learn something from her and her methods even yet, for life would be pleasanter with some of the strain removed—if it were no longer true, as someone has said, that "things are in the saddle and rule mankind."

Here is a good New Year's resolution for us all to make: To simplify our lives as much as possible, to overcome that feeling of haste by remembering that there are just as many hours in the day as ever, and that there is time enough for the things that matter if time is rightly used.

Then, having done the most we may here, when we reach the limit of time, we will sail on over the horizon rim to new beauties and greater understanding.

Mother
September 1921

The older we grow the more precious become the recollections of childhood's days, especially our memories of mother. Her love and care halo her memory with a brighter radiance, for we have discovered that nowhere else in the world is such loving self-sacrifice to be found; her counsels and instructions appeal to us with greater force than when we received them because our knowledge of the world and our experience of life have proved their worth.

*The truths of life are taught by precept,
and, generation after generation, we
each must be burned by fire before we
will admit the truth that it will burn.*

The pity of it is that it is by our own experience we have had to gain this knowledge of their value, then when we have learned it in the hard school of life, we know that mother's words were true. So, from generation to generation, the truths of life are taught by precept, and, generation after generation, we each must be burned by fire before we will admit the truth that it will burn.

We would be saved some sorry blunders and many a heartache if we might begin our knowledge where our parents leave off instead of experimenting for ourselves, but life is not that way.

Still, mother's advice does help, and often a word of warning spoken years before will recur to us at just the right moment to save us a misstep. And lessons learned at mother's knee last through life.

But dearer even than mother's teachings are little, personal memories of her, different in each case but essentially the same—mother's face, mother's touch, mother's voice:

*Childhood's far days were full of joy,
So merry and bright and gay;
On sunny wings of happiness
Swiftly they flew away.
But oh! By far the sweetest hour
Of all the whole day long
Was the slumber hour at twilight
And my mother's voice in song—
"Hush, my babe; be still and slumber,*

Holy angels guard thy bed,
Heavenly blessings without number
Gently resting on thy head."

Though our days are filled with gladness,
Joys of life like sunshine fall;
Still life's slumber hour at twilight
May be sweetest of them all.
And when to realms of boundless peace,
I am waiting to depart
Then my mother's song at twilight
Will make music in my heart.
"Hush, my babe, lie still and slumber;
Holy angels guard thy bed."
And I'll fall asleep so sweetly,
Mother's blessings on my head.

"Mother Passed Away"*
June 1924

"Mother passed away this morning" was the message that came over the wires, and a darkness overshadowed the spring sunshine; a sadness crept into the birds' songs.

Some of us have received such messages. Those who have not, one day will. Just as when a child, home was lonely when mother was gone, so to children of a larger growth, the world seems a lonesome place when mother has passed away and only memories of her are left us—happy memories if we have not given ourselves any cause for regret.

---

*What a joy our memories may be or
what a sorrow!*

Memories! We go through life collecting them whether we will or not! Sometimes I wonder if they are our treasures in Heaven or the consuming fires of torment when we carry them with us as we, too, pass on.

What a joy our memories may be or what a sorrow! But glad or sad they are with us forever. Let us make them carefully of all good things, rejoicing in the wonderful truth that while we are laying up for ourselves the very sweetest and best of happy memories, we are at the same time giving them to others.

---

*Caroline Quinter Ingalls ("Ma") lived from 1839 to 1924.